CONTEMPORARY AFRICAN SOCIAL AND POLITICAL PHILOSOPHY

This book explores what constitutes contemporary African social and political philosophy with regard to its meaning, aims, sources, and relevance for today's Africa. Kasanda denounces conventional approaches, considering these either as a subcategory of general philosophy or as the ideological attempts of individual African leaders and professional philosophers, such as Nkrumah, Nyerere, Senghor, Fanon, Hountondji, and Towa. On the contrary, Kasanda defines contemporary African social and political philosophy as an inclusive reflection of African communities with regard to power and equitable modes of social and political organization in order to promote human excellence for everyone. This perspective also includes the criticism of social and political concepts in use within African communities.

The author postulates that contemporary African social and political philosophy relies on the legacy of precolonial African societies, as well as on the contribution of the diaspora throughout the world. Contemporary African social and political philosophy is rooted in the daily lives of African people, and it expresses itself through multiple modalities including, for example, art, religion, literature, music, and the policy of urbanization of African cities.

This book sheds new light on debates concerning topics such as ethnophilosophy, negritude, pan-Africanism, democracy, African civil society, African cultures, and globalization. It aims to ward off the lethargy that strikes African social and political philosophy, taking a renewed and critical approach.

Albert Kasanda is a Researcher in African social and political philosophy at the Centre for Global Studies, Institute of Philosophy of the Czech Academy of Sciences, Czech Republic.

CONTEMPORARY AFRICAN SOCIAL AND POLITICAL PHILOSOPHY

Trends, Debates and Challenges

Albert Kasanda

LONDON AND NEW YORK

First published 2018
by Routledge
2 Park Square, Milton Park, Abingdon, Oxon OX14 4RN

and by Routledge
711 Third Avenue, New York, NY 10017

Routledge is an imprint of the Taylor & Francis Group, an informa business

© 2018 Albert Kasanda

The right of Albert Kasanda to be identified as author of this work has been asserted by him in accordance with sections 77 and 78 of the Copyright, Designs and Patents Act 1988.

All rights reserved. No part of this book may be reprinted or reproduced or utilised in any form or by any electronic, mechanical, or other means, now known or hereafter invented, including photocopying and recording, or in any information storage or retrieval system, without permission in writing from the publishers.

Trademark notice: Product or corporate names may be trademarks or registered trademarks, and are used only for identification and explanation without intent to infringe.

British Library Cataloguing in Publication Data
A catalogue record for this book is available from the British Library

Library of Congress Cataloging in Publication Data
Names: Kasanda Lumembu, Albert, author.
Title: Contemporary African social and political philosophy : trends, debates, and challenges / Albert Kasanda.
Description: New York : Routledge, 2018. | Includes bibliographical references.
Identifiers: LCCN 2017053096 | ISBN 9780815381655 (hardback) | ISBN 9780815381662 (pbk.) | ISBN 9781351209922 (ebook)
Subjects: LCSH: Social sciences--Philosophy--Africa. | Political science--Philosophy--Africa.
Classification: LCC H61.15 .K3645 2018 | DDC 300.1--dc23
LC record available at https://lccn.loc.gov/2017053096

ISBN: 978-0-8153-8165-5 (hbk)
ISBN: 978-0-8153-8166-2 (pbk)
ISBN: 978-1-351-20992-2 (ebk)

Typeset in Bembo
by Taylor & Francis Books

For Alena Tshala and Ela Keta, my daughters

For Alena Tebala and Lia Kata, my daughters

CONTENTS

Acknowledgements *viii*
Introduction *x*

1 Approaching contemporary African social and political philosophy 1
2 Sources of contemporary African social and political philosophy 11
3 Exploring the antecedents and precursors of contemporary African social and political philosophy 23
4 Reviewing the African identity discourses: Ethnophilosophy and negritude 40
5 The pan-African movement: From race-based solidarity to political unity and beyond 63
6 African democratic turn 88
7 Approaching African civil society: Paradigms and philosophical backgrounds 106
8 African cultures and globalization 128
Conclusion 141
Epilogue: A struggle for the right to live Mandela, in defence of pluralism and democracy 145

Bibliography *158*
Index *169*

ACKNOWLEDGEMENTS

This book owes to both decisive support and happy collaboration with different institutions and individuals. First, I would like to give thanks to the Institute of Philosophy at the Czech Academy of Sciences, Prague, and particularly to its Director, Ph.Dr. Ondřej Ševeček, Ph.D., for the warm and unwavering support provided to this research project.

This book is published thanks to the financial support of the Institute of Philosophy of the Czech Academy of Sciences, Prague.

I also would like to express my deep gratitude to Doc. Ph.Dr. Marek Hrubec, Ph.D., Director of the Centre for Global Studies at the Institute of Philosophy of the Czech Academy of Sciences. For me, consulting with him has been invaluable. Without his enthusiasm, support and friendship, this book would most likely have remained unfinished. I also extend my gratitude to colleagues and friends at the Centre for Global Studies at the Czech Academy of Sciences for their useful comments and encouragement during seminars in which different steps of my research were presented and debated. Thanks go especially to Doc. Ph.Dr. Oleg Susa, CSc., and Doc. Ph.Dr. RNDr. Milan Kreuzzieger, Ph.D.

While working on this book, I had the privilege of being invited as guest lecturer to the inaugural seminar of a conference on African philosophy at the School of Oriental and African Studies (SOAS), University of London. This conference was entitled *Asixoxe* (Let's Talk) and it took place on 1–2 May 2014. It was launched by Alena Rettová, Ph.D., Senior Lecturer in Swahili Literature and Culture at SOAS. The *Asixoxe* conference represents an innovative project in the field of African studies at SOAS. May Dr. Rettová find here the expression of my warm gratitude.

On the occasion of this seminar and through other opportunities at SOAS, I met and had discussions with many colleagues, friends, researchers and students from SOAS and elsewhere on the issue of African social and political philosophy. These debates were stimulating for me as they helped me to focus better and clarify my topic. I express my appreciation to every one of them, particularly to Benedetta Lanfranchi and Sara Marzagora, both doctoral students in philosophy at SOAS. With the former, I discussed Arendt's political philosophy and its potential implications for today's African communities, especially regarding alternative procedures of justice, such as *Gacaca*, that were set up in the euphoria of expiation of the Rwandan genocide of 1994. With the latter, I discussed the issue of African modernization, particularly the Ethiopian experience of the early twentieth century, known as the Ethiopian Japanization. I also express my warm gratitude to Carli Coetze whose valuable observations helped me to improve my approach to pan-Africanist theories.

Last but not least, a loving thought for Alena Tshala, Ela Keta and Alena, my companions every day and a source of unparalleled joy to me! At times, the writing of this book imposed on us asceticism and periods of retreat. Both the understanding and generosity with which you assumed these moments constitute, for me, a great sign of your love and encouragement. With all my heart, I express my gratitude to each one of you! I also extend this acknowledgement to Babička Alenka and Dědeček Vítězslav, without whom your life would lack its current flavour. Their presence at your side can be considered a godsend.

This book is published thanks to the financial support of the Institute of Philosophy of the Czech Academy of Sciences, Prague.

INTRODUCTION

Prague. Autumn 2012. I met with Dr. Marek Hrubec, Director of the Centre for Global Studies at the Institute of Philosophy of the Czech Academy of Sciences, to explore potential topics of interest concerning our cooperation on African philosophy. After considering various issues, Dr. Hrubec suddenly interrupted the conversation and said: "And what if we concentrate on African social and political philosophy? I have the feeling that this field of study counts amongst the lesser explored areas of African philosophy." This impromptu suggestion stimulated my curiosity to know more about the issue. I took note of it and decided to explore the topic further. In the time it took for me to carry out an overview of the question, the results were encouraging enough to confirm Dr. Hrubec's intuition. In this respect, Martin observed the following in introducing his own book on African political thought:

> As a distinct field of study, African political thought is a relatively new discipline. It was only in the late 1960s that it emerged as different and distinct from other ... systems of thought. ... To say that *"the history of African political thought is a neglected field of studies" is a major understatement.*
>
> *(2012, 1, emphasis added)*

In my exploratory survey, I discovered an important set of raw materials on the issue; these are hidden and scattered in speeches of African leaders, African traditional legacy, literature, art, music, books, and articles along with many other sources. So, I decided to continue my exploration of this topic. At first, I roughly drafted an attempt which was developed during 2012–2013 and, later, published in the *Journal of East-West Thought*, under the following title: "Analyzing African Social and Political Philosophy: Trends and Challenges".[1] Materials gathered during the preparation and writing of this paper prompted me to take a step forward and move on to the work of this book.

From the outset, it was, and still is, my challenge to identify African social and political philosophy through analysis of its specificities, sources, main topics and debates. Thus, I have kept a distance from common approaches that present this philosophy as nationalist ideology or merely as a set of theories elaborated by African leaders and professional philosophers. Although largely shared, those approaches seem to me to limit what this philosophy is, and they appear ignorant of its diversity, richness and modes of expression. I personally rely on the idea that this philosophy represents an autonomous attempt to think rationally about African people's daily life, power and paradigms of governance, as well as an intent to clarify political concepts to promote excellence in human beings.

I take the Act of the Berlin Conference (1884–1885) as a starting point of this philosophy because this represents the founding moment of contemporary African states, at least in terms of their current borders and configuration. Relying on this point of reference, I distinguish African precolonial societies from those that follow the division of the African continent. The former can be said to reflect original African values, while the latter are viewed as having been altered due to Western influence and colonization. This option also explains the use of the concept of "contemporary" in the title of this volume. As already mentioned, this concept refers to the founding moment (*Kairos*) of today's African states, but it also avoids having to engage in the complex debate about terms such as "modern" and "modernity", often used to speak of current African states and politics.[2]

The present volume consists of eight chapters and a conclusion followed by an epilogue. Chapter 1 addresses the definition of contemporary African social and political philosophy. It divides into three sections. The first focuses on the nature and purposes of this philosophy. Contrary to a shared propensity to view this philosophy as a subcategory of general African philosophy or reduce it to an ideological attempt or a single thought of African professional philosophers, this section considers African social and political philosophy as a reflexive process rooted in African daily reality and aiming at two purposes: first, the criticism and the evaluation of concepts in use in African social and political philosophy's sphere in order to ensure their common meaning; and second, support of rational understanding of power and the search for alternative forms of social and political organization that can enable excellence in the performance of humankind.

The second section explores the distinction between contemporary African social and political philosophy and ontology. From the outset, I consider that this philosophy doesn't coincide with ontology as they both have very different purposes: ontology searches for the quintessence of being, while African social and political philosophy is anchored in African daily realities. In other words, the latter cannot be locked into the search of the essence of being, because it must deal with issues, such as poverty and development, that cannot be reduced to ontological concerns.

The last section concentrates on the relationship between African social and political philosophy and ideology. It maintains that despite having a common interest in the life of ideas, these concepts are not automatically synonymous.

Understanding the equivalence between them requires an extension of each of the concepts as well as a rigorous methodology of interpretation. It is my feeling that African social and political philosophy does not systematically refer to ideology, and vice versa. Each concept includes its own semantic content as well as social and political references.

Chapter 2 focuses on sources of contemporary African social and political philosophy. It outlines the fact that this philosophy has multiple sources, many of which are neglected to the benefit of written and so-called philosophical texts (Houtondji 1983, 32). It identifies sources such as literature (written and oral), music, religion, art, or even the architecture of African cities.

Chapter 3 stands on the premise that contemporary African social and political philosophy does not arise *ex nihilo*. This chapter explores antecedents and legacies of this philosophy. It divides into two sections. The first section analyzes the legacy from African precolonial communities, shedding light on notions such as communal mind, solidarity, consensus, and democracy, to mention a few. The second section explores the contribution of the African diaspora through its struggles for recognition and efforts to protect the dignity of black people. It outlines the thought of some outstanding personalities from Negro-African diaspora including, for example, J. B. Africanus Horton, Edward W. Blyden and J. E. Casely Hayford. Through this exploration, this section also highlights some relevant debates concerning, for example, the formation of modern African states, African regeneration, self-governance and development.

Chapter 4 addresses the discourse of African identity through paradigms of ethnophilosophy and negritude. It is divided into two sections. The first section analyses ethnophilosophy as a fundamental category through which issues of identity and otherness are often approached. It explores the origin and interpretations given to this concept in the framework of African philosophy. Nkrumah is considered the first to make use of this word in African philosophy. Hountondji and Towa used it in a rather pejorative and restrictive context of criticism and denial of the status of philosophy to discourses that, in the wake of Tempels's thought, mixed ethnology and philosophy and thereby presented ethnological findings as African philosophy. In addition to this debate, this section outlines the concern for a broader sense of the concept of ethnophilosophy that goes beyond the context of the African philosophy debate.

The second section concentrates on the negritude movement, which counts amongst the most sophisticated discourses on African identity and otherness. My approach to this movement refers mainly to Senghor's theory. The choice to discuss Senghor's approach relies on two premises. First, Senghor was an outstanding poet and intellectual, but he also acted as a Senegalese statesman and was an important leader of pan-Africanism. Second, Senghor represents a kind of ideal-type of leader combining both of the qualities of a leader imagined by Plato – namely, philosopher and king (*The Republic V*). He was committed as both an original African thinker and a statesman.

This section also examines criticism of Senghor by thinkers such as Adotevi and Fanon. They both denounce the fact that Senghor identifies black people with emotion and also that he reproduces and adopts racist clichés inherited from colonialism. They criticize Senghor's containment of black people in their past and in self-contemplation. For the two of them, by his attitude, Senghor avoids political debate and also ignores cultural diversity characterizing the black African world in favour of his essentialist quest for black people's identity. The chapter concludes by highlighting the revolutionary dimension of Senghor's theory and its political implications: the assertion of the right to be different and the relevance of the negritude strategy of endorsement, consisting of inverting stigmas to relativize Western discourse and remove it from its pedestal.

Chapter 5 approaches pan-Africanism as a call for racial solidarity among black people all over the world and as a concern for African political emancipation and unity. This develops in four sections. The first section deals with the idea of pan-Africanism as a call for solidarity among black people that was launched by the African diaspora in the late nineteenth century as part of the struggle against their domination and exploitation at the hands of white people. This call spread out all over the world and took different forms, such as trans-Atlantic pan-Africanism, trans-American pan-Africanism, sub-Saharan pan-Africanism, to name a few.

The second section explores the personalities and theories of some of the founders of pan-Africanism. Booker T. Washington, for example, is considered for his promotion of the idea of black empowerment through vocational education, work and black people's accommodation theory. Marcus Garvey encouraged the return of black people to Africa. A. J. Cooper is illustrious by way of both her "theory of value" and her struggle for access to higher education for black students. Through his life and work, W. E. B. Dubois has established himself as the epitome of pan-Africanism.

The third section concentrates on African heirs of pan-Africanism. This movement's passing on of the torch from its founding fathers to its African heirs at the Fifth Pan-African Congress in Manchester, in 1945, ushered in an important change: the quest for emancipation and unity of African countries had eclipsed the racial claim that characterized the original approach of the founding fathers. The Concern for African unity was driven by two opposing tendencies: supporters of the creation of a state superstructure called the "United States of Africa" and defenders of a progressive realization of this entity that takes into consideration the needs of African people. The creation of the Organization for African Unity (OAU) in May 1963 allowed the controversies between these two tendencies to be overcome. In 2002, the African Union (AU) was established as a replacement for the OAU.

The fourth section examines some important figures amongst African heirs of pan-Africanism, including Nkrumah, Fanon, and Gaddafi and briefly explores various debates about the future of African unity. The chapter concludes with a short evaluation of the potential grounds for a contemporary search for African unity. The effects of globalization and the emergence of new social and political configurations bring new challenges for pan-Africanism thought, particularly through ideas such as Afropolitanism (Mbembe 2005; Selasi 2005) and cosmopolitanism (Appiah 2007).

Chapter 6 concentrates on democracy in Africa. It is divides into three sections. The first section covers briefly the etymology and general history of democracy. This concept came from the contraction of two Greek words: *demos* (people) and *kratos* (power), and it referred, in Ancient Greece, to a specific form of governance that was based on equality of rights and participation of people in public affairs. After a long eclipse, this form of governance has returned thanks to social contract theorists including Hobbes, Locke, and Rousseau, among others. Nowadays this concept implies more than a simple reference to a mode of governance, because it includes a normative reference concerning political organization. This change of meaning took place thanks to the growing awareness both of rights and the capacity of individuals to create by themselves their own forms of social and political organization, regardless of their religious and metaphysical backgrounds.

The second section looks at African experiences of democracy. It rests on the premise that liberal democracy was the original mode of governance inherited from the Berlin Conference and colonization. First accepted by the majority of African countries, soon after their emancipation this system was rejected in favour of a variety of principles of governance, including single-party rule, diarchy rule, no-party rule and multiparty rule. Changes that occurred throughout the world in the last decades of the twentieth century contributed to the development of a new political awareness among African people regarding their rights and struggle for a humanized living. The emergence by the 1990s in various African countries of Sovereign National Conferences can be considered as illustrative of this process.

The third section examines the (re)discovery of liberal democracy by African people. It concentrates principally on the debate between supporters of a universalistic approach to democracy and protagonists of a local approach. For the former, democracy is a universal process which is valid for people and cultures all over the world regardless of their history and cultural peculiarities. For the latter, it is important to emphasize the particular values and experiences of democracy within every people and culture. This debate highlights the dilemma of African intelligentsia: the choice between the global market paradigm and the preservation of African values and traditions of governance. This chapter pleads for the promotion of constructive values for humankind from every concerned culture.

Chapter 7 explores the idea of African civil society. It addresses the use of the concept of civil society to refer to African social and political realities. A range of thinkers and scholars argue that this usage isn't appropriate because of the concept's Western origin and trajectories. In addition, the African social and political context is far from that of the Western reality. Defenders of the idea of African civil society support two assumptions: the universalism characterizing civil society and, subsequently, its role as an indication of progress achieved concerning the process of democracy.

The chapter goes on to analyze the theoretical background of African civil society. For a range of thinkers, this dynamic emerged as an result of the recommendations and policies of international funding institutions such the World Bank and International Monetary Fund (IMF). For another category of thinkers and activists, this movement results from people's own consciousness and aspiration to democracy. Beyond those two considerations, there is the fact that civil society has, in Africa, its own modes of expression and action. According to the context, it can be viewed either as a mode of resistance to colonialism or as a means to struggle against the postcolonial state, for example.

The third section analyzes some paradigms of African civil society, including the resistance against colonial rule, the platform for civilized (Westernized) people, the expression of African nationalism, among others. The fourth section focuses on the question of the future of African civil society. Regardless of theoretical differences, civil society constitutes the core of African social and political life. Beyond the conventional organizations forming part of civil society, the emergence of new civic organizations can be observed, such as Balai citoyen, Y en a marre, Filimbi, and LUCHA, supporting a new approach to political practice in Africa. Those movements are essentially linked by young people regardless of their ethnic origin, gender, or religious beliefs. They rely on people's political consciousness, and they make claims for the respect of their respective country's fundamental laws or constitutions, political alternation, and the full achievement of human rights.

Chapter 8 discusses the issue of globalization and its social, cultural, and political implications for contemporary Africa. It is divided into two sections. The first section examines the hypothesis that globalization is a threat – due to homogenization and clash of civilizations – to cultures of humankind. It denounces this premise as being based on the illusion of cultural purity, which subsequently neglects cultural diversity and specific modes of development of cultures, particularly through contact and exchange within them. This section also raises the existence of new technologies concerning African development and the requirement for new and constructive policies.

The second section expands on the development of an African state under the influence of the global market. This section outlines the effects of international funding institutions on both African states and African people, particularly through their requirements for financial supports and measures – such as structural adjustment programmes – aiming at securing global market balance to the detriment people's well-being. As a result, African states have been deprived of their sovereignty and are dependent on foreign will.

The general conclusion of this volume is in the form of an epilogue which focuses on one of the most emblematic and outstanding African political personalities and activists: Nelson Mandela (1918–2013). This examines the strategies and philosophical background of Mandela's struggle against apartheid as a denial of democracy and equality of human beings. It is divided into three sections. The first evokes the general context of Mandela's struggle for the right to live, while the second briefly explores his first steps and commitments. The last section concentrates on Mandela's political philosophy and strategies, including collective action and democracy, African nationalism, and pluralism.

The back and forth between philosophical intuitions and contemporary African reality formed the basis of my methodological background. I relied on philosophical premises as well as on historical, sociological, and cultural approaches to identify the traits of this philosophy and to lay out its rational basis.

Chapters are designed as autonomous units of reflection. Beyond their common concern for innovative and emancipating African political thought, each chapter can be discussed independently from the others. I use concepts such as polis, city and country interchangeably. I go beyond their respective and common interpretations to focus on the idea of an organized political community, or a city-state (Held 2006, 11). In writing this volume, it is my desire to invite readers to join the debate on contemporary African social and political philosophy, enriching the topics and aspects of this volume that are not yet sufficiently entangled.

Notes

1 Kasanda, Albert. 2015. Analyzing African Social and Political Philosophy: Trends and Challenges, *Journal of East-West Thought*, 2(5), 29–50.
2 Concerning the debate on these concepts, see *American Historical Review*, June (2009); Wagner (2015).

1

APPROACHING CONTEMPORARY AFRICAN SOCIAL AND POLITICAL PHILOSOPHY

Introduction

Notwithstanding the increasing number of treaties and textbooks on African philosophy, it is distressing to note that most of these publications pay very little attention to contemporary African social and political philosophy.[1] At best, the few that deal with this issue enclose it in categories such as "ideological thought" (Smet 1980, 277–282; Lopes 2001, 13–16; Ngoma-Binda 2013), "nationalist-ideological philosophy" (Lajul 2013; Serequeberhan 1991), or "liberation philosophy" (English and Kibujjo 1996, 6). In addition, many people confine this philosophy to the thinking of individual leaders such as Nkrumah (1909–1972), Nyerere (1922–1999), Senghor (1906–2001), and Fanon (1925–1961). As a result, they limit this philosophy to the exclusive preoccupation of professional thinkers and politicians, regardless of the commitment of African people to searching for a better mode of social and political organization.

This chapter denounces the scarcity of publications in this area of study. It also rejects the propensity to reduce African social and political philosophy to the status of an ideology, a single theory or individual thought of an African leader or professional philosopher. To state this positively, this chapter addresses African social and political philosophy as a common and inclusive quest for better paradigms of social and political organization on behalf of African people, their scholars and leaders. It also perceives this philosophy as aiming at the clarification of concepts in use in the African social and political sphere.

This chapter is divided into three sections. The first deals with both the nature and duties of African social and political philosophy. It maintains that this philosophy is a rational search for better modes of social and political organization and governance on behalf of African people and their leaders and intellectuals. This search not only includes theoretical debates and the clarification of concepts, but also deals with African people's daily challenges for a better life and creating a humanized community (*faire société*).

The second section analyzes the relationship between contemporary African social and political philosophy and ontology. For a range of African thinkers and Africanists, the search for African quintessence is essential to characterizing African philosophy. This section introduces some light and shade, showing that African social and political philosophy is not merely a subcategory of a general philosophy, nor is it exclusively concerned with metaphysical issues. On the contrary, this philosophy also deals with matters related to people's daily lives, such as diseases, poverty, and social and political organization. Based on this observation, this volume postulates the lack of concordance between African social and political philosophy and ontology.

The last section concentrates on the relationship between contemporary African social and political philosophy and the concept of ideology. It denounces the opinion that these notions are synonymous with each other. Subsequently, this section argues that despite their theoretical proximity, these concepts cannot be used to stand in for one another as they both include a slight difference in meaning and practice.

1.1 The idea of contemporary African social and political philosophy

A range of African scholars and Africanists define contemporary African social and political philosophy in terms of national and ideological thought. Scholars such as Nkombe and Smet (1980), for example, think that this philosophy has developed as an antithesis of racist assumptions justifying the black slave trade and colonialism as well as the denial of human dignity to black people. For them, this philosophy developed into various trends including the African personality, pan-Africanism, negritude, African socialism, and African humanism, to mention those few. In addition, Nkombe and Smet (1980, 278) observe that

> Nous sommes ici en présence d'une littérature de combat, *qui n'est que rarement élaborée en philosophie systématique et explicite,* dont l'objectif est la libération des Noirs. Cette libération est politique, économique et culturelle.
>
> *(Emphasis added)*

> (We are here in the presence of a literature of combat, which is rarely developed as a systematic and explicit philosophy, whose concern is the emancipation of black people. This emancipation refers to political, economic and cultural spheres.)

It is my feeling that this approach gives rise to a set of questions concerning, for example, the precise concept of political philosophy to which Nkombe and Smet refer. In other words, what do they mean by "systematic and explicit philosophy"?

Are the known formulations of what they call national ideological philosophy not systematic and explicit enough to match their expectations? This questioning is central because it refers to a major debate concerning both the genesis and the development of African philosophy, as illustrated by thinkers such as Hountondji (1983, 33), Bodunrin (1991), Wiredu (1991), and many others. It is not the purpose of this section to excavate this debate. So let us leave it aside and concentrate instead on defining contemporary African social and political philosophy.

Lajul (2013) thinks that national ideological philosophy stands for contemporary African political philosophy. This philosophy is viewed as specific to some African states and statesmen. It is thought to have roots in the African precolonial legacy which was adapted to match contemporary African challenges. Concretely, according to him, this philosophy is "represented by the works of politicians like Nkrumah, Nyerere and Senghor. [It] involves an attempt to evolve a new and, if possible, unique political theory based on traditional African socialism and family-hood" (Lajul 2013, 48).

In the same way of thinking, Serequeberhan (1991, 20) considers that national ideological philosophy can be viewed as

> embodied in the assorted manifestos, pamphlets and political works produced by the African liberation struggle. The writings of Nkrumah, Touré, Nyerere, Fanon, Senghor, Césaire, and Cabral, and the national liberation literature as a whole, harbor differing politico-philosophical conceptions that articulate the emancipatory possibilities opened up by the African anticolonial struggle.

In addition to that, Serequeberhan also thinks that there is a very thin difference between national ideological philosophy and other trends of African philosophy including philosophic sagacity and professional philosophy. In this respect, he notes that national ideological philosophy "might be seen as a special case of philosophic sagacity, in which not sages but ideologues are subjects. Alternatively, we might see it as a case of professional political philosophy" (quoted in Lajul 2013, 47).

These approaches identify contemporary African social and political philosophy with the anti-colonial struggle. They confine this philosophy to the status of single and individual theories set out by African thinkers and freedom fighters such as Nkrumah, Nyerere, Senghor, Cabral, and others. It is my feeling that anti-colonial thought is a legitimate part of the African intellectual legacy and an important contribution to African political thinking. But I can hardly imagine this legacy as embodying all of the African social and political issues of today. It is also my belief that the above-mentioned perceptions rest on the mistaken logic of taking a part to represent the whole. They reduce this philosophy to problems concerning African emancipation and safekeeping of African traditions. Such a reductionism is hardly sustainable nowadays. It is my feeling that in order to be relevant, every approach to the African social and political situation must take into consideration the dimensions of both time and space. In this respect, it can be observed that the definitions of African social and political philosophy discussed here pay very little attention to mutations occurring in African societies. They pass over or ignore new challenges faced by African people and their constant creativity in tackling them. On the contrary, these approaches concentrate on the restoration of pristine and precolonial forms of indigenous cultures as a solution to the challenges of contemporary Africa. They can be viewed as reductive of the horizons of African social and political philosophy.

It is also my feeling that the equivalence established by Serequeberhan between national ideological philosophy, philosophic sagacity and professional philosophy needs a bit of clarification and criticism. The idea of philosophic sagacity was introduced by Odera in his attempt to identify African philosophy's trends. He thinks that

> philosophic sagacity is a reflection of a person who is a *sage and a thinker*. ... *As sages, they are versed in the belief and wisdoms of their people*. But *as thinkers, they are rationally critical and they opt for or recommend only those aspects of the beliefs and wisdoms which satisfy their rational scrutiny.*
>
> (Odera 1991, 51, emphasis added)

From this definition, it can be outlined that philosophic sagacity is a philosophy of individual African wise men. In this view, the most important thing is the "philosophical wisdom", regardless of the topic at stake. This makes it different from social and political philosophy, whose concern is defined in terms of critical analysis of political concepts, the search for people's well-being, and reflection on the management of power and better organization of the city. In other words, the former can be viewed as a general approach to the problems of daily life, while the latter can be considered a specific and specialized view on any social and political issue.

Professional African philosophy stresses the universality of philosophy through its technical dimension. It relies on professionally trained philosophers (Odera 1991, 48). This philosophy can be considered as a meta-philosophy, because it addresses various claims as to whether some given thoughts qualify or don't qualify as philosophy. This approach is so general that it evokes a feeling of standing far from the nature and central preoccupations of contemporary African social and political philosophy. Resting on these observations, I believe that contemporary African social and political philosophy cannot be assimilated into this approach, because it has its own characteristics and duties including the clarification of concepts and providing a justifiable rationale for institutions in charge of organizing the polis and the promotion of people's excellence.

The duty to clarify political concepts aims at ensuring common understanding of shared concepts and their normative implications. A common understanding of political concepts is important because those concepts are contestable and their meaning often depends on the contexts in which they are formulated. For instance, the concept of democracy has a variety of meanings; thus it is imperative to clarify, each time it is applied, from which perspective and for which purpose it is being used so that the accurate meaning can be pointed out. The use of this word by the ancient Greeks differs from its use by communist and liberal thinkers, for example. From this perspective, it can be argued that clarification of concepts helps to avoid anachronism and amalgam in the presentation of political ideas and related principles. It can be also observed that the notion of democracy, for example, describes a form of organization of the polis but refers also to an ideal and set of values structuring the polis, such as freedom, plurality, and people's participation. Democracy, as many other political concepts, is not a single idea to be used without any epistemological precaution. It includes a multitude of meanings whose philosophical backgrounds rely on both the history and context of their production.[2]

The idea of providing a justified rationale for ruling institutions refers to the fact that contemporary African social and political philosophy deals with both the setting up and the management of the common world. It is its duty to scrutinize people's everyday experiences of alliances and collective actions (Matthieu 2004; Fillieule and Pechu 1993; Jordan 2003) to establish rational frameworks and sustainable policy. It is my belief that the reference to the common world constitutes the nourishing sap, the lifeblood, and the compass of contemporary African social and political philosophy. I owe the idea of common world to two theoretical backgrounds. First, I rely on Arendt's analysis of the human condition, in which common world refers to the political sphere where people reveal themselves to each other as equal as well as mutually commiting to create a political community together. This sphere is characterized by the propensity of human beings to act (*actio*) together (Arendt 1994).

Second, I refer to the African notion of *Ubuntu*. Tutu (1999, 34–35) thinks that the concept of *Ubuntu* includes more than a mere description of African traditions, as it refers to the normative requirements for a good life. Such a life is characterized by strong humanistic feeling and balanced relationships between individuals and community as well as with nature. In sum, this concept highlights the requirement for equity and better life for everyone. It is my feeling that the planting of contemporary African social and political philosophy in such a soil accounts for the way by which this philosophy has been able to specify its objective and forge its own identity.

The search for excellence and well-being of citizens is a permanent concern of any social and political philosophy. From ancient times up to now, nobody has ignored this topic, even if every thinker assigns to it a specific content and sketches differently its modalities of achievement. Socrates, Plato, Aristotle, Rousseau, Locke, Hobbes, Rawls, and many others have explored this issue in different ways and according to their respective context. On this basis, it is my belief that African thinkers also must deal with the range of challenges facing the continent, including poverty, human rights, gender, democracy and equity (Appiah 1992; Gyekye 1997; Odera 1997).

The issue of power is also fundamental for contemporary African social and political philosophy. The first generation of African leaders considered the conquest of political power as a duty and founding principle of their political commitment.

Nkrumah's aphorism is illustrative of this aspiration: "seek ye first the political kingdom, and all else shall be added onto you". Nevertheless, it is worth noting that in postcolonial Africa, power is still a burning debate. Political leaders, activists, and scholars hardly agree concerning its nature, justification, and management. For all of them, questions regarding who governs the polis and by which principles does he/she perform such a duty, for how long and according to what modalities does he/she have to rule, constitute a major point of protest. This debate is illustrated through theoretical analysis but also by upheavals that have shook African countries in recent decades (Appiah 1992; Wiredu 1997; Gyekye 1997). Recall, for example, the events following the presidential election in Ivory Coast with candidates Gbabo, going for another term as president, and Ouattara, the opposing candidate, when results were contested by Gbabo (2010–2011); the fall of Compaoré in Burkina Faso (2014); as well as current social and political upheavals in Burundi (2015) and the Democratic Republic of Congo (2016). This context illustrates the need for a deeper and more critical reflection aiming at improving both the civic and political cultures of the African people and their leaders.

1.2 Contemporary African social and political philosophy and ontology

Consideration of the relationship between contemporary African social and political philosophy and ontology raises the question about the relevance of ontological assertions in the sphere of political thought and vice versa. On the one hand, a range of African thinkers view the search for African quintessence as an unavoidable background to the analysis of issues of the polis; on the other hand, some of them consider the political sphere as a space of empirical attitudes and pragmatism. This makes the issue complex, since it involves two opposing perceptions of philosophy: the idea of philosophy as *theoria* and the perception of philosophy as *praxis* (Kasereka 2015, 312–321). Beyond this antagonism, questions about the identity and the role of African philosopher can be detected (Kasanda 2003, 16–17).

The debate around Tempels's work *Bantu Philosophy* (1947) contributed to denouncing the Western epistemological and cultural imperialism denying the existence of any specific philosophy outside of that inherited from the Greek tradition. This debate also highlighted the difficulty for African thinkers themselves in providing a consensual definition of African philosophy (Bell 2002, 21–22; Hountondji 1983, 33–46). However, it is agreed – at the expense of the concept of philosophy itself – that African philosophy exists and it is even anterior to Tempels's work and its subsequent debates (Bidima 1995, 9). This statement can also be considered as valid concerning African social and political philosophy, because the search for better management of power and social matters has always been the concern for African societies, even before colonization. Theories of African humanism and African socialism, for example, rest on this legacy. For many scholars and political leaders, the *Bantu*'s ontology as described by Tempels constitutes an invaluable *vade mecum*. The idea of Senghor on African peculiarity and the theoretical postulates of

Nyerere about *Ujamaa* can be viewed as relying on the same background, which means the search for African quintessence (Bidima 1995, 13).

This ascendancy of ontology in African social and political thought raises suspicion concerning two stumbling blocks of political philosophy, formerly denounced by Strauss in his famous lecture, *Qu'est-ce que la philosophie politique?* (Strauss 1992). First, there is a temptation to consider political philosophy as an application, a case study or a subcategory of general philosophy, by transposing problems and concepts of the latter into the sphere of politics. The search for African quintessence characterizing the political reflection of various African thinkers made this temptation more than likely. Theories such as negritude, African socialism, and African humanism, for example, are among those most affected by this criticism, because they seem to put more emphasis on ontological speculation than on daily struggles of African people (Adotevi 1998, 51–80).[3] This attitude can be compared to what Arendt denounced in her criticism of Plato's political philosophy: the withdrawal of the thinker from the common world and the subsequent hierarchy between *theoria* and *praxis* (Arendt 1994, 115). According to Arendt, Plato's attitude created a deep misunderstanding about the relationship between philosophy and politics. For her, the concept of the world refers to a common world which includes factors that cannot be reduced to the metaphysical; for instance, the issues of poverty, social exclusion, and gender, among others.

The second stumbling block concerns the propensity to perceive African social and political philosophy as a systematization of opinions that are already present in the polis. This perception is the Achilles' heel of trends in African social and political philosophy relying on both the exhumation of African past and the rehabilitation of African cultures. The risk of transforming opinion into philosophical discourse is permanent in a context where, in the name of African traditions, the words of (political, religious, or other) hierarchies are viewed as expressing wisdom and truth, and consequently they are very seldom questioned and debated. It is my belief that contemporary African social and political philosophy should be aware of both stumbling blocks discussed here.

1.3 Is contemporary African social and political philosophy an ideology?

The identification of contemporary African social and political philosophy with the notion of ideology seems to be a common practice within both the African and Africanist intelligentsia. Works such as those of Thomas (1965), Bénot (1969), Langley (1979), Young (1982), Mbonimpa (1989), Smet (1980), and Ngoma-Binda (2013) attest to this trend. Such a pattern cannot be taken for granted. On the contrary, it raises the question of the epistemological basis of this trend, which requires the theoretical extension of the concepts and the conditions for such an equivalence. In other words, the issue at stake consists of clarifying the meaning given to each of the two concepts as well as the nature of the bond uniting them.

Let us focus on the notion of ideology. From an etymological point of view, the authorship of this notion is attributed to Destutt de Tracy (1754–1836). This French thinker and politician coined this term from two Greek words, "*eidos*" and "*logos*", to refer to "the science of ideas". He aimed at the elaboration of a discourse on the genesis, the development, and the decline of ideas. In other words, it can be argued that for him, the notion of ideology can be understood in the same way as disciplines such as zoology (science of animals), cosmology (discourse on the cosmos), and theology (discourse on god), and so on. Thus, the aim is to identify what the notion of ideology includes, particularly for our times and concerning African social and political reality.

Napoléon Bonaparte made use of this expression to mock thinkers who, according to him, were unrealistic speculators whose studies were disconnected from reality, particularly concerning social and political issues. From this perspective, the concept of ideology refers to false theories or ideas based on a mistaken perception of realities. Karl Marx, in his famous work *The German Ideology*, made use of this concept to denounce the Hegelian philosophers who, in his view, were not able to see reality correctly because they walked headlong into it. These philosophers were accused of reversing the relationship between consciousness and material life as they were incapable of understanding that it is not the consciousness that determines material life but rather the opposite (Colas 1996, 380–381).

According to Foulquié (1992), the concept of ideology refers to

> un système plus ou moins cohérent d'idées, d'opinions ou de dogmes, qu'un groupe social ou un parti présente comme *une exigence de la raison*, mais *dont le ressort effectif se trouve dans le besoin de justifier des entreprises destinées à satisfaire des aspirations intéressées et qui est surtout exploité pour la propaganda*.
>
> *(Emphasis added)*

> (a roughly coherent system of ideas, opinions or dogmas, that a social group or a party presents as a requirement of reason, but its last purpose is the need to justify structures aiming at the satisfaction of interested aspirations and which is mainly exploited for propaganda.)

Beyond these multiple evocations, it should be emphasized that the notion of ideology refers to a set of ideas and beliefs that ground and modulate the action of a collectivity within a given spatio-temporal framework. The use of this concept in African social and political philosophy implies specific nuances to outline its specific features. A first feature is the consideration of this notion as an antithesis of the colonial ideology of domination and exploitation of black people. This approach is noticeable through works such as those by Bénot (1969, 1975), Smet (1980), Thomas (1965), and Young (1982). It evokes, for example, the Negritude movement as an ideology of self-affirmation in opposition to the colonial ideology that considers black people to be savage and barely a caricature of human beings. In this respect, the already mentioned postulates of Nkombe and Smet (1980, 278) can be viewed as largely confirmed.

The second feature concerns the development of politico-religious movements as a mode of resistance to spiritual domination. Religion, especially through the emergence of African messianisms such as Kimbanguism, Kitawala, and Matsouanism, assumes an ideological role in order to justify the beliefs of African populations and to legitimize and modulate their actions (Ngoma-Binda 2013; Gérard 1969; Gilis 1960). Finally, the third feature is the struggle for political emancipation. This aspiration was expressed through mass movements, but also through social and political theories such as *Ujamaa*, consciencism, and theories of dependence and unbalanced relationships between the centre and the periphery.

All those theories are also placed, regardless of their respective nuances and aims, in the same category of African ideological thought. An awareness of the diversity of meaning attached to the notion of ideology in the African context leads to the questioning of the very relevance of any equivalence established between the concepts of ideology and philosophy. For Ngoma-Binda (2013), for example, this practice can be justified to the extent that, on the one hand, an ideology can be viewed as a philosophy as far as it is open to universal values. It is thought to be critical and flexible. On the other hand, a philosophy can be considered as ideological as soon as it assumes a dogmatic and rigid behaviour and becomes deviant, militant, uncompromising, and probing of consciousness.

Ngoma-Binda's explanation is easy to understand as he defines circumstances under which both African social and political philosophy and ideology can stand one for the other. It is my view that the idea of equating those concepts without any epistemological precaution relies on rather hazardous and reductive assumptions about the very meaning of political philosophy and ideology. Both the concepts refer to different realities, and subsequently they cannot replace each another. In other words, African social and political philosophy cannot be reduced to the concept of ideology. In his study of main ideologies of the twentieth century, Faye (1996) highlights the difference between both the concepts as well as denouncing fallacies and mistaken use of philosophical discourses in support of ideologies such as Stalinism and Nazism. Following the analysis by Faye (1996, 9–13), I maintain that contemporary African social and political philosophy is not reducible to ideology. This philosophy should use its critical vigilance and sense of freedom to oppose both the blindness and the authoritarianism that characterize the notion of ideology.

1.4 Conclusion

This chapter discussed the definition of contemporary African social and political philosophy as well as its relationship to ideas of ontology and ideology. Contrary to widely shared opinion, this chapter considered this philosophy as a rational search for the clarification of social and political concepts, better management of political power, and the achievement of better modes of governance.

The search for African quintessence is at the core of African philosophy. A wide range of African leaders and thinkers consider African social and political philosophy as also being concerned with this search. This chapter denounced this point of view, arguing that this philosophy cannot be reduced to a subcategory of a general philosophy nor to an ontological search. It deals with issues such as poverty and social exclusion, power and democracy, to name but a few.

The previous section explored the relationship between African social and political philosophy and ideology. This distinguished different uses of the concept of ideology in the African context, and it denounced the reductionism of making both concepts stand one for the other. Subsequently, it reinforced that the idea that African social and political philosophy doesn't coincide with the notion of ideology as it relies on critical vigilance and a sense of freedom, whereas ideology involves blindness and authoritarianism.

Notes

1 The review by Ngoma-Binda (2013) of publications on African political philosophy during the last five decades can be viewed as illuminating in this respect. See also Boele van Hensbrock (n.d., 9).
2 See Held (2006).
3 For more comments on African ontology, see, for example, Brown (2004).

2

SOURCES OF CONTEMPORARY AFRICAN SOCIAL AND POLITICAL PHILOSOPHY

Introduction

The previous chapter began with an observation about the scarcity of studies and publications on contemporary African social and political philosophy. This observation might lead one to believe that this philosophy is conceived and expressed only by professional philosophers[1] and political leaders. To think in this way can give rise to a misunderstanding of this philosophy, particularly to a failure to acknowledge the diversity of its protagonists, sources, and forms of expression. Mazrui's observation is relevant in this respect:

> *there is a tendency in the study of African political thought to rely almost entirely on political ideas that have been captured in writing.* A major underlying assumption is that thought is not thought unless it is also written. Because of this assumption *there has been a relative disregard of the oral tradition in political thought, and almost complete obsession with political writers and with the written speeches of political leaders.*
>
> *(2001, 99, emphasis added)*

Following Mazrui (2001, 99), it can also be observed that "there are three major sources for the student of political though in Africa – the oral, the written and the political behavior of Africans".

It is my feeling that Mazrui's range of sources of African social and political philosophy is not exhaustive. Many traditions of thought have been ignored, silenced, and excluded from the mainstream and predominant thought. I can speak of silenced subaltern voices and agencies. This chapter aims at exploring those traditions as well as finding out their relevance to contemporary African social and political thought.

The chapter is divided into five sections. The first section addresses the relationship between creative writing, particularly African literature, and African social and political philosophy. It denounces the philosophical tradition based on Plato's approach in which creative writers, since they are dealing with shades of grey, cannot access real and political knowledge. Therefore, they are disqualified from taking part in the management of the polis. To put things positively, the section highlights some common points between African literature and African social and political philosophy as well as emphasizing the relevance of the former for the latter.

The second section examines a range of African political behaviours and their relevance for the development of African social and political thought. It discusses different paradigms and their inherent philosophical views as well as associated modes of governance such as gerontocracy, the warrior paradigm of governance, the oneness paradigm, and the wisdom paradigm.

The third section explores urbanization policy in Africa as an indicator of policies set up by the ruling authorities. The proliferation of townships and the increasing poverty of the African population cannot be viewed as neutral. On the contrary, they are indicative of political strategies and policies set up in many African countries.

The fourth section focuses on religious phenomenon as a mode of social and political resistance. This section denounces the premise restricting religion to the role of the opium for the people. On the contrary, it stresses the ambiguous role of religion concerning social and political change as well as insisting on the revolutionary potential of religion in Africa. The last section analyzes the contribution of both African art and music to the awakening of African people's political consciousness and commitment. It approaches African music texts that go beyond emotions and require hermeneutic tools for an accurate interpretation. In sum, this chapter calls for more attention to neglected African ways of making and thinking politics.

2.1 African social and political philosophy and literature

The relationship between social and political philosophy and literature conveys a great debate regarding the capacity of creative writers to produce philosophical discourse in accordance with the African context. In this respect, it seems important to know whether African creative writing can offer a critical appraisal of the political crisis confronting African societies. In other words, can an African creative writer set an ideal standard for African states? (Okolo 2007, 1). If so, what can be his/her impact on African political thought and people's daily lives? Exploring the ideal state, Plato denies political and ruling status to creative writers because, for him, their works are superficial, subjective and untrue (*République V; X*). This premise relies on the view that literature is simply a shadow or a pale copy of reality. As Melberg (1995, 10) reminds us,

> poetry delivers a poor and unreliable knowledge ... since it is a second-hand imitation of an already second-hand imitation [while] the philosopher comes

closest to first-hand knowledge of real reality: he can see the form or ideal form of things and can therefore disregard imitations.

According to Plato's view, reality belongs to the world of ideas which is accessible only to the philosopher. The philosopher has access to first-hand knowledge because he can see ideal forms of things and therefore disregard their imitation. A range of African thinkers assimilated this view, assigning to areas of study such as art, literature, and music the exclusive role of entertainment and subsequently disqualifying them from expressing philosophic challenges. Aristotle denounced this attitude toward creative writers. For him, fiction is unfettered by accidents and randomness of everyday life, and it can be better than facts at getting to the heart of the matter. There is no evidence that mimetic art and literature overstimulate emotions and enclose reality in the emotional sphere. Aristotle pleads for both the recognition and the inclusion of imaginative writers and artists as active agency in social and political life. Contrary to Plato, he considers prudence as the most important political virtue (Politics).

More and more studies outline the relationship between African social and political philosophy and literature. Scholars such as Appiah (2004), Bidima (2004), Okolo (2007), and Rettová (2013a) denounce the prejudice confining literature to the sphere of entertainment and consequently denying its ability to conceive and express philosophical ideas. Bidima (2004, 557), for example, observes that

> both literature and philosophy have a number of intertextual relationships, particularly as regard three domains: namely, political philosophy, philosophy of history, and aesthetics. One illustrative fact in particular should be emphasized. The political tendency of the critique of ethnophilosophy among African francophone philosophers ... owes a great deal to numerous passages in *Discours sur le colonialisme* by the poet Aimé Césaire; which is yet another confirmation of the extent to which philosophy and literature both journey along similar paths.

Along the same lines, Mudimbe (1988) illustrates the relationship between literature and political philosophy through his analysis of ups and downs of African approaches to Marxism. He considers that African creative writers understand this political perspective in terms of three strands: the domestication of political power, the criticism of colonial life, and the celebration of African sources of life. In this respect, he notes that

> In [African] literature, this position is expressed in three major ways: first, in terms of domestication of power (E. Mphahlele, Mongo Beti, and Sembene Ousmane); secondly, in a criticism of colonial life (Chinua Achebe, D. Chraïbi, F. Oyono); and thirdly, in the celebration of the African sources of life (A. Loba, A. Sefrioui, Cheikh Hamidou Kane).
>
> *Mudimbe (1988, 91)*

Relying on the existentialist philosophy developed by Sartre (1905–1980), for whom theatre was the main mode of broadcasting ideas, Rettová (2013a) shows both the capacity and the relevance of literature in expressing philosophical questions, reaching the public, and calling them to an interactive debate. She illustrates this challenge through her study of Swahili Congolese songs by Sando Marteau[2] who, writing and singing in African language (Swahili), explored topics such as poverty, social and political violence, the concept of time, the situation of African women, migration, development, and peace (Rettová 2013b).

In the same vein, Okolo (2007, 13–22) examines the relationship between African literature and political philosophy. For her, both these disciplines are equally interested in dealing with ideas. The affinity between them is noticeable in areas such as their moral influence on human behaviour, their effect on language, their contribution to development, their social incidence, and their political criticism. In this regard, she observes that

> Essentially, philosophy and literature are theoretical disciplines. *The interest of the philosopher is in ideas*; by examining and clarifying ideas philosophy affects mankind and the world in a critical way. … *The concern of the imaginative writer is equally with ideas. By using words* to invent characters, dialogue and plot, *the imaginative writer can challenge traditional views as well as offer prophetic insights into human life*.
>
> (Okolo 2007, 13, emphasis added)

The interest of African creative writers themselves on political issues has become more noticeable than ever in recent decades. The majority of writers have become aware that their own relevance depends on how far they are engaged in social and political debates. As Achebe reminds us, "An African creative writer who tries to avoid the big social and political issues of contemporary Africa will end up being completely irrelevant" (quoted in Okolo 2007, 2).

It is my feeling that various creative works including, for example, those of Sembene Ousmane (1970, 1972), Soyinka (1976), Brink (1979), Ngugi wa Thiongo (1993), Kourouma (1998), Ouloguem (2003), Dovey (2008), and Bofane (2008), among many others, attest to the relationship between African literature and African social and political philosophy. They defy conventions by promoting interdisciplinarity between African political philosophy and literature. The awareness of new configurations and interdependencies at work in the world can be evoked in support of this development which, as already suggested, leads to a broader, more inclusive, and more emancipatory approach to African social and political philosophy.

2.2 African political behaviour and precolonial traditions

A range of African scholars and Africanists postulate the existence of indigenous cultures prior to the infusion of Islamic, Judaic, and Christian ideologies (Brown

2004, 158; Mbiti 1970). These cultures constitute a precious legacy for contemporary Africa. Works such as those of Wiredu (1996), Karp and Masolo (2000), Appiah (1992, 2007), Gyekye (1997), and Lajul (2013), to quote just those few, can be viewed as illustrative in this respect. The propensity to exhume the African precolonial past also characterizes both the political theories and the practice of leaders such as Nkrumah, Nyerere, Senghor, Kaunda (1924–), and Cabral (1924–1973). They all assert the existence of valuable precolonial traditions, and they claim to dig them up and to rehabilitate them for the sake of the contemporary African state.

Analyzing the political legacy of African precolonial times, Mazrui (2001, 99) outlines a set of paradigms serving as theoretical background to the behaviour of various African leaders: the elders' tradition, the warrior's tradition, the wisdom tradition, and the monarchical trend. The elders' tradition considers age as the archetypal criterion for legitimacy and moral and political authority. Elders and ancestors are given a central position in the social and political hierarchy. This attitude rests on two premises: loyalty towards traditions and elders as well as resistance to change, or conservatism. A range of African leaders have claimed that they benefit from their membership in the "elder" category through, for example, the possibility to stay in power endlessly in the name of alleged elder virtues such as moral authority, continuity, and stability. Some proclaimed themselves members of the social category of elders regardless of their real age. This was the case with leaders such as Kenyatta, Houphouët Boigny, Mobutu, and Banda, among others. They granted themselves titles like *Mzee* (ancient), *Vieux* (old), and *Tata* (father) to legitimate their own authority (Mazrui 2001, 103) and to gather respect for themselves from the people.

The warrior's paradigm insists on obedience and submission to orders rather than on respect based on age and regard for traditions. This model relies on the rejection of any kind of criticism or democratic debate. Proponents of this paradigm put emphasis on hierarchic spirit and automatic obeyance of those who rule. In the history of African political ideas, personalities such as Idi Amin Dada (1923–2003) and Bokassa I (1921–1996), among others, can be viewed as representative of this paradigm (Mazrui 2001, 104).

The paradigm of wisdom stands on a binary reasoning structured around two ideas: from one side, the master, the teacher, the wise knowledge holder, whose duty is to guide, to instruct, and to initiate his ruled; on the other side, the people, who are viewed as disciples, apprentices, ignorant, and powerless. It is my feeling that to some extent, this paradigm includes a paternalistic attitude. Nyerere, for example, called himself *Mwalimu*, the Swahili concept representing teacher and knowledge holder.

Monarchic behaviour privileges the principle of oneness (*monos*), or singleness. Various features based on this paradigm have been used in African modes of governance. Recall, for example, calls for worship of the leader and respect for the consecration of power as well as the ostentation and pretention of rulers in their claims to stand apart from common genealogy, having a particular destiny arising from their divine or royal ancestry. Personalities such as Nkrumah (Appiah 1992, 161) and Banda (Englund 1996), for example, can be viewed as embodying such a practice. For many long decades, this theoretical model dominated the one-party regimes in Africa.

These paradigms reveal the role given to African cultures and traditions by African postcolonial leaders in their management of the *res publica*. These cultures and traditions were perceived as an alternative to Western hegemony. Apart from the seductive appearance of this argument, two potential deficits should be noted. First, this way of thinking includes the risk of anachronism concerning contemporary African reality, because it pays very little attention to changes actually happening in Africa. The idea of homogeneity of cultures and people is, in reality, contested thanks to the current globalization process and outwards and inwards migratory flows as well as concerning the new self-representations of African people (Appiah 2007; Mbembe 2005).

Second, even though referring to African traditions, this approach to power reflects a surprising convergence with the colonial view, as it includes a glaring dualism putting to one side the elite, the holders of power, knowledge, and wisdom, and to the other side, the powerless and the common people. This convergence constitutes a challenge for African thinkers, particularly at this time when the continent is in search of new ways of being and alternative modes of governance.

2.3 African cities and urbanization policies

Gordon (2008, 220) considers that African political philosophy differs from Western political thought because it deals with the legacy of both colonization and racism. This legacy is noticeable in the discourses of African leaders and through policy and urbanization of African cities. The development of shanty towns in the majority of African countries and the existence of racialized areas, such as Soweto or Alexandra in South Africa, reveal the poverty of the population, but it also shows the limits of national policies and the want of political will to fight this scourge. This context can be viewed as a source of information about contemporary African social and political challenges, particularly poverty, solidarity, and social justice.

Fanon came to the fore in African political thought through his struggle against colonization. He was attentive to the living conditions of a colonized people. He also paid close attention to the urbanization and configuration of African cities. For him, their division into poor and racialized areas cannot be viewed as something spontaneous and politically neutral. This division expresses the will of ruling authorities to keep people dominated and in conditions of poverty and misery with the effect of reinforcing their dependence and submission. Fanon (1979, 67) thinks that the lack of infrastructure that characterizes the majority of African countries is one of the reasons why they depend so much on the metropolis, but this also serves as an indicator of policies and strategies set up by the ruling system. He thinks that colonization relies itself on the petrifaction of African countryside by considering the people as being opposed to progress and by promoting urban cities which, in their turn, are structured according to racial, economic, tribal, or ethnic segregation (Fanon 1979, 65).

It is my feeling that this configuration of African cities is not exclusively the outcome of colonial rule. It is also the expression of the political and economic attitudes of African postcolonial rulers. Achebe's novel *Anthills of the Savannah* (1987), for example, denounces the extent to which African leaders themselves impede the development of the African people for the sake of their own privileges. The work of De Boeck and Plissart, *Kinshasa: Tales of the Invisible City* (2004), reveals the same preoccupation: street children accused of witchcraft, poor accomodation, lack of salubriousness in the Democratic Republic of Congo's capital city, to mention a few. Paradoxically, this state of affairs puts the spotlight on the (lack of) responsibility of people in charge to promote better living for everybody.

In sum, it is my belief that the gap between the poverty and lack of salubriousness which characterize highly populated zones and the luxury of other residential areas constitutes a sign of, and can be considered a source of information about, the everyday experience in Africa as well as the political strategies needed to bring into reality a more human and humanizing society.

2.4 Religion

In *L'avenir d'une illusion*, Freud (1995) makes a bet on the extinction of religious activity thanks to the progressive triumph of reason. The analysis of both Marx and Engels considers religion as an ideology whose purpose is to contribute to the alienation of the people. They famously approach religion as the "sigh of the oppressed creature, the soul of a heartless world, ... the opium of the people". Current debates on secularization and disenchantment of Western societies (Gauchet 1989) also stand on this theoretical background owing largely to thinkers such as Durkheim (2008) and Weber (1994). While the latter explores the role of religious cultures concerning the development of industrial civilization and Western people, particularly the interaction between religion and economy, the former approaches religion as self-representation and a fundamental link between every society.

Contrary to the premise of secularization, the Latin American theology of liberation, for example, postulates a positive role for religion concerning social and political development. Instead of viewing religion as the opium of the people and a backward cause, protagonists of this way of thinking consider it as the ferment for social and political change, particularly in favour of the poor and the most disadvantaged. Therefore, they rely on the postulate that every human being is both the creature of God and in his image. In the name of God's kingdom, proponents of this theological view stand against all kind of injustice, structures, and attitudes that destroy this image (Houtart 2006; Dussel 1995).

Parallel to this *theological* movement, there is also the Latin American *philosophy* of liberation. According to Sanchez (1999, 46),

> En America latina oficialmente a principio de la década de los setenta en Argentina, y … va a dedicarse a desarrollar una serie de temas comunes entre sus miembros, relativos a los conceptos de dependencia, liberacion, pobreza, ética de la alteridad, humanismo e identidad, entre otros.[3]
> (Officially this philosophy emerged at the beginning of the 1970s in Argentina, … and its protagonists concentrate on a range of common topics related to concepts such as dependence, liberation, poverty, ethics of the otherness, humanism and identity.)

The founders and main thinkers of this philosophical trend, including Dussel and Zea, for example, denounce every kind of discrimination and oppression of Latin American people. As Sanchez (1999, 47–48) observes,

> Zea, por medio del analisis de les ideas filosoficas, densemascara la ideologia subyacente de aquellos grupos dominantes que dirigen los destinos de sus naciones. Dussel apela a la *Exterioridad* como aquelle instancia critica que toda forma de pensamiento y todo modelo de vida rechaza, olvida e ignora.
>
> *(Emphasis original)*
>
> (Through the analysis of philosophical ideas, Zea denounces the ideology of the ruling groups leading the destiny of nations. Dussel focuses on the exteriority as the critical instance that is refused, forgotten, and ignored by several paradigms of life.)

Consideration of both the theology and the philosophy of liberation makes me think of what Foucault qualified as "political spirituality" (Kintges 2011, 106–107), which means the ability to sustain the imbrication between social and political claims and religious aspirations. Standing on this premise, I believe that religion cannot be perceived as a socially and politically neutral phenomenon or, to put it another way, an attitude concerned exclusively with issues of the hereafter. On the contrary, it is called to actively engage in the transformation of the present world. Now the issue becomes about which principles and world views guide this transformation.

In this respect, I can note three paradigmatic discourses or ways of thinking: attesting speech, contesting thought, and protesting discourse. Attesting speech focuses on legitimizing the status quo. This attitude aims at the integration of people into the existing regime, praising the virtues of the ruling regime and its achievements. The existence of political parties that have affinities with religious denominations illustrates this category of discourse.

Contesting thought includes two opposite trends: on the one hand, it involves a critique of tradition, which is considered as decaying and conservative, and on the other hand, it evokes a fundamentalist attitude contesting any innovation deemed harmful. Current debates on discrimination against women, homosexuality, and the wearing of the veil, for example, show how far this thinking influences not only the social and political spheres, but also the religious domain.

Protesting discourse implies radical breaks ranging from secession to subversion. The secular conflict between Catholics and Protestants reveals disagreements concerning religious dogmas and theological views, but it also provides information about the different social and political conceptions being implemented by the ruling authority. In the same way, it would be wrong to ignore the effects of current Islamic activism on the political thinking and policies of our societies (Rivière 1997, 176).

African history is filled with ups and downs in the relationship between religious belief and social and political struggle (Ela 1980, 2003; Mbembe 1988; Diagne 2001). The emergence of African messianism and the current proliferation of various religious movements can be viewed as illustrative in this respect. The effect of African messianism on social and political thought is one of the most explored case studies. The concept of messianism refers to the fact that the founders of the (new) African religions were viewed as prophets and God's messengers who, like Jesus, were persecuted righteous. Many of them proclaimed the imminent end of the world of injustice and exploitation of black people. They announced instead the beginning of a heavenly city where injustices suffered by black people no longer exist. They are convinced that African religion will be led by a "black Messiah" or a *sui generis* God, totally different from the one announced by white people. Kimbanguism and Matsouanism are, in this regard, eloquent examples (Mwene-Batende 1982; Ngandu Nkashama 1998; Rivière 1997, 158–166). These religious movements can be viewed as part of black people's resistance against colonial authority. They consider colonization as a negation of the social, political, moral, or religious principles that governed precolonial African societies. They cannot accept such a loss of autonomy and power. Therefore, religion served as a platform to mobilize against the enslavement and acculturation of black people (Rivière 1997, 160–163). Apart from the traditional religions and conventional faith communities, including the Catholic, Protestant, Jewish and Muslim faiths, there is an impressive proliferation of religious sects and communities in contemporary Africa. They all played an ambiguous social and political role in the postcolonial state, and they are still performing this role today. By their doctrines and practices, several religious groups dissuade believers from all civic and political commitment to the benefit of their spiritual prosperity and life beyond. The role of the Catholic Church, for example, in the process of peace, justice, and democracy building in recent decades can be viewed positively as it illustrates both the new consciousness of citizens and the place of religion in African society. In addition, recent development of Islam in Africa, including the emergence of extremist trends, constitutes an important issue concerning tolerance and democracy.

It is my feeling that religion represents an important source for social analysis and political thinking in Africa. This represents a great challenge for African scholars and Africanists in identifying the real borderlines between religion and political philosophy as well as to address and clear up their ambiguities and sophisms.

2.5 African art and music[4]

African music constitutes the aesthetic background of African daily life. It has been the subject of a variety of commentaries and studies.[5] A range of people speak of it in high terms, while some others despise it. Monga (2009), for example, illustrates both these attitudes in his essay on the arts of living in Africa. From the outset, he distinguishes two kinds of African music: popular music, and subliminal or transcendental music. He describes popular music as successful and oriented to common people. This music resonates warmly throughout the African continent and beyond. It mimes and arouses collective dizziness more than it expresses subtleties; it is

> insipide, construit sur un tempo binaire et lancinant, dénué de subtilités harmoniques mais acérée sur une mélodie vaguement charmeuse et des hululements enroués d'un vocaliste qui chante faux sans donner le sentiment d'en éprouver le moindre complexe.
>
> *(Monga 2009, ebook location 799)*

(often tasteless, built on a binary and throbbing tempo, devoid of harmonic subtlety ... [this music is] anchored on a vaguely charming melody and hoarse hoot of a vocalist who sings out of tune without any complexity.)

Transcendental music is based on a sophisticated and technical work aiming at symmetry, harmonic subtleties, and the elevation of the soul. As an illustration, Monga evokes the work of the artists Lokua Kanza and Richard Bona. Concerning the latter, he notes that

> Son style se démarque résolument du minimalisme technique qui réduit trop souvent cette musique [africaine] à une gesticulation répétitive, aride et lancinante. Sa musique est ponctuée de fulgurance et constamment traversée du souffle de l'universel.
>
> *(Monga 2009, ebook location, 1309)*

(His style is marked resolutely by technical minimalism that often turns [African] music into a repetitive, arid, and throbbing gesture. His music is marked by flashes and constantly refers to universal breath.)

It is my feeling that Monga's approach to African music ignores the variety in African music production in concentrating only on these two categories of popular music and transcendental music. This approach can be viewed as reductive of African music. Monga's analysis includes a real dichotomy, opposing emotion on one side and reason on the other. It is my belief that a strict separation between emotion and reason is not sustainable since they both are part of our human identity and attitudes. Emotion cannot be reduced to the expression of low instincts and negative performances. On the contrary, it can be viewed as a source of great artistic and intellectual creativity, even concerning political commitment.

Contrary to Monga's approach, it can be argued that African music includes a variety of trends and genres as it forms the accompaniment to the various circumstances of life from birth to death. This music can also be viewed as an important source of African political thinking. My hypothesis is that there is a fruitful relationship between musical performance and African philosophical thought. This fertility is noticeable, for example, through the use of music as a text, a kind of written down speech – *parole consignee* – that is thus protected against the erosion of time as well as submitted to both explanation and interpretation by human beings.

The performative and narrative paradigms are viewed as two modes of expression used in Africa (Rettová 2013b, 158). According to Drewal, in this continent, perfomance is

> a primary site for the production of knowledge, where philosophy is enacted. ... [P]erformance is a means by which people reflect on their current conditions, define and/or, re-invent themselves and their social world, and either re-enforce, resist, or subvert prevailing social orders.
>
> *(Quoted in Rettová 2013b, 159)*

Performance is rooted in social life and African politics so that it expresses the complex power relationship at work between various social and political agents. Concerning music particularly, it should be recognized that African music is not a narrative or an argumentative discourse in the way philosophic discourse can be. Beyond melodies and subtleties of harmony, it performs its role of production of knowledge and philosophical inquiry through "entextualization"; that is to say, through the process of making the musical discourse "an entity from which fragments can be extracted and language produced as a unit – a text – which can be removed from the scope of interaction" (Rettová 2013b, 161). This way of thinking allows music to be treated as text rather than stressing the inherent harmony and melody (Rettová 2013b, 171). Such an attitude implies a meticulous hermeneutic work of explanation and interpretation, which African thinkers and Africanists should be aware of.

2.6 Conclusion

This chapter explored a range of often neglected sources of contemporary African social and political philosophy. It pointed out the contribution of African creative writers to this philosophy, and it discussed a variety of African traditional paradigms determining the behaviour of African leaders, including gerontocracy and the warrior and wisdom modes of governance.

This chapter also examined the role of religion as a ferment of social and political change. Based on Latin American philosophy as well as theology of liberation, it was argued that religion is not a neutral process. As such, it plays an important social and political role that can be viewed as a support, a critique, or a full rejection of ruling institutions. The experience of African messianism and the current proliferation of religious movements as well as the role of conventional churches in the development of African countries and their policies can hardly escape the attention of the African political thinker.

Music is present in every context of African daily life. Approached as a text, it represents an real support for social and political thought. This observation is also true concerning urban policy in African cities. The increasing poverty of African cities reflects policies at work not only during colonial times, but also under postcolonial regimes. The increasing number of townships illustrates the poverty of African people and at the same time calls for a deep understanding of the real causes and consequences of such a situation. In order words, it calls for a rigorous social and political analysis.

Notes

1 According to English and Kibujjo (1996, 7), the concept of professional philosophers refers to African scholars that are "identified not only by their credentials as doctors of philosophy ... but also by a common conviction that philosophy, in the strictest academic sense, is a universal practice. ... It essentially involves reflection, criticism, argument, and written peer review." This expression was used principally in the debate about the existence of African philosophy to oppose proponents of ethnophilosophy (Mudimbe 1988, 160; Odera 1991; Bodunrin 1991). It is used here just to refer to the institutionalization of African (social and political) philosophy.
2 Sando Marteau is the stage name of Jean Papy Kabange Numbi, a Congolese artist and singer living in Lubumbashi, Democratic Republic of Congo whose work is entirely in Swahili. For further details, see Rettová (2013b, 43–53).
3 See also Cerutti Guldberg (1997, 11–23).
4 This section concentrates particularly on African music. For comments on African art and political thought, see, for example, Bidima (1997); Diagne (2011).
5 See Tchebwa (1996) and Stewart (2003).

3

EXPLORING THE ANTECEDENTS AND PRECURSORS OF CONTEMPORARY AFRICAN SOCIAL AND POLITICAL PHILOSOPHY

Introduction

Contemporary African social and political philosophy doesn't emerge *ex nihilo*. It has various antecedents, including the legacy of African precolonial societies, the painful experience of slavery and colonization, the struggle for emancipation, and the emergence of African postcolonial states. This chapter relies on the premise that those antecedents represent a relevant background to the understanding of major trends characterizing this philosophy today. Therefore, it develops a survey of some important thinkers and theories as well as outlining their implications for today's African social and political thought.

This chapter is divided into two sections. The first section concentrates on the African precolonial legacy. It explores a range of values and practices of African precolonial societies viewed as being of interest for contemporary Africa, including ideas such as political participation, consensus, and communitarian mind. These ideas are evoked by a range of African thinkers in order to improve current African political institutions and build alternative social and political paradigms (Gyekye 1997; Wiredu 1996).

The second section focuses on the contribution of the black diaspora. It analyses the theories of personalities such as Africanus J. B. Horton (1835–1883), Edward W. Blyden (1832–1912) and J. E. Casely Hayford (1886–1930). In addition, this exploration puts emphasis on the relevance of those theories for today with respect to African political challenges such as African modernization, African revival, self-governance, and democracy.

3.1 The legacy of African precolonial communities

A range of African scholars and Africanists including Gyekye (1997), Wamala (2004), Wiredu (1996), Brown (2004), and Odera (1991), to name a few, affirm the existence of a philosophical and political legacy from African precolonial societies. Their statement echoes the postulates already formulated by the first generation of African leaders and fighters for independence – such as Nkrumah, Nyerere, Senghor, Cabral, and others – in this respect. First, this statement denounces both Western ethnocentrism and the evolutionist view that considers African societies as savage and uncivilized; that is communities without rules or social and political organization (Kodjo-Grandvaux 2013, 196; Mudimbe 1988, 1–23). Second, it expresses the desire of African leaders to build new institutions according to the people's expectations and cultural paradigms. In other words, they wanted to set up institutions that match African people's desire for emancipation and development.

The interpretation of this legacy still constitutes a burning debate amongst African scholars and Africanists. Thinkers such as Kabou (1991), Etounga-Manguelle (1991), and Smith (2003) think that the claim for African traditions is useless as those traditions constitute a huge handicap to African development. The fathers of African independence and a range of contemporary African scholars are opposed to this view because they consider the legacy as an important and unavoidable tool in the building of new African nations. For them, African traditions include values and practices that can be viewed as revealing the democratic spirit of African precolonial societies. Let's briefly explore some of those values.

3.1.1 Democracy: The people's will and political participation

Democracy is commonly considered as the rule of the people by the people and for the people (Held 2006; Odera 1998). This approach to democracy puts emphasis on the people's role concerning the management of the polis and the articulation and legitimation of power. Based on this definition, it seems paradoxical to speak of democracy in precolonial African societies, because those societies did not have any structure of democracy as is known today. In other words, they were to some extent monarchical, and their political organization did not include an elected parliament or separation of powers. In this respect, Wamala's questioning on the issue can be viewed as relevant:

> Would we be using the concept of democracy in the commonly accepted sense when we apply it to social and political organizations that seemingly did not have any ideas about the separation of powers and checks and balances, and, moreover, in a sociocultural milieu that lacked political parties in which there were no periodic elections? *Could traditional African societies have been democratic unconsciously, i.e. without elaborately worked out ideas of democracy?*
>
> *(2004, 435, emphasis added)*

Various African scholars including Gyekye (1997), Wiredu (1997, 2004), and Wamala (2004) approach this debate on the premise that democracy involves multiple definitions and different modes of articulation. They emphasize various elements from African traditions that they think of as fairly representing African democratic spirit. Gyekye (1997), for example, postulates that although they realized democratic principles in a specific way, African precolonial societies were indeed democratic. For him, while contrary to Western practices incorporating structures such as multiparty rule, an electoral system, parliamentary government, separation of powers, and accountability, African precolonial societies applied different modes of functioning, these also guaranteed the participation of people in power and their ability to control and to legitimate their ruling authorities and social and political structures. Gyekye's statement relies, first, on a range of testimonies and African proverbs. Second, it stems from the political experience of the Akan ethnic group from Ghana.

Concerning testimonies, Gyekye refers to British anthropologists, such as Fortes and Evans-Pritchard, for whom

> The structure of an African state implies that *kings and chiefs rule by consent. A ruler's subjects are as fully aware of the duties he owes to them as they are of duties they owe to him*, and are able to exert pressure to make him discharge these duties.
>
> *(Quoted in Gyekye 1997, 117, emphasis added)*

He also mentions testimony from Dugald Campbell, who noted that in Africa

> [all] government is by the will of the people, whether it be the choice and coronation of a king; the selection of a man to fill a new chieftainship; the framing, proclamation, and promulgation of a new law; the removal of the village from one site to another; the declaration of war or the acceptance of terms of peace: everything must be put to the poll and come out stamped with the imprimatur of the people's will. No permanent form of negro government can exist save that based four square on the *people's will*.
>
> *(Quoted in Gyekye 1997, 117, original emphasis)*

Gyekye thinks that in the African context, the contract uniting the leader and the led can be established in both ways: with the framework of formal political structures and through established relationships. This contract can also be shaped by the awareness of the leader that his authority derives from the people. Consequently, the rulers and the ruled have a mutual contractual bond between them. Gyekye also thinks that numerous maxims express this reciprocal bond. In this respect, he points out a series of maxims from different African ethnic groups in which the link between a chief and his people is viewed as sacred. For Basoko people, for example, "A chief is a chief by the people". The Lovelu people of Transvaal consider that "chieftainship is people", while for the Ndebele from Zimbabwe, "The king is the people. ... He who praises [the] king praises [the people]" (Gyekye 1997, 117).

Similar proverbs and reasoning can also be found in many other African societies. In the Luba community (Democratic Republic of Congo), for example, people perceive the relationship between the ruler and the ruled in the same way. For them, political leadership is not compatible with a split between the ruler and the ruled. The following proverbs can be considered as illuminating in this respect:

> *Mukalenga wa bantu, bantu wa mukalenga.*
> (The leader depends on his own people just like the people depend on him.)
> *Bukalenga budi tshinsangasanga, mukulu mukuata, muakunyi mukuata.*
> (Power is union, the support of everyone, the elders and the youngers, is necessary.)

Based on these testimonies, Gyekye postulates the existence of democratic spirit in precolonial African societies. For him, in those societies, people participated in political power and also had the faculty to sanction their rulers. Thus, those societies can be viewed as democratic. Gyekye notes that

> It may be inferred from the observations so far made that *the principle of popular government is firmly established in the traditional African political practice, for the chief has to rule with the consent of the people*. In the event of the chief's failure to make his rule reflect the popular will, he could be defied or deposed.
> *(Gyekye 1997, 117, emphasis added)*

Wamala (2004) goes in the same direction in his discussion of an alternative form of democratic government based on the idea of consensus. Commenting on the precolonial society of Ganda, he sees the existence of ideas and practices such as the principle of subsidiarity as reflecting the democratic nature of this community. For him, this principle is central to Ganda's democratic system as it rests on the complexity of their social relationships. It is expressed in the following proverbs:

> *Obukulu Ndege, tezivugira mumazi.*
> (Authority is like an ankle bell: it doesn't ring in water.)
> *Omukulu takulira mpya bbiri.*
> (A master cannot rule two homesteads.)
> *(Wamala 2004, 436–437)*

For this society, responsibility at the family level must not be taken away by the city; neither should that of the city be taken by the state. Behind this is the idea that higher social and political units have legitimate authority to promote the well-being of the lower units, helping them to achieve good lives as well as to reach their potential (Wamala 2004, 437).

The statements of both Gyekye and Wamala appear seductive because they highlight other possible approaches to democracy. For these two thinkers, the idea of democracy is not univocal, because it has multiple modes of expression and interpretation. However, it is my feeling that their reasoning comes across a range of problems. First, their statement includes a risk of anachronism, since they both refer to societies that don't exist anymore. In the best of cases, they speak of communities that are presently undergoing a process of change due to globalization and its subsequent effects concerning the inwards and outwards flows of people as well as the new cultural, social, and political configurations (Mbembe 2005, 1–2; Appiah 2007, 101–113). In this regard, it is hardly possible to speak of African traditions and values, because those traditions and values are not, like unmovable stones, realities that are out of the reach of any change. It is my feeling that no culture is a static reality. Every culture evolves and transforms itself through contact and exchange with others (Kasanda 2013b, 226–234). This mobility allows, as Nouss (2005) observes, the emergence of new cultural, social and political paradigms.

Second, Gyekye and Wamala ignore various deficits of precolonial African societies concerning democracy, equality of rights, and gender parity, for example. In this respect, attitudes of precolonial African societies can be compared to the practice of democracy in ancient Greece, where discrimination of slaves, children, and women was accepted as part of the rules. However, it is worth asserting that this perception of democracy is hardly sustainable as practices of democracy have themselves largely improved (Held 2006). Premises related to equality of human beings and their equal participation in political life are nowadays better articulated and more established in various countries than in the past. Based on this observation, it is my feeling that it is necessary to mitigate the postulate describing African precolonial societies as democratic. Democracy is a complex process that includes, on the one hand, a range of fundamental norms and practices and, on the other hand, the daily struggle for all people to bring this ideal into reality.

3.1.2 The African communitarian spirit

Searching for an alternative to capitalism, various African leaders have opted for African socialism. Their choice relied on the perception that socialist views characterized African precolonial societies. Those societies represent the matrix and the prefiguration of modern socialism. According to Senghor, for example, the communitarian spirit represents the very nature of Negro-African societies. In this respect, he wrote that "Negro-African society is collectivist or, more exactly, communal, because it is rather a communion of souls than an aggregate of individuals. ... *We had achieved socialism before the coming of the European*" (quoted in Gyekye 1997, 146, emphasis in the original).

Nyerere also considers socialism as being anchored in precolonial African societies. He thinks that African socialism is both the expression and the recognition of African cultural heritage. He perceives the African state as an extension of a fundamental project: the familyhood. He sees the rehabilitation of this paradigm as a fundamental challenge for the construction of new African society. Thus, he developed his political project of African socialism, better-known as *Ujamaa*, the Swahili expression for familyhood or community spirit. According to Nyerere, *Ujamaa* is an attitude of mind through which African people's aspirations for unity, identity, equality, and human dignity can be achieved (English and Kibujjo 1996, 295).

Nkrumah shares this line of thought. For him, the matrix of socialism can be found in African traditional societies, particularly through African communalist thought. He declares in this respect that

> If one seeks the social-political ancestor of socialism, one must go to communalism. Socialism has characteristics in common with communalism. ... In socialism, principles underlying communalism are given expression in modern circumstances. ... Socialism is a form of social organization which, guided by the principles underlying communism, adopts procedures and measures made necessary by demographic and technological developments.
>
> *(Nkrumah 1970, 73)*

It is worth stating that the alleged socialist nature of African traditional societies served as a pretext in support of socialist ideology in Africa. This option emerged in the context of antagonism between the East and the West, better-known as the cold war. This context generated various cleavages and alliances between African countries. Regardless of their reference to African roots and traditions, postcolonial African countries divided themselves into two opposing blocs. The countries on the side of African socialism constituted one bloc, under the leadership of the Soviet Union, and the countries supporting capitalism formed another under the rule of both the USA and Western Europe. The majority of African leaders served as intermediate agents in this global antagonism, fighting and killing each other in the name of foreign ideological interests. Both the Angolan (1975–2002) and the Mozambique (1977–1992) civil wars can be viewed as proxy battles in the cold war. It is my feeling that this context revealed the weakness of the hypothesis that communitarian thought is a fundamental characteristic of African people. In addition, the rapacity of African leaders concerning power as well as their submissiveness toward world ruling powers can be viewed as the main hidden agenda behind the mention of African communalist thought (English and Kibujjo 1996, 253–320).

3.1.3 Consensus making and good governance

The idea of consensus is often evoked as characterizing African precolonial societies. This is very present in the studies of many African leaders and scholars who have analyzed those societies. Gyekye (1997, 118), for example, attests to the centrality of consensus in conducting public affairs. It is based on both freedom of expression on public issues and consensual discussion among members of the community. Drawing on Sithole's observations in this respect, he notes that

> "[in Africa] things are never settled until everyone has had something to say. [The traditional African] council allows the free expression of all shades of

opinions. Any man has full right to express his mind on public questions" and "to carry out any program required the sanction of the whole clan or tribe".

(Gyekye 1997, quoting Sithole, 118)

Gyekye also evokes Nyerere's perception of a traditional mode of governance in Africa which privileges both popular discussion and the subsequent agreement between everybody: "in African society *the traditional method of conducting affairs is by free discussion*" (quoted in Gyekye 1997, 118, emphasis added).

For Gyekye, this freedom of speech implies that despite the lack of political parties and democratic conventional structures such as a parliament, for example, African traditional societies provided a specific forum through which everyone – including those with opposing views – could express their own opinions on public issues. The imperative of such a public debate was to conclude with some form of general agreement between all the members of the community. Describing the process which is controlled by elders, Nyerere himself notes that "elders sit under the big tree and talk until they agree. *This talking until you agree is essential to the traditional African concept of democracy*" (quoted in Gyekye 1997, 118, emphasis added). In other words, it can be deduced that this "talking until you agree" aims at ensuring harmony in the community.

However, Gyekye (1997) also points out that for a range of thinkers – such as V. G. Simiyu, for example – precolonial African societies were not democratic because they were hierarchical, gerontocratic, non-egalitarian, and even ignorant of women's rights. This criticism can be compared to the one often raised concerning Athenian democracy in which women, children, and slaves were not considered as citizens and were thus deprived of the right to take part in the management of public affairs. It is my belief that democracy is always a process. Some values that are important today have not always been so. Concerning women rights, for example, it is not only the ancient Greek that did not recognize them, but also our modern democracies if we consider the development of women's rights in countries such as the UK, France, the USA, and many others. The concern for women's rights developed progressively, and there is still a lot to do. It is a long-term process. The history of democracy continues to develop, and new social and political axiology are created thanks to the progress of human consciousness and the emergence of new configurations. It would be prejudicial to restrict the idea of democracy to a narrow and limited approach. Therefore, following Gyekye (1997, 118–119), I recognize the existence of elements of democracy in precolonial African societies. But I do not lose sight of the risk of anachronism, the propensity to blindly graft attitudes of the past onto today's African societies. This is one of the stumbling blocks of ethnophilosophy as denounced by Eboussi-Boulaga (1977).

The resort to the idea of consensus raises questions concerning both its purpose and its philosophical background. At first, it is my feeling that there is a need to dismiss the generalization underlying the issue since there is a big difference between African political systems, which means that the political systems of the past were not all the same. These systems promoted different attitudes about the value of consensus as social and political practice. Wiredu, for example, states that

> It is ..., perhaps, easier in the context of the less centralized social orders to appreciate the necessity of consensus. Where the exercise of authority ... rested purely on moral and perhaps, metaphysical prestige, it is obvious that decision by the preponderance of numbers would be likely to be dysfunctional. But it is more interesting to observe that the habit of decision by consensus in politics was studiously cultivated in some of the most centralized [groups]. ... By a somewhat paradoxical contrast, the authorities in some of the comparatively less militaristic of the centralized societies ... seem to have manifested less enthusiasm for consensus in political decision making.
>
> *(1997, 304–305)*

The idea of consensus implies more than a political expedient aiming at avoiding and preventing crisis. It refers to social and interpersonal relationships based on two premises: the existence of common interests and the epistemological idea that knowledge is both dialogical and social progress. According to Wiredu (1997, 303), consensus is the expression of an inherent view of social interaction and interpersonal relationships between adults. It is an axiomatic paradigm concerning collective action. In the context of the struggle for democracy, for example, the most important aspect of this paradigm is awareness of the community's interests and their relation to the ambitions of individuals. Wiredu uses the metaphor of a crocodile having two heads and just one stomach to illustrate his reasoning. His argument develops as follows:

> this adherence to the principle of consensus was a premeditated option. It was based on the belief that ultimately the interests of all members of society are the same, although their immediate perceptions of those interests may be different. This thought is given expression in an art motif depicting a crocodile with one stomach and two heads locked in [the] struggle for food. If they could but see that the food was, in any case, destined for the same stomach, the irrationality of the conflict would be manifest to them.
>
> *(Wiredu 1997, 306)*

Wamala (2004, 437–438) thinks that consensus relies on the epistemological idea that no one has a monopoly on knowledge and political wisdom. Everyone needs the acknowledgement and opinions of others. Social and political issues must be addressed until a general agreement is reached as to what should be done. Relying on this background, I suggest that the idea of consensus as "an endless discussion between elders" constitutes a misleading metaphor that emphasizes the authority of elders, or the gerontocracy mode of governance, to the detriment of the whole community. This approach doesn't take into consideration evoked ideas of mutual recognition and dialogue.

The illusion of unanimity and harmony that underlies this approach constitutes another stumbling block. People think of unanimity and harmony as characterizing African traditional societies, and subsequently they think of both these values as being equivalent to consensus. This perception seems totally illusory and intrinsically contradictory, as the idea of consensus always presupposes a dissension calling for deliberative debate between all concerned members of the society. As Wiredu (1997, 304) notes, "[consensus] usually presupposes an original position of diversity. However, this doesn't mean that consensus was always attained. Nowhere was African society a realm of unbroken harmony."

Conflicts among lineages and antagonism between social and ethnic groups have always existed and are still prevalent in Africa. In this regard, "people's know-how" remains the main tool for addressing social bonds, exploring underlying conflicts and identifying opportunities to settle on one opinion rather than the other without alienating anyone.[1] This "know-how" consists of the patience and political convictions of African people, but it also includes the capacity for African traditional systems to include everyone, be they groups or individuals. In other words, nobody is kept in a minority position, excluded or permanently reduced to silence. If the idea of consensus is accepted, there is a great challenge to contemporary African social and political philosophy to include the powerless into its dynamics, making real use of a policy of consensus.

3.2 Modern precursors of contemporary African social and political philosophy

Contemporary African social and political philosophy is also rooted in African history, particularly the painful experiences of slavery and colonization. These events can be viewed as inaugural indices of African modernity. Contrary to a widespread belief, modernity began for Africa with the denial to its people of all its constitutive and recognized values, including the rational capacity and dignity of human beings. Africa and black people were considered as a negative for modernity and a symbol of backwardness (Thomas 2011, 727–728; Mbembe 2013).[2] Various voices from the Negro-African diaspora have denounced this situation since the second half of the nineteenth century. Contributions of thinkers such as Crummel, Africanus J. B. Horton, Edward W. Blyden and Casely Hayford are still relevant even for today's African social and political debate. Let's explore some of their main arguments.

3.2.1 Africanus J. B. Horton: The plea for the constitution of modern African states

The interdiction of the slave trade propelled England to the rank of the most active marine police in tracking recalcitrant slave traders. The concern to assure a land of freedom for freed slaves and to relocate slaves captured in the triangular trade led British authorities to establish, in 1787, the colony of Sierra Leone, whose capital city took the name of Freetown (Wesseling 1991, 142). According to Iliffe (1998,

203), approximately 74,000 freed slaves were deported to this colony, which they came to dominate soon after thanks to the education received from the Church Missionary Society – an education based on the British cultural model. On the basis of this education, many people from Sierra Leone dreamed about their political freedom and development. Horton is one of those who embodied this aspiration.

Horton was born from parents of Igbo origin who had been captured by the British police on their crossing to slavery and relocated in Sierra Leone. He studied at King's College London and at the University of Edinburgh, where he received his doctorate in medicine. During his stay in London and Edinburgh, he adopted the nickname of Africanus, associated with both his identity and his political commitment. This choice presented great challenges in a context where to be different – that is, to be "someone coloured" – was not the best asset. It was during this period that pseudoscientific racist doctrines, of which Gobineau was one of the most striking proponents, were expanding (Delacampagne 2000, 164–174).

A report of the House of Commons from 1865 proposing the disengagement of the British from Western Africa provided the opportunity for Horton to express his political concerns. This report stipulated that British policy

> should be to encourage in the native the exercise of those qualities which may render it possible for us more and more to transfer to the natives the administrations of all the Governments, with a view to our ultimate withdrawal from all, except probably Sierra Leone.
>
> *(Boele van Hensbroek 1998, 39)*

In reaction to this report, Horton published *West African Countries and Peoples* in 1868. This work includes a description of Western British African communities and proposals for the implementation of African institutions. Horton aimed at the creation of autonomous West-African British colonies built according to the example of Australia and Canada. Concerning his own native land, he wanted, for example, a constitutional government that

> forms the basis of his administration, consisting of House of Assembly which should be composed of men elected by the people, as it will be difficult for his Government to stand without popular confidence, and the only means by which that can be secured is by giving the people the power to elect one branch of the Legislature. … Each member should have landed property, be over the age of twenty-two, and be properly educated.
>
> *(Boele van Hensbroek 1998, 44).*

Horton was persuaded of the possibility to modernize African states in agreement with the principle of self-government. According to him, the model of a modern and tested state represented a guarantee for the successful modernization of African countries. Therefore, he insisted that British authorities should consider the task of promoting and overseeing the advent of modern African states as fully part of their duty.

People viewed Horton either as a paternalist thinker or as echoing the voice of British domination because of his favourable attitude towards a British protectorate. The idea of a British protectorate relies on an unspoken scepticism concerning African people's capacity to carry out their own development by themselves. The fear of ethnic antagonism and the epistemological prejudice that considered Europe as the exclusive source of reference for both knowledge and development fed popular imagination in this respect. Non-Western people, particularly black people, were viewed as children needing paternal protection and assessment.

Horton's attitude about a Western protectorate anticipates and illustrates a bone of contention amongst African emancipation fighters in the second half of the twentieth century. Some of those fighters considered Horton's idea as a good strategy towards emancipation, while some others opposed such a proposal. As an illustration, two cases can be evoked: the Congolese and Guinean emancipation processes. Concerning Congolese emancipation, for example, in 1956 a Belgian scholar, Joseph Van Bilsen (1913–1996), suggested that the Belgian government postpone the emancipation of Congo for around 30 years, the period of time estimated as being adequate to prepare and make the Congolese people ready to rule on their own (Van Bilsen 1994).[3] This proposal was received differently in the Congolese community. Some leaders, such as members of an African consciousness group led by the Congolese Christian wing led by Reverend Malula, supported this project; while some others, particularly those moving under Kasa-Vubu's leadership contested this deadline, which they thought too lengthy. Social upheaval and the creation of Lumumba's political party (the Congolese National Movement) inverted the course of events, and Congolese emancipation took place earlier than thought on 30 June, 1960 (M'Bokolo 1985, 201). Taking into account the current bankruptcy of this country after more than 50 years of emancipation, many people wonder whether Van Bilsen's proposal was not the right one.

French African colonies also underwent a twisted process in their moves towards emancipation. The Guinean leader Sékou Touré was one of the symbols of resistance to French manipulation and desire to postpone emancipation. In the late 1950s, he rejected the staged route to emancipation suggested by French president Charles De Gaulle, voting "NO" in a French referendum on the issue. For him, this choice should be grounded on the desire of Guinean people for freedom and dignity; as he declared, "We prefer poverty as free men to riches as slaves" (quoted in Martin 2012, 92). As a result, the relationship between France and Guinea was disturbed, and Guinea became isolated among African French colonies (Martin 2012, 92). Thinkers such as Césaire, for example, celebrated the courage of Sékou Touré's actions (Mudimbe 1988, 91).

The struggle for sovereignty remains up to this day a crucial negotiation for African people, whose development seems to rely on foreign vectors such as international aid and science and technology in addition to the effects of the predominant neo-liberal globalization process. So, the issue at stake is knowing how to break both African dependency and Western hegemony while living under such a model? This can be viewed as a long-term process. The emergence of new African social and political consciousness regarding, for example, human rights and democracy constitutes a stimulating starting point in this regard.

3.2.2 Edward W. Blyden: The African revival

Blyden is a native of Saint Thomas in the Danish Antilles. He was born to black, free, educated parents. In 1850, he went to the USA to study theology. Unfortunately, he was never admitted to any American university because of racial discrimination. Blyden migrated to Liberia in 1851, thanks to the support of the New York Colonization Society. This new direction for his life derived from his passion for Africa, which he considered as his fatherland, and wanting to contribute to its regeneration.

According to Mudimbe (1988, 129), Blyden was "a strange and exceptional man, who devoted his entire life to the cause he believed in". His intellectual legacy can be viewed as an articulation of three consecutive oppositions: first, the racial opposition between white people and black people; second, a cultural confrontation between civilized (the Western world) and savage (Africa); third, the religious antagonism between Christianity, paganism, and Islam.

To begin with, Blyden defended the abolitionist view in which slavery, including the deportation of black slaves to America and the return of former slaves or their descendants to Africa, was part of a project of divine providence. God allowed these tragedies to happen in order to promote the regeneration of Africa. Thanks to the return of former slaves – now civilized and indoctrinated in the Christian faith – to Africa, sons of Cham that had remained in African darkness could have access to these benefits also.

Blyden improved his knowledge of Africa through his work within African communities and his journeys inside the continent as well as his studies of African cultures and history – including the study of Arabic and Islamic culture. This allowed him to make an epistemological breakdown of his original perception of Africa. He rejected the Christian abolitionist hypothesis that relied on a pejorative image of African cultures to justify their removal. Paradoxical to his position as a Presbyterian minister, Blyden no longer considered Christianity as a universal paradigm and as a suitable tool to regenerate Africa.[4] On the contrary, he thought Islam was the best option in this respect. For him, as Mudimbe (1988, 115) observes, this religion was

> [an] excellent means of promoting an African consciousness and of organizing communities. Unfortunately ... the historical facts badly contradict Blyden's belief in the positive capabilities of Islam. Throughout the nineteenth century in Central Africa, Islamic factions represented an objective evil and practiced a shameful slave-trade.

It was Blyden's conviction that African cultures must not be annihilated for the benefit of Christianity and Western culture or even under the pretext of regenerating Africa. These cultures must be protected because they hold values that don't exist anywhere else and which are essential to African identity. He was opposed to the imposition in Africa of Western ideology, which he considered as irrelevant for African authenticity. Thus, he developed a perception of African regeneration that excluded the purification of black Africa of its alleged paganism. For him, to be reliable, regeneration had to be rooted in African cultures.

To achieve such a purpose, Blyden proposed a course of action consisting of three principal methods, all based on the capacity for learning. First, emphasis should be put on Africa's past and the current objective African reality. This attitude relies on his rejection of Western methods of education that, according to him, were more concerned with books than reality, the result being that knowledge consists of knowing what other men (principally foreigners) have said about things, even about Africa and the African people themselves. The objective was to become familiar not with reality, but with what is printed. This entailed a huge gap between reality and subjective interpretation and led Africans into an absurd situation (Mudimbe 1988, 121).

Second, Blyden denounced black people's mimicry of social behaviour. For him, the imitation of white men by black people revealed their psychological domination and dependence. It also showed a secret desire to become white.[5] To tackle this attitude, Blyden recommended that all debate and research on this topic should take into consideration African culture and create stimulating proposals for its future. Concerning black youth, he insisted that

> new and vigorous canons should be initiated ... to "assist their power of forgetfulness ..." by increasing "the amount of purely disciplinary agencies" and reducing "to its minimum the amount of distracting influences" ... "to study the cause of Negro inefficiency in civilized lands; and, so far as it has resulted from the training they have received, to endeavour to avoid what we conceive to be the sinister elements in that training".
> *(Mudimbe 1988, quoting Blyden, 122)*

Third, Blyden recommended a new policy of formal education that would contribute to the transformation of Africa. He suggested the creation of a balanced curriculum combining classical (Western) education and African-focused education at the same time. According to Mudimbe (1988, 123), Blyden's proposal can be summed up as follows: "in addition to the critical presentation of history from an African point of view, he insisted on the study of classics – the Greek and Latin languages and their literatures – mathematics, and the Bible".

This attitude relies on two things. First, Blyden thinks that the learning of ancient languages contributes to strengthening and disciplining the mind; it subsequently enables the student to master any business to which he may turn his attention. Second, the study of classics lays the foundation for successful pursuit of scientific knowledge. In this respect and following Mudimbe (1988, 123), I can observe that more than 90 years later, the majority of the African elite, including Senghor, for example, rely on the same argument in support of teaching Greek, Latin, and classical literature in Africa. This way of thinking can be viewed as suitable in the context of a standardized approach to social organization and development. However, taking into consideration the process of globalization, this approach seems hardly sustainable, as both the diversity and mobility characterizing social and political organization require flexibility and multiple competencies. In addition, the focus today on development of sciences, economics, and new technologies calls for a dismissal of the idea of prioritizing the study of classical literature in Africa.

The idea that black people all over the world are a single nation and consequently they must unite is one of Blyden's main legacies. It also constitutes the background of movements such as pan-Africanism and negritude. For Blyden, every race is a natural unit with its own territory and specific mission. He was black and he was proud to be so. He exhorted his fellow black men to behave in the same way, because he saw consciousness and pride in being black as essential to the progress of black people. In this regard, he focused on the virtues of black civilization, and he promoted ideas of blackness and Negro personality that resulted in the invention of positive myths on race and black personality (Mudimbe 1988, 131). In this regard, Blyden is celebrated by Senghor and many scholars as the foremost precursor of both negritude and African personality theories (Mudimbe 1988, 98–99).

Following his abandonment of the Christian abolitionist view, Blyden became critical about the mixing of races and opposed the idea of identifying as black someone having a drop of black blood (Semprini 1997, 10). He equated purity of race or purity of blood with purity of personality. This accounts for his racist position towards mulattoes. He was against the introduction of the blood of the oppressor among its victims. Relying on this premise, he denied even the possibility of union between pure Negroes and mulattoes. Moreover, he disparaged those negroes who he saw as being as white as some white men. In this respect, his attitude seems rather close to a theory of racial purity. To put this positively, he developed a rigorous anti-racist racism whose purpose was the negation of power relationships based on racial discrimination, exclusion, and exploitation of black people (Mudimbe 1988, 119).

African renaissance was the purpose of many African leaders and intellectuals. In addition to claims related to pan-Africanism and negritude, it is worth remembering the commitment of people like Cheik Anta Diop and Thambo Mbeki, for example, who insisted that African nations must overcome their current challenges and access a viable cultural, scientific, and economic renewal. Diop studied the African past and searched for cultural and technological foundations for the development of Africa. Succeeding Mandela as the head of state in South Africa, Mbeki sought the economic renaissance of the continent. He considered South Africa as the spearhead of this project and dominant neoliberalism as its philosophical underpinning. In short, it can be observed that the idea of African renaissance was echoed within the African intelligentsia and that its achievement still a long-term undertaking.

3.2.3 J. E. Casely Hayford: The claim for native self-governance and African development

African colonization and its subsequent economic exploitation could not impede the awakening of the resistance of local communities. Such was the case, for instance, in Sierra Leone, concerning a colonial law from 1890 that aimed at the distribution of idle lands to the Crown (*Waste lands, crown lands*). This law offended the patriotism of Sierra Leone's leaders because, aside from the land concern, it targeted the foundation of their culture and social organization. As a result, it can be noted that "West Africans felt cheated of their land, deprived of their right of self-government, defrauded of their economic resources and stripped of the very essentials of their culture and way of life" (Boele van Hensbroek 1998, 63).

In reaction to this law, Sierra Leone intelligentsia set up an association – the Aboriginals Rights Protection Society (ARPS) – to defend their rights and protect their social and cultural assets. This association also developed political ambitions as it claimed the right of indigenous people to their own educational system and self-government. According to Boele van Hensbroek (1998, 62), their claim can be formulated as follows: "We want our education to enable us to develop and to improve our native ideas, customs, manners and institutions".

Casely Hayford, a journalist and Cambridge-trained lawyer, is counted among the important leaders of the ARPS. Contrary to a widespread prejudice considering African cultures as conservative, he was optimistic and believed in their potential for modernization. For him, there was no contradiction between modernization and African cultures. He thought that like Japanese traditions, African traditions would also able to meet the requirements of modernization should such an opportunity be offered to them. In this respect, I note that Casely Hayford was opposed to the idea of cultural purity as developed by Blyden. He believed in the beneficent virtues of encounter and exchange between different cultures.

The desire to follow the Japanese paradigm for African development rests on a dual observation: on the one hand, the consciousness of African stagnation and foreign domination and exploitation; on the other hand, the belief in a potentially different African society based on prosperity and competitiveness. However, fascination for the Japanese model of development raises questions concerning, for instance, the relevance and compatibility of this model to the African cultural and political context as well as the question of what development represents to African people in terms of its purpose and methods.

The attempt at modernization in Ethiopia in the 1930s took Japan as its model. This choice was based on Japan's success story with respect to development, but also on the relationship between the two countries and their common opposition to Western dominance. This trial can be viewed as an illustration, in the history of African ideas, of ambiguities and mistakes that such a project can make. Due to criticism from its own elite, imperial Ethiopia decided to take path of modernity resting on the Japanese reformist model of the Meiji era. The choice of this paradigm of development was guided by a rough comparison of the dynasties of Ethiopia and Japan. They both were part of the "Alliance of coloured people" in search of emancipation from European domination. After a long period of being isolated from the world, Japan quickly achieved both technological and economic development as well as the education of its people. The idea is that what was possible for Japan could also be feasible for Ethiopia. Unfortunately, this argument failed to take into consideration factors such as cultural differences between the two countries and Western manumission on the African continent through colonization, geostrategic interests, and financial twists (Calvitt Clark 2011). In addition, I can also mention the failures of the African elite themselves. The only noticeable effect of the cooperation between the dynasties was the new Ethiopian constitution, which had a striking similarity to the Japanese constitution in that both texts consecrated the authority of the Emperor as well as strengthening the submissiveness of the people (Zewde 2008).

As already suggested, this experience calls for the attention of the African political elite and scholars in their search for strategies for African development. It constitutes a relevant case for today's African leaders in terms of knowing whether their choices meet the interests of African people or serve dictatorships and foreign powers. Current social and political upheavals taking place in various African countries illustrate how crucial this challenge is.

3.3 Conclusion

This chapter stood on the premise that contemporary African social and political philosophy doesn't emerge *ex nihilo*. It must have a range of antecedents, which can be classified into two categories: the African precolonial legacy and the contribution of the black diaspora.

The analysis of the African precolonial legacy focused on a set of values and traditions including concepts such as consensus, communal thought, people's participation in power, dialogue, and the subsidiarity principle. Protagonists of this legacy claim for its rehabilitation in order to improve current African social and political organization. This analysis called attention to a double risk of essentialization of the African past and anachronism.

The exploration of the contribution of the black diaspora outlined the struggle of this diaspora for the recognition and rehabilitation of black people's culture and rights. Ideas of thinkers such as Africanus J. B. Horton, Edward W. Blyden and J. E. Casely Hayford, on, respectively, the creation of African modern states, African regeneration, and African development were examined. It was observed that despite changing context, most of the issues that were faced by the African diaspora are still present in today's Africa. They constitute a crucial challenge for contemporary African leaders and thinkers and Africanists.

Contemporary African social and political philosophy can hardly be viewed as being oriented towards the past. This philosophy refers to the African past in order to better understand its challenges today and, subsequently, to consider its future by taking into account changes taking place within the continent.

Notes

1 Concerning the relevance of kinship and social relationships in African politics, see Bayart (1989), Smith (2003), and Dovey (2008).
2 Regarding the debate on modernity, see the *American Historical Review*, 116(3) (2011).
3 It is worth remembering that Belgian colonial policy did not promote higher education for colonized people in order to keep them under control and take advantage of a cheap rate of labour. See Coquery-Vidrovitch (1994); Ngoma-Binda (2013).
4 Mudimbe (1988, 127) thinks that at the end of his life, "Blyden was quite pessimistic about missionary activities. In 1910, in a letter to R. L. Antrobus, assistant under-secretary at the British Colonial Office, he complained about 'teaching mistakes' that created 'a gulf between aborigines and colonists.'"
5 See also Fanon (1975).

4

REVIEWING THE AFRICAN IDENTITY DISCOURSES

Ethnophilosophy and negritude

Introduction

The preoccupation with African identity can be considered from two points of view in the context of contemporary African social and political philosophy. First, this preoccupation expresses itself as the antithesis of racist premises attempting to justify the denial of humanity to black people. Second, this concern developed as a mobilizing ideal aiming for the rehabilitation of both black people and their culture, but also the acceleration of African emancipation. A range of theories emerged in this context, mixing cultural claims and political constraints. Such was the case concerning, for example, the negritude movement; the search for African socialism by Nyerere, Senghor, and Nkrumah; the paradigm of African humanism developed by Kaunda; as well as the pan-Africanist movement (Smet 1980; Mbembe 2005). Because of their great impact on the development of African social and political philosophy, this chapter aims to review main postulates structuring the paradigms of ethnophilosophy and negritude. Therefore, it takes into consideration factors such as the current process of globalization, the mobility of worlds, and subsequent new social and political configurations.

This analysis is provided in two sections, each dealing with one of the two topics in question. The first section focuses on the origin, development, and major debates concerning the concept of ethnophilosophy. From the outset, this section denounces the approach, attributing the creation of this word to Hountondji and Towa. Based on Hountondji's own reflection, this term in fact belongs to Nkrumah who, while studying at Pennsylvania University, submitted a doctoral thesis proposal including the concept of ethnophilosophy. In the American context at that time, the application of this concept was concerned with recognition and rehabilitation of ethnic or cultural peculiarities. Hountondji and Towa used the concept pejoratively in the debate related to origin and development of African philosophy in order to denounce a philosophical practice based on ethnological methods to the detriment of argumentative rigour. Nowadays a wide range of thinkers recognize and also support the ethnophilosophical character of all philosophy as well as arguing for both constructive and universalist use of this concept.

The second section examines the issue of negritude. This analysis relies on the idea that the negritude movement is not reducible to Africa, even though this continent is the only region of the world with a major concentration of black people. This movement deals with a fundamental claim related to the disregarded alterity not only of black people (who are here only a paradigmatic figure), but also concerning every human being and his/her right to be themselves. In other words, the negritude movement struggles for everyone's right to be different and equal.

Senghor's thesis, according to which emotion is the fundamental characteristic of black people, provoked a huge (also violent) wave of criticism. While recognizing the theoretical framework in which this reaction emerged, this section highlights the positive and constructive role of emotion in human life, as it is part of the human condition. This section also emphasizes the fact that far from deserting the political field, negritude is still politically committed to black people through its specific strategy of endorsement, the most important element of which is not violence but the downplaying of Western values and topics.

4.1 The idea of ethnophilosophy

4.1.1 The word and the thing

The concept of ethnophilosophy was successfully used in the debate concerning the existence of African philosophy (Van Parys 1993, 89–95). For many African scholars, the discourse of ethnophilosophy was and still is based on the assumption that

> there is a *metaphysical system, and an ideology*, embodied in the traditional wisdom, the institutions and the languages of Africa; and consequently it aims at thrashing out from myths, folktales, beliefs, proverbs, and languages, "*the quintessential African approach to the world*".
>
> *(Kaphagawani 2000, 89, emphasis added)*

Scholars such as Appiah (1992, 94), Bidima (1995, 12–15), Odera (1991, 47, 49), Kodjo-Grandvaux (2013, 26), and Van Parys (1993, 90), for example, attribute the origin of this concept to Hountondji and Towa. It is my feeling that this is a mistaken belief because, as Hountondji himself later recognized, the earliest usage of this concept in African philosophy was due to Nkrumah. After receiving his Master's in Philosophy in 1943, Nkrumah intended to present a doctoral thesis on ethnophilosophy at the University of Pennsylvania in the USA. He drafted a proposal for his doctoral dissertation that was entitled "Mind and Thought in Primitive Society: A Study in Ethno-Philosophy with Special Reference to the Akan Peoples of the Gold Coast, West Africa" (quoted in Hountondji 2004, 533).

Unfortunately, Nkrumah never gave any comment nor did he provide a meaning concerning his usage of the concept of ethnophilosophy. Considering this lack of explanation, Hountondji formulated a hypothesis to search for the meaning of this word in the domain of ethnic sciences, noting that at the time when Nkrumah was setting out his doctoral research project, those sciences and their aim of establishing the specificity of the languages and cultures of American Natives were in fashion in USA. In this respect, Hountondji (2012) notes that

> On aurait pu s'attendre à ce que ce terme soit ... historiquement situé et justifié dans le corps de la thèse. Mais on ne trouve rien de tel ... Je devais donc formuler l'hypothèse que l'ethnophilosophie ... était une de ces disciplines nées au Etats-Unis dans la foulée des ethnosciences, qui s'étaient elles-mêmes développées à partir de l'étude ethnolinguistique des langues et cultures amérindiennes: ethnobotanique, ethnozoologie. ... L'originalité [de] ... Nkrumah était donc d'appliquer à sa propre société la théorie et la méthodologie de cette discipline déjà reconnue.[1]

> (One would expect that this term was ... historically explained and justified in the thesis. But there is nothing like that ... I should therefore make the hypothesis that ethnophilosophy ... was one of the disciplines produced in the United States in line with ethnosciences, and it developed on account of ethnolinguistic studies of the languages and cultures of American Natives: ethnobotany, ethnozoology ... Nkrumah's originality consisted of applying both the theory and methodology of this already recognized discipline to his own society.)

Relying on this context, Hountondji interprets the potential meaning which Nkrumah would have provided to this concept, highlighting the centrality given to people's world views. For him, it seems that

> L'objectif de Nkrumah était clair. L'anthropologie doit pouvoir ... au-delà de ses thématiques traditionnelles, mettre en place "une ethnophilosophie synthétique" par laquelle elle "s'efforcerait de pénétrer les significations les plus fondamentales et les plus profondes qui sous-tendent toute culture, en sorte qu'elle atteigne une *Weltanschauung* culturelle de base par laquelle l'humanité reconnaîtrait que, malgré les différences de race, de langue et de culture, elle est une en ce sens qu'il n'y a qu'une race: l'*Homo Sapiens*".
>
> *(Hountondji 2012)*

> (By this expression, Nkrumah sought to promote the idea that anthropology should, by going beyond its traditional topics, set up "a synthetic ethnophilosophy" through which "(it) will penetrate the most fundamental and deep meanings underlying every culture so that it reaches a basic cultural *Weltanschauung* by which humankind would recognize, despite the differences of race, language, and culture, that there is only one race: The *Homo Sapiens*".)

This attempt to trace the genesis of the concept of ethnophilosophy helps to clarify two things. First, it clearly establishes the anteriority of this concept in relation to the debate on African philosophy. In this respect, it is worth observing that questions concerning both the origin and meaning of the concept of ethnophilosophy had already been raised by Smet (1980, 161–162) years before Hountondji's attempt at definition. This specialist in the history of African philosophy considers the concept of ethnophilosophy as one of the "neologisms" used by various Africanists (in the post-war era) to refer to auxiliary sciences of anthropology and ethnology, as for example ethnohistory, ethnomusicology, and ethnopsychology. Relying on Doutreloux's work, he stresses the search for the specific "*Weltanschaung*" of non-modern societies (Smet 1980, 161–162). Beyond raising the issue and offering this general indication, Smet doesn't explore further the evolution of this concept and the reasons why it impacts African philosophy. He just calls for more investigations in this respect.

> [Les] publications comme celles de Doutreloux mériteraient une analyse plus détaillée. ... Il faudra rechercher advantage l'origine veritable du terme "ethno-philosophie" pour caractériser une partie importante de la littérature philosophique de (ou sur) l'Afrique.
>
> *(Smet 1980, 162)*

> (Publications such as those of Doutreloux deserve a more detailed analysis. ... The very origin of the expression "ethnophilosophy" must be sought to characterize an important part of African philosophical literature.)

Second, Hountondji's attempt to trace the genesis of the concept of ethnophilosophy sheds light on the very contribution that Towa and Hountondji himself made and to the widespread usage of this word in African philosophy. Both these philosophers diverted this expression from its original and positive meaning, and they assigned to it a pejorative and restrictive interpretation to denounce an approach to philosophy which was based on confusion between the disciplines of philosophy and ethnology. The approach relies on describing collective world views, and in doing so, it truncates the main purpose of philosophy, which consists of rational demonstration and argumentation. According to Hountondji and Towa, African philosophy is not reducible to the description of African traditions and the reconstitution of African past. It is and should be a process of taking a position on/ and rationally justifying issues at stake. In his own words, Hountondji defines their very contribution to the usage of the concept of ethnophilosophy as follows:

> Le mot existait bien avant les années soixante-dix. *Towa et moi ne l'avons pas forgé. Notre seule originalité était de l'utiliser dans un sens péjoratif et polémique pour stigmatiser une pratique que nous rejetions,* alors qu'il était jusque-là, quand il était employé, le nom d'un projet consciemment revendiqu.
>
> *(Hountondji 2012, emphasis added)*

(The word already existed before the 1970s. Towa and myself didn't coin it. Our originality consisted of using it in a pejorative and controversial way to denounce an approach to philosophy that we rejected, although it had been used up until then to refer to a consciously claimed project.)

4.1.2 Rehabilitating the concept of ethnophilosophy

Following his recognition of Nkrumah's usage of the word ethnophilosophy, Hountondji rectified his original approach to it. Thus, he wonders about the relevance of his own critique for today:

> *devons-nous toujours, aujourd'hui, maintenir cette connotation?*
> (Hountondji 2012)

> (should we still maintain this connotation nowadays?)

In answer to this self-questioning, he thinks that the concept of ethnophilosophy can be positively interpreted in today's African philosophy debate, but only under certain conditions, including, for example, the extension of the concept of philosophy and the adjustment of the idea of ethnophilosophy itself. In this way, he writes that

> on ne peut nier l'existence d'un ensemble d'idées littéralement pré-conçues, d'un ensemble de « pré-concepts » et de « prejudges » véhiculé par une culture collective, pas plus qu'on ne peut refuser toute légitimité à une étude qui entreprendrait d'identifier, d'examiner méthodiquement ce système de « pré-concepts ». ... *[J]e ne vois pas d'inconvénients à ce qu'une telle étude soit appelée ethnophilosophie, à condition de reconnaître que dans ce mot composé, le vocable « philosophie » est employé dans un sens un très large,* pour désigner la composante intellectuelle d'une culture que l'on se contente de décrire ou de restituer sans prétendre en aucune façon la légitimer, à la différence de *la philosophie stricto sensu qui s'entend comme une discipline rigoureuse, exigeante, toujours soucieuses de justifier ses affirmations.* Il y a donc place pour une ethnophilosophie comprise en ce sens très général.
> (Hountondji 2012, emphasis added)

> (we cannot deny the existence of a set of literally preconceived ideas, "pre-concepts" and "prejudices" of a collective culture; neither can we deny legitimacy to a study aiming at systematically identifying, methodically examining this system of "pre-concepts". ... *I don't see any problem with naming such a study ethnophilosophy as long as it is recognized that the concept of "philosophy" underlying this compound word is used in a broad sense* to refer to intellectual components of a culture, that can be described, restored, regardless of legitimizing it, contrary to *philosophy in its strict sense, conceived as a rigorous and*

demanding discipline that is always concerned to justify its assertions. Thus, the idea of ethnophilosophy is acceptable on account of this general meaning.)

Various scholars have approached ethnophilosophy in different ways. According to Lajul (2013, 35), for example, today's major arguments about ethnophilosophy include three main interpretations: ethnophilosophy as a philosophy of values, of metaphysics, and of cultural philosophy.[2] Bell (2002, 22–23) distinguishes two important trends of ethnophilosophic discourse: the universalistic approach and the particularistic perspective. Both those trends share the metaphysical principle asserting the uniqueness of being. They differ from each other in that the former universalizes its statement on cultural unity, while the latter emphasizes the peculiarity of single African cultures. Thinkers such as Tempels (1949), Mbiti (1970), Kagame (1956), and Senghor (1995) can be viewed as illustrating the universalistic trend, while scholars like Gyekye (1987), Imbo (1998), and Wiredu (1992, 1996) can be considered as representing the particularistic approach.

Mora (2004) supports the idea that ethnophilosophy should be free from pejorative connotation. He thinks that this concept should be given new and broader interpretation and that it deserves value in philosophical debates because it refers to a set of raw materials and contexts on which any thinker (regardless of his or her own identity and world view) can rely to develop philosophical arguments.[3] For him, ethnophilosophy performs more than a descriptive role or an ethnological mandate. It is a philosophical discourse that can be viewed as valid for philosophers all over the world. In addition to its descriptive duty, this philosophical trend can also serve as an argumentative horizon from which philosophers can participate in all kind of philosophical debates. He describes ethnophilosophy as follows:

"Etnofilosófica" es toda filosofía ..., en tanto ella presente características étnicas o culturales y se diferencie en ello de la filosofía de otros grupos cultural o ... étnicamente determinados.

(Mora 2004, 4)

(Ethnophilosophy refers to every philosophy ... as far as it has its own ethnic or cultural characteristics on which it stands as different from philosophy of other ethnic and cultural groups.)

Defining the very role of ethnophilosophy, he insists that

este concepto de "Etnofilosofia" ... describe formalmente un aspecto de la filosofia, a saber: si de la apelación a las tradiciones, de la reflexión sobre las particularidades de una lengua o de las especificidades comparables y culturalmente determinadas, *se pueden extraer argumentos en cuestiones filosóficas.* ... [E]n tanto se cumpla con el mencionado criterio, Hegel o Heidegger pueden argumentar etnofilosóficamente tanto como N'krumah o Oluwole, Zea o Freire.

(Mora 2004, 4, emphasis in the original)

(this concept of ethnophilosophy ... formally describes an aspect of philosophy: whether taking a stand on traditions, reflecting on the peculiarities of a language or culturally defined and comparable specificities, arguments for philosophical debates can be deduced. ... [A]s far as these requirements are achieved, thinkers such as Hegel or Heidegger can be involved in ethnophilosophy as much as N'Krumah or Oluwole, Zea, or Freire do.)

4.1.3 Ethnophilosophy: A literature of struggle

A range of African scholars recall the marginalization and contempt that came with slavery and colonization. For them, the debate on ethnophilosophy is about more than the speculative issue regarding use of this concept. They view ethnophilosophy as a platform from which to tackle racist discourses and related prejudices. According to them, ethnophilosophy aims at asserting the presence of reason in Africa, and consequently the existence of African people as fully human. In other words, ethnophilosophical discourse opposes racist theories justifying the exploitation of black people and excluding Africa from world history (Eze 1997, 8–10; Bidima 1995, 29). From this perspective, this concept implies a variety of disciplines and protagonists. Defenders of ethnophilosophy focus on different specialized areas and methodologies to tackle this challenge. Kagame (1956), for example, relies on Aristotelian categories to show that Bantu languages can express philosophic and complex ideas just as well. Laléyê (1970) relies on the method of phenomenology to introduce the subtleties of African philosophy and to explore issues such as African development. Mbiti (1970) makes use of African religions to develop his thinking on African otherness through the concept of time. Scholars such as Obenga (1990, 1993) and Diop (1979) focus on African history and linguistics to build their theory of black Egypt, refuting Hegel's assertion that black Africa is not important in world history nor does it exhibit any movement or development (Kebede 2004, 51; Bidima 1995, 29–32; Imbo 1998, 56–60).

African leaders of the first generation such as Kaunda, Senghor, Nyerere, Nkrumah, to name a few, can be viewed as pragmatic ethnophilosophers. They made use of ethnophilosophical methodologies and theories to implement their political views and projects, principally their common dream for an emancipated and prosperous African continent. Therefore, they searched for African quintessence through the exhumation of precolonial African traditions. Theories such as that of familyhood (*Ujamaa*), African socialism, and African humanism can be viewed as illuminating in this respect.

The idea that ethnophilosophy represents a theoretical background to fight Western racism is fairly criticized by various African thinkers including Adotevi (1998), Hountondji (1983), Eboussi-Boulaga (1977), and Towa (1971), among others. Adotevi (1998), for example, concentrates his criticism on the negritude trend developed by Senghor. He thinks that it is unrealistic to argue that this movement can serve as a counterpoint to Western racism and colonial exploitation, because the discourse of negritude endorses the premises of colonization. It views

African people as objects as well as considering them as cannibals and primitive. In sum, negritude is a duplication of Western clichés on African primitivism and marginality, the only difference being that this time it is developed by black people themselves. Adotevi (1998, 43–80), for example, concentrated his criticism on the negritude trend developed by Senghor.

Adotevi's criticism can be viewed as seductive because it stresses the ambiguities of the strategy of endorsement developed by proponents of negritude to tackle Western racism and colonization. These thinkers emphasize the concept of emotion, as opposed to reason, as characterizing black people. Considering that reason or the capacity for rational thought is the criterion by which Europe discriminates and classifies peoples as advanced or as backward, the endorsement strategy is understandably viewed as ambiguous and questionable. Developing this further, I can already observe that, in this context, it may be convenient to keep in mind the distinction between colonial strategies and African perspectives on the struggle for emancipation. It is my feeling that African freedom fighters by no means pretend to justify colonialism. On the contrary, they are worried for themselves and for their fellow countrymen. The most important challenge for them consists of being aware of Western domination and its subsequent alienation of black people.

To achieve this duty, they make use of the strategy to dismiss attitudes and values that Western civilization considered fundamental. They oppose the valuing of reason over emotion, but they also claim their right to be different. The claim for respect of difference and diversity constitutes, for the proponents of negritude, a legitimate way to relativize the central position of Europe and to deprive this continent of its main criterion for segregation, the possession of reason. Through this claim, they highlight the fact that Africa is not and should not be viewed as a failed copy of Europe. It stands as a different but equal continent. Negritude's proponents are proud of their identity.

4.1.4 Ethnophilosophy and African social and political philosophy

Ethnophilosophy was and still is a source of burning debate in contemporary African philosophy, as attested to by various scholars including, for example, Appiah (1992, 185–196), Bell (2002, 22–26), Eboussi-Boulaga (1977, 28–32), Mudimbe (1988, 154–161), and Lajul (2013, 33–39). In this respect, it is worth noting two ideas whose implications are important to African social and political philosophy: the premise that African philosophy is a collective and anonymous thought, and the ascendancy of the search for ontology in African philosophy.

One of the main criticisms of ethnophilosophy is that this approach refers to African philosophy as spontaneous thinking, which means both anonymous and collective thought. As already suggested, Eboussi-Boulaga (1977, 30) is one of the main and more rigorous African critics of ethnophilosophy. He highlights that according to the approach of ethnophilosophy,

> Le philosophe ... est *un révélateur,* au sens chimique du mot; il rend visible ce qui est, il appelle d'un nom nouveau ce qui a toujours été. *Mais le vrai sujet de la philosophie, celui qui la fait, c'est l'ethnie anonyme et éternelle.*
>
> (The philosopher ... is a revealer, in the chemical sense of the word; he makes visible what exists, he calls by a new name what has always been. But the real subject of philosophy, whoever is doing it, is the anonymous and eternal ethnic group.)

Eboussi-Boulaga (1977, 31) also criticizes the method used by protagonists of ethnophilosophy. For him, those thinkers consider philosophy to extend and universalize local realities and related concepts.

> *Par la généralisation extensive*: l'ethnie se dilate jusqu'à la grande ethnie négro-africaine, plus abstraite, qui n'existe que comme sommation des traits, de constantes. ... [Cette] philosophie est celle de l'ethnie, puis celle de tous les négro-africains qui peuvent proclamer: "nous avons des philosophies, nous aussi".
>
> (By extensive generalization: the ethnic group expands to the great Negro-African ethnic group, more abstract, which exists only as a summation of traits and constants. ... [This] philosophy is that of the ethnic group, then of all Negro-Africans, who can proclaim: "us too, we have philosophies".)

This view includes various effects concerning African social and political thinking. In this respect, consider, for instance, the occultation of individual thinkers and the exemption of political agency as well as the refusal of pluralistic political debate by virtue of what I can qualify as "ethnic metaphysics". In the name of those metaphysics, various conservative political paradigms and behaviours have been sustained in Africa, including, for example, modes of governance such as gerontocracy and the warrior and wisdom paradigms. In other words, as a background for political philosophy, the approach of ethnophilosophy includes the risk of anachronism and elimination of political thinking. It is my belief that beyond the debate on the rehabilitation of ethnophilosophy, the application of this way of thinking requires both vigilance and criticism.

I addressed already the relationship between African social and political philosophy and metaphysics. It is my feeling that the search for quintessential Africa that characterizes ethnophilosophy allows philosophers to avoid confronting people's real lives and the everyday world. This attitude can be compared to what Arendt (1994) referred to as the withdrawal of the thinker from the world. Césaire (1976, 36–37) also denounces this attitude in his critique of Tempels's work, which he qualifies as the search for ontological satisfaction. In his "Discours sur la négritude", Césaire (1987) insists on the importance of paying attention to people's daily struggle and local experience as opposed to abstract ideas of universalism.

As already mentioned, the resort to ontology constitutes a permanent temptation and the Achilles heel of African thinkers. It is important to call their attention to such a trap, particularly concerning social and political thinking. The increasing interest in human rights, gender, poverty, and civil society can be viewed as an opportunity for them to concentrate more on real social and political challenges than on the search for the African quintessence (Odera 1997, 81–93; 115–125; Graness 2012, 32–33).[4]

4.2 Negritude, African identity and politics

4.2.1 Negritude and African peculiarity

The negritude movement is one of the best-known movements struggling for both the recognition and rehabilitation of black identity. For its protagonists, it is essential to assume being black, to cultivate pride in one's self. That is the reason why, being themselves in a situation of despair, contempt, and powerlessness, founders of this movement didn't have any choice other than to have courage to free themselves from [their] loaned clothes, those of assimilation, and to assert their own being, that means [their] negritude.[5] In other words, it can be noted that from its conception, the negritude movement contained germs of resistance. Sartre views this movement as a paradoxical dynamic expressing the negation of the negation of black people.[6] He thinks that negritude implies a revolutionary project because not only does it comment upon a *Weltanschauung*, but it also interprets a given world, unveils the universe, and gives a significance to it (Mudimbe 1988, 87).

The claim to recognize and to rehabilitate black peculiarity propelled the issue of identity to the heart of negritude, as it implies the statement of the constituent features of such a peculiarity. Senghor remains one of the most enlightening thinkers on the issue. For him, contrary to Western people, for whom reason constitutes a fundamental characteristic, black people are characterized by emotion. Emotion defines their epistemology and configures their world view (Senghor 1995). The famous aphorism according to which "emotion is as Negro as reason is Hellenic" (Senghor 1964) can be viewed as the best synthesis of this perception of African peculiarity (Kasanda 2013b, 213).

Senghor's assertion about African identity provoked a general outcry among African intelligentsia. Many African scholars and Africanists considered negritude as a duplication, by African thinkers themselves, of Western racism towards black people. Adotevi (1998, 59), for example, observes that Senghor's perception excludes black people from all reason-based competition with white people, particularly on issues of science and technology. For him, Senghor supports the marginalization of black people in a world controlled by white people through the predominance of reason. In this perspective, he wrote that

> en faisant de lui un mystique et un émotif, la constitution biologique du Nègre senghorien lui interdit ... "tout espoir de pouvoir jamais rivaliser avec le Blanc sur le terrain de la raison et la science ... Le Nègre tant qu'il demeure

tel, n'a pas de place, en tout cas, pas de place d'égale à celle du Blanc, dans un monde fondé sur la raison et la science".

(Adotevi 1998, 61)

(By considering black people as mystic and emotional beings, Senghor's biologically based perception of black people ... "impedes all possibility of competition between black people and white people about science and reason. ... As far as black people are like that, they cannot be considered equal to white people in a world which is regulated according to reason and science.")

It is my feeling that Adotevi supports the idea that the theory of negritude, as developed by Senghor, is determinist and essentialist (Adotevi 1998, 45–46). He thinks that Senghor ignores diversity and plurality of African cultures and traditions. He puts all black people across the planet in the same single category of the *black race*, regardless of their specific trajectories, social groups, and individual histories.[7] Senghor is aware of this set of criticisms, and he makes the following observation in this respect:

Some ... Negro intellectuals ... have reproached me for having reduced the knowledge of the African Negro to pure emotion, and for having denied that African Negro is endowed with reason and technical knowledge.

(Senghor 1995, 121)

In his own defence, Senghor argues that reason is common to everybody, but he suggests that its articulations and modes of application depend on the psychological and physiological features of every race. Therefore, he maintains his idea that the West is characterized by its reference to analytical reason, whereas the African universe is based on intuitive and participative reason. He explains himself as follows:

They have read me absent-mindedly. ... Reason has always existed. ... Reason is one, in the sense that it is made for the apprehension of the Other, that is, of objective reality. Its nature is governed by its own laws; but its modes of knowledge, its "forms of thought" are diverse and tied to the psychological and physiological make up of each race. ... The reason of classical Europe is analytic through civilization, the reason of the African Negro, intuitive through participation.

(Senghor 1995, 121)

Senghor's reaction is far from calming down criticism of his perception of African peculiarity. A range of his critics consider the antagonism that he establishes between both emotion and reason as harsh. To negate this antagonism, thinkers such as Ochieng'-Odhiambo state that reason and emotion do not exclude one other in Senghor's thought. Emotion is viewed as being the force, while logic is considered as the sight that gives the direction which force should follow (Lajul 2013, 35). I personally share the desire to dismiss antagonism between emotion and reason, but for different reasons. I think that every human being possesses capacity for both emotion and reason, regardless of their skin colour. Both those virtues constitute our human condition, and they cannot be in sharp opposition to each other because of the colour of one's skin. Various studies including that of Bourdieu (1994, 39–57), for example, have demonstrated that the development of both abilities doesn't depend on skin colour, but rather on external factors such as social, cultural, and financial "capital", to use Bourdieu's term. According to this approach, the lack or the inadequacy of these capitals can be viewed as an obstacle, while their acquisition can be viewed as an asset and stepping stone.

In addition, it can be observed that the concept of emotion, for example, must not be confined to the realm of low instinct. It is as humanizing a trait as reason. This category can also be viewed as a source of high spirituality and of the deep sense of wonder we can experience from appreciation of artistic creativity (Mosley 1995, 219). I hardly support the dichotomy between, on the one hand, defenders of "pure reason", viewed as a Kantian expression of objectivity, and, on the other hand, the protagonists of emotion, conceived of as a Spinozist manifestation of human subjectivity. As already observed, both reason and emotion are valuable features of every human being. Thus, it is my feeling that it is meaningless to interpret the idea of emotion in a pejorative way.

Coming back to the point, I must recognize that Senghor put less emphasis (if any) on criticizing concepts of race and racism than he did on the claim for the right to be different and on the specification of this difference. In the first half of the twentieth century, Europe was under the influence of racist theories inherited from nineteenth-century thinkers (Delacampagne 2000). The main philosophic principle leading this set of theories was the idea of identity defined according to Parmenide's notion that this expresses the coincidence of the being with itself; and subsequently this principle implies the ignorance of the "not being". According to this approach, A is equivalent to A (A = A), and everything which is not A is considered as "not being" and subsequently "excluded". Concretely, this principle regulated relationships between Europe and the rest of the world, colonizer and colonized, white people and black people, for example (Kasanda 2013b, 202–209).

Senghor was aware of these theories as well as he was aware of his own condition as a victim of racism and as a fighter for equality and recognition of black people. As already suggested, his originality can be viewed in terms of the reversal of stigmas and the claiming for the right of black people (and all non-Western people) to be different, to be recognized as such, and to live as all equal human beings do. His very worry concerned the issue of alterity. In this respect, as far as I understand his thinking, he tries to move the centre;[8] that is, to change the centre of gravity of the Western discourse and paradigm of domination, opposing phenomena such as reason and emotion, individual and community, analytic and participative, exclusive logic and inclusive reasoning, and so on. More than a mere reversal of stigmas, the strategy of negritude aims at moving the centre and promoting new social and political configurations and relationships.

The concern for emancipation of African cultures is still relevant nowadays, as numerous studies postulate a potential disappearance of cultural diversity because of globalization (Barber 1996; Fornet-Betancourt 2011). It is worth observing that for Senghor and most proponents of negritude, the defence of black people and African cultures is not an end in itself. They claim for both the recognition of the diversity of humankind and the defence of otherness regardless of the colour of the skin. In this respect, Mudimbe (1988, 88) states that "the other is resistance to colonialism, whether passive or violent".

It may be relevant to note that Senghor doesn't consider difference as a sign of exclusion nor as an expression of antagonism. On the contrary, for him, difference is and should be the link between peoples and cultures all over the world, because it contributes to their mutual enrichment. From this perspective, he pleads for a civilization of the universal: "*Le rendez-vous du donner et du recevoir*". Such a civilization doesn't absorb other people and cultures, but calls for knowledge of the values of the other, his cultural and geographical legacies, through mutual dialogue (Senghor 1995; Shutte 1998). Relying on this premise, I think that the idea that negritude ignores African diversity loses its relevance. Essentially, this movement is based on claims for both recognition of diversity and respect for difference. The search for the peculiarities of every culture as well as the defence of everyone's right to be different constitute its "trade mark". This is still valid concerning the relationship between Europe and the rest of the world, white people and black people, but also among African people themselves.

Reacting to the observation that negritude is a past-oriented theory that drapes African people in their particularism and conservatism and, therefore, does not answer the Western challenge embodied through reason, science and technology, Senghor considers it out of question to renounce both the industrial world and scientific knowledge. He thinks that the most important duty consists of living a life that is at the same time original, African, and Western. He doesn't claim the past for its own sake, but for better living conditions in Africa. As he writes: "There is no question of reviving the past, of living in a Negro-African museum; the question is to inspire this world, *here and now*, with the values of our past" (quoted in Kebede 2004, 61, emphasis in the original).

4.2.2 Negritude and politics

Mudimbe (1988) observes that from its inception, negritude has been essentially a political movement. This movement aims at the recognition of black personality, but in turn it also supports black people's claim for social and political rights, African emancipation, and nationalist pride. He sums up its development as follows:

> in the wake of *negritude … is the affirmation of African political thought*. It aimed initially at recognizing the black personality … and obtaining certain

sociopolitical rights. Only later, in the 1950s, did it really serve projects for African independence. *It is commonplace to see in it one of the important elements of African nationalism.*

(Mudimbe 1988, 87–88, emphasis added)

The anchoring of the negritude movement in literature, particularly in poetry, raises the already mentioned debate on the aptitude of the creative writer to express political experience and to adequately shape the political views of African people. In other words, the question is to know to what extent negritude – as creative discourse – can embody the philosophical and political concerns of black people. According to Bidima (2004, 557), Césaire's poetic work, for example, has had a great impact on African political thought. It is worth noting that Senghor places negritude on a theoretical basis including notions such as emancipation (Marx) and existence (Sartre), for example, whose impact on political philosophy is noticeable (Bidima 2004, 551). Let us explore the criticisms of both Adotevi and Fanon to highlight the political dimension of negritude and its relevance for today's Africa.

4.2.3 Adotevi: Emancipatory negritude and truncate negritude

Adotevi introduces his work *Negritude et Négrologues* (1998) with a report that views negritude as the original period of African renaissance, which he considers to be essentially a political process. For him, this poetry is not simply satiric or imprecatory, but rather it is a way of becoming aware of African struggle for emancipation. Thus he states that

> Point n'est besoin de solliciter les textes pour affirmer que la négritude est politique avant d'être poétique. Pratique, elle l'était avant d'être lyrique. En d'autres termes, c'était hier une des formes possibles de la lutte d'émancipation: le premier moment de l'exigence actuelle. ... Nous devrions la considérer comme le temps primitif de la Renaissance africaine.
>
> *(Adotevi 1998, 31)*

(There is no need to rely on texts to assert that negritude is first political, and later a poetic attitude. It is pragmatic before being lyrical. In other words, it was in the past one of the potential forms of struggle for emancipation: the first step of the current requirement. ... We should consider it as the primitive time of African regeneration.)

Adotevi distinguishes two forms of negritude: the original negritude and the truncate negritude. He defines the former as an emancipatory project focusing on the struggle for emancipation of black people. It takes roots in the painful experience of both slavery and colonization. It aims at rehabilitating Negro-African cultures. Black pride and black rehabilitation are important attitudes in this respect. For

Adotevi, Sartre's preface, *Black Orpheus*, illustrates the fundamental logic of this trend of negritude. Quoting Sartre himself, he notes the following:

> Qu'est-ce donc que vous espériez, quand vous ôtiez le bâillon qui fermait ces bouches noires? Qu'elles allaient entonner vos louanges? Ces têtes que nos pères avaient courbées jusqu'à terre par la force, pensiez-vous, quand elles se relèveraient, lire l'adoration dans leurs yeux? Voici des hommes débout qui nous regardent et je vous souhaite de ressentir comme moi le saisissement d'être vus. Car sans qu'on le voie, il était regard pur, la lumière de ses yeux tirait toute la chose de l'ombre natale, la blancheur de sa peau c'était un regard encore, de la lumière condensée. L'homme blanc, blanc parce qu'il était homme, blanc comme la vertu, éclairait la création comme une torche, dévoilait l'essence secrète et blanche des êtres. Aujourd'hui ces hommes noirs, à leur tour, éclairent le monde et nos têtes blanches ne sont plus que des petits lampions balancés par le vent.
>
> *(Quoted in Adotevi 1998, 36)*

(What did you expect when you removed the gag that was muzzling these black people's mouths? That they would sing your praises? Did you think that you would read adoration in the eyes of those heads that our fathers had been forced to bend down when they come to be raised up? Here are (black) men standing up, looking at us, and I wish you to feel, as I do myself, the shock of being seen. Because, without being seen, (the white man) was only a look, the light from his eyes drawing everything from native shadow, the whiteness of his skin was another look of condensed light. The white man was white because he was man, white like virtue, (he) lit up creation like a torch and unveiled the secret and white essence of beings. Today, in their turn, these black men light up the world, and our white heads are no more than Chinese lanterns swinging in the wind.)

The truncate negritude corresponds, for Adotevi (1998, 33), to the corrupt and perverted kind of negritude which is a contemporary echo of racist ideology of the nineteenth century and its subsequent policies of domination, colonization, and racial segregation. Adotevi (1998, 100) thinks of Senghor as one of the main black representatives of this version of negritude, and, according to him, Senghor's theory of negritude is an overhang made up of determinist clichés and empty neologisms about black people. One of the failures of this thought is that it ignores the social, political, and economic diversity characterizing the universe of black people. As already mentioned, Adotevi views Senghor's approach to negritude as fixed and determinist. In this respect, he observes that

> Tout dans cette théorie de la négritude [senghorienne] est une mascarade, une cavalcade de clichés grotesques et ridicules, une chevauchée de néologismes creux à traits d'union. ... la négritude telle qu'on la brade repose sur des

notions à la fois confuses et inexistantes, dans la mesure *où elle affirme de manière abstraite une fraternité abstraite des Nègres.* Ensuite parce que *la thèse fixiste qui la sous-tend est non seulement anti-scientifique mais elle procède de la fantaisie.* Elle suppose une essence rigide du Nègre que le temps n'atteint pas. A cette permanence s'ajoute une spécificité que ni les déterminations sociologiques, ni les variations historiques, ni les réalités géographiques ne confirment. *Elle fait des Nègres des êtres semblables partout et dans le temps.*

(Adotevi 1998, 45–46, emphasis added)

(Everything in this theory of negritude (of Senghor) is a masquerade, a cavalcade of grotesque and ridiculous stock phrases, a mix of empty neologisms. ... [T]his trend of negritude relies on ambiguous ideas that don't exist, and it asserts in a confusing way the abstracted brotherhood of black people. Next, because the underlying thesis is anti-scientific, but also a fantasy. This negritude supposes a strong Negro essence resistant to change. In addition, there is a specificity that doesn't rely on any sociological determination, historical changes, geographical realities. This negritude considers black people as all similar everywhere and in whatever time.)

Adotevi also evokes the idea that Senghor evades social and political issues for the benefit of the ruling system and its prevailing theories. In other words, he criticizes Senghor of supporting colonialism, domination, and backwardness of African people despite his own declarations for African emancipation. He wonders,

Faut-il entendre par là que pour le Nègre de la brousse la question raciale ne se pose pas? Non, assurément! A l'exploitation simple ... s'ajoute constamment pour tout Noir le mépris racial. Mais si le Nègre de la brousse souffre, ce n'est pas dans son cerveau, mais dans sa chair. La violence faite à ce Nègre est d'ordre économique et musculaire. Aussi, c'est en bandant ses muscles qu'il réclame sa liberation.

(Adotevi 1998, 90)

(Based on that, can it be considered that the question of race doesn't exist for black people from the bush? Certainly not! In addition to mere exploitation ... there is a permanent racial contempt for every black person. But if black people from the bush suffer, it is not in their mind but in their own body. Violence done to them can be viewed as both economic and physical violence. Thus, it is through their physical force that they claim for their emancipation.)

It is my feeling that Adotevi's observations rely on an unsaid postulate that as a groundswell, prompts his own thought: the comparison between the fathers of the negritude movement, Césaire and Senghor. He aims to present the former as a revolutionary mind, one committed politically to the emancipation of black people, and the latter as a romantic mind, one playing with words, more invested in poetry than engaged in the everyday world of African people. This perception is based on an illusion that considers the thought of both fathers of negritude as antagonistic. Césaire and Senghor were two different personalities, and they had very different intellectual tones and literary styles. There is a gap between the observation of those differences and the assertion of antagonism between the thinkers.[9] Césaire and Senghor were hardly antagonistic to each other; on the contrary, their respective thoughts seem to be mutually illuminating on several points, including the relationship between black cultures and Western civilization, modernization, humanism, diversity, and dialogue between cultures. Concerning the above-mentioned antagonistic relationship between reason and emotion, for example, Kebede (2004) observes that both the poets, Césaire and Senghor, converge to some extent in their approach to negritude and social and political issues. He formulates this synergy in the following terms:

> Senghor is not alone in pleading for the association of the discursive logic of [the] West with Africa's gift of emotion. Césaire too wants a "rejuvenated world with its balance restored" by the cooperation of all peoples, who will then say we "have helped to found the universal humanism".
>
> *(Kebede 2004, 66)*

Based on Adotevi's assertions against Senghor's approach to negritude, I have the feeling that from time to time Adotevi himself makes the same mistakes that he denounces in Senghor's thought, including, for example, articulation of the opposition between cultural struggle and political fight. His own passion for political emancipation and his admiration for Césaire's thought and commitment made him oblivious to potential interactions between culture and politics; this led him to neglect how fruitful such an interaction can be, as already demonstrated by Bourdieu through his studies on cultural and symbolic capital (Bourdieu 1994; Accardo and Corcuff 1986). In this regard, I think it is important to keep in mind that all emancipatory projects would remain incomplete if they fail to take into consideration the constant interaction between economy, culture, and politics.

4.2.4 Fanon: Return to the source, African emancipation and violence

Scholars such as Mudimbe (1988, 92) consider Fanon as a solid Marxist, but also as a good student of Hegel, Kierkegaard, Nietzsche, and Sartre. Gordon (2008, 81) thinks that Fanon is one of the canonical figures of African-American philosophy and one of the true founders of postcolonial theory. For Gordon, the impact of Fanon on African-American philosophy and Afro-Caribbean and African thought is so vast that he can rightly be compared to W.E.B. Du Bois. These testimonies aim at stating Fanon's philosophical background and insights on contemporary African social and political philosophy, particularly his approach to negritude (Gordon 2008, 89; Keucheyan 2010, 281).

Fanon's interest in African social and political thought is based on his struggle against colonization. His written works, for example, *Peau noire, masques blancs* (Fanon 1975) and *Les damnés de la terre* (Fanon 1979), illustrate this preoccupation. The recognition of Fanon as one of the precursors of postcolonial theory emphasizes how far his thought has gone beyond the strict issue of colonization and expanded to denounce all social and political rationales of conquest, domination, and exclusion (Mbembe 2005; Bhabha 2007).

Fanon includes negritude in the framework of discourses relying on the theoretical paradigm of otherness, which he also considers as the antithesis of colonial alienation (Mudimbe 1988, 83–92; Kebede 2004, 51–128). Those theories aim at tackling the basic reasoning of colonization and its subsequent exploitation through the paradigm of alterity, putting emphasis on African peculiarity as well as inverting colonial stigmas. They attempt to revive the African past and to sketch a brilliant and promising future for black people. Protagonists of those theories seem themselves committed to persuading black people that they have no reason to be ashamed of their past. On the contrary, they must be proud of it, and they should approach their own history and cultural legacy with a curious attitude. The claim to "return to the source" constitutes one of the fundamental premises for this line of thought. In this respect, Fanon observes that for proponents of this way of thinking,

> there was nothing to be ashamed of in the past, but rather dignity, glory, and solemnity. The claim to a national culture in the past does not only rehabilitate that nation and serve as a justification for the hope of a future national culture. In the sphere of psycho-affective equilibrium it is responsible for an important change in the native.
>
> *(Quoted in Kebede 2004, 95)*

From this perspective, Fanon considers negritude as the answer of intellectuals to the dehumanizing and contemptuous behaviour of colonizers. For him, this movement constitutes the logical antithesis of the insult of white people to black people because of its glorification of the African past and through its emphasis on African peculiarity, which is mainly described in terms of emotion. Thus Fanon considers the concept of negritude as

> *l'anti-thèse affective sinon logique de cette insulte que l'homme blanc faisait à l'humanité.* ... A l'affirmation inconditionnelle de la culture européenne a succédé l'affirmation inconditionnelle de la culture africaine. Dans l'ensemble les chantres de la négritude opposeront la vieille Europe à la jeune Afrique, la raison ennuyeuse à la poésie, la logique oppressive à la piaffante nature, d'un côté raideur, cérémonie, protocole, scepticisme, de l'autre ingénuité, pétulance, liberté, pourquoi pas luxuriance. Mais aussi irresponsabilité.
>
> *(Fanon 1979, 146, emphasis added)*

(the affective and logical antithesis to the insult of white people to humankind. ... The unconditional affirmation of African culture replaced the unconditional affirmation of European culture. Globally, protagonists of negritude will oppose old Europe to young Africa, boring reason to poetry, oppressive logic to swaggering nature, from one side, stiffness, ceremony, protocol, scepticism, and on the other side ingenuity, liveliness, freedom, as well as luxuriance. And irresponsibility.)

Fanon thinks that negritude aims at a radical change in the relationship between the colonizer and the colonized. It initiates a revolution that it cannot succeed in because of its own method, the strategy of endorsement. Through ideas such as the return to the past and racialization, this theory endorses colonial stereotypes of black identity, but it also limits black people according to a fixed and ahistorical attribute of race. In this respect, Kebede (2004, 95) notes that for Fanon,

> Neither the racialization of Africans nor the return to the source can bring about the promised bright future. Instead of understanding black identity as an outcome forged by the process of the actual struggle, the negritude movement resorts to a fixed and ahistorical race attribute, even at the expense of endorsing colonial descriptions of black entity. The result is the definition of African identity in terms antagonistic to modern requirements.

Fanon considers that this situation enlarges the gap between Africa and Europe, and it makes improbable the achievement of black people's emancipation. The only way out would be to resort to violence. This option raises a range of questions such as: What does violence mean in Fanon's view? How can violence be emancipatory in the African context of domination and colonization? Can violence be considered compatible with the philosophical premises of theories of otherness? If so, under what conditions can such a perspective be considered feasible? Before examining those questions, it is important to keep in mind that Fanon's approach to violence rests on two things: on one hand, the Hegelian paradigm of dialectical relationship between master and slave and, on the other hand, his perception of the African struggle for emancipation (Gordon 2008, 80–90).

The Hegelian dialectic rests on the premise that both the master and the slave are engaged in the struggle for recognition. The idea of recognition refers to every individual's desire to be viewed and accepted as a free being. Both master and slave have in common the idea that each one is a human being. From the outset, they both share a common human condition. As they struggle for life or for death, the one who aggrees to work in exchange for the preservation of his life becomes slave, while the one who feels ready to sacrifice his life is considered master. Concretely, the distinction between the master and the slave relies on their respective courage (or lack of) and their freedom or their aptitude to lay down their life.

For Fanon, this paradigm doesn't develop in the same way concerning the African colonial context, because the relationship between colonizer and colonized doesn't rely on an assumption of their equality as human beings. Contrary to the Hegelian dialectic, the colonial context assumes the inferiority of colonized people to the colonizer. Contrary to the Hegelian situation where the loss of freedom results from a defeat in the fight between the two contenders, in the colonial context, one of the contenders is viewed as subhuman or, better said, not a real human being. The colonial paradigm relies on an unbalanced relationship between contenders and expresses both the alleged inferiority of the colonized and the superiority of the colonizer. Concerning this lack of balance, Fanon considers the strategy of endorsement developed by the negritude movement as useless and inefficient. For him, only violence can contribute to undoing the drawbacks of colonial rule and to dissolving the inferiority complex from which the colonized suffer. Thus, he can proclaim the emancipatory virtue of violence in the following terms: "Violence alone, violence committed by the people, violence organized and educated by its leaders, makes it possible for the masses to understand social truths and gives the key to them" (quoted in Kebede 2004, 98).

What then does violence mean to Fanon? This is a complex question concerning Fanon's general approach to African liberation. Considering this context, it is worth keeping in mind that for Fanon, violence expands two spheres at a time: political struggle for emancipation and clinical process of healing. It can be viewed as a means to fight colonial domination, but also as embodying therapeutic and creative value consisting of liberating colonized people from their inferiority complex. Fanon distinguishes three forms of violence: colonial violence, emancipating violence, and the violence of the international relationship.

Colonial violence refers to inaugural violence achieved by the colonizer in bringing into reality and perpetuating his project of domination and exploitation of other people. This form of violence follows three dimensions: first, it inaugurates and legitimates the colonial system; second, it promotes both the control and subjugation of colonized people; and third, regardless of the principle of dialectical recognition and all moral argument, colonial violence becomes plural and endless (Fanon 1979).

Emancipating violence represents the reaction of colonized people towards colonial attitudes. It expresses their determination to invert the paradigm of the colonial relationship and to free themselves from colonial domination and exploitation. For Fanon, this form of violence is the only way out for colonized people to rehabilitate their human dignity and to come back to humanizing life (Fanon 1979). The violence of the international relationship results from the framework of unbalanced global relationships and unjust ruling structures against which the "wretched of the world" fight.

It is easy to see the seductive power of Fanon's theory on violence. It is my feeling that this theory relies on a Manichean approach to social and human relationships, dividing human beings into antagonistic and hermetic categories of colonizer versus colonized, elite versus peasant, powerful versus powerless. The hypothesis behind this perception is that conflict, especially when it seems to be in favour of the powerless and the most disadvantaged, constitutes a source of social and political change. This attitude raises the question of whether human beings, and subsequently their daily relationships, can be fit into such a fixed and antagonistic frame. Progress made in human and social sciences nowadays allows a renewed approach to human and social class relationships, taking into consideration both recognition of the other and the fluidity characterizing social and political relationships. Bayart (1989), for example, outlines how complex the relationship between people and the state in Africa can be, particularly concerning the political field. In this respect, he spoke not only of the *"politique du ventre"*, but he also qualified the African state as a *"Etat rhizome"* due to its complex purposes and subterranean connections.

This recognition does not imply any exoneration of the colonial system and its subsequent effects. As Fanon (1979) himself demonstrates, there are several reasons for this system to be rejected. The struggle for human dignity and the right to be different (otherness) and to think in different way count amongst those reasons. The proponents of theories of otherness rely on these rights. The strategy of endorsement aims at removing Western civilization from its pedestal and considering it equal to other cultures and civilizations. By rejecting the world system of rule, this method questions both the relevance and the legitimacy of colonial rule. In this regard, it is my feeling that Fanon's idea that "endorsement strategy is useless" needs to be rejected. The endorsement strategy is not as severe as violence. It proceeds differently, though aiming at the same purpose as protagonists of the strategy of violence. In this respect, the endorsement method can be viewed as a different and subtle process, asking more for patience than violence. Thus, to perceive it as a useless strategy seems to be a hasty conclusion given the complexity of the issue.

It is also my belief that Fanon's premise that colonialism instilled negative prejudices and stereotypes in colonized people is relevant (1975, 11). Now the question is whether violence is the right strategy to root out such a legacy. It is my feeling that the resort to violence can hardly be defended in this regard, particularly given Gandhi's theory of non-violence by which violence always generates violence and leads to the creation of an inextricable circle of violence, a vicious circle! Fanon himself seems aware of this indefinite counter-reaction of violence and the potential imbalance of power between contenders (Fanon 1979). Out of that, my feeling is that it is hard to explain how guns and wars might root out the inferiority complex, which is fundamentally a psychological attitude. I feel right in thinking that a pedagogical approach to violence seems more effective than Fanon's suggestion of answering violence by violence. Both the recognition of the other and the rehabilitation of people's memory seem to be, among other things, relevant in this case.

Otherwise, it is my impression that Fanon's analysis of violence is a seminal contribution to the framing of the encounter between Africa and Europe, particularly concerning colonization and struggle for emancipation. It is important to note that despite African emancipation, violence remains the daily experience of African people. These people suffer from all kinds of violence including structural violence from African states themselves and cultural, social, and economic violence. They are involved in an endless circle of violence. In this respect, Africa can be compared to a boiling pot or land of apocalypse where all is in danger of extinction and no future can be expected. Unfortunately, very few African thinkers and Africanists address this issue critically. Thinkers such as Odera (1976) and Wiredu (1986), for example, explore the issue in a rather formalistic tract, while Monga (2009) develops a nihilist description of this phenomenon. Concretely, Odera introduces an analytic discussion on crime and punishment from the perspective of a curative and pedagogical approach to villainy, while Wiredu offers a tactical discussion on the relevance of violence regarding the struggle for African emancipation. Based on Cameroonian experience of the struggle for democracy, Monga describes both the use and abuse of violence by African postcolonial rulers towards their political opponents and their own people.

It is my feeling is that this topic requires closer attention than it has received up to now by African thinkers, not only concerning the memory of the experience of colonization and the struggle for emancipation, but also, and mainly, concerning the current African context in which not only do financial and international institutions generate violence and poverty, but African leaders themselves also resort to violence for the sake of their own interests (Achebe 1987; Serequeberhan 1994, 55–56). In this regard, the leading purpose should be a rigorous identification of real causes and mechanisms of violence and a subsequent search for appropriate solutions. A relevant diagnostic is always better than a blind and approximate healing.

4.3 Conclusion

This chapter explored African theories of identity, focusing on the paradigms of ethnophilosophy and negritude. The idea of ethnophilosophy is perceived as a global background on which African discourses on identity and otherness emerged as both the antithesis of racist theories of black people and as the mobilizing ideal for African emancipation. This concept was used for first time, in African philosophy, by Nkrumah. Thinkers such as Hountondji and Towa gave it a pejorative and restrictive meaning to denounce the tendency to consider ethnographic descriptions as constitutive of African philosophy. A wide range of scholars argue for a broader interpretation of this concept that allows for its multiple usages outside African philosophy. For this category of scholars, every philosophy can be viewed as ethnophilosophy as long as it refers to cultural peculiarity.

The chapter also concentrated on the negritude movement as developed by Senghor. It examined the criticism of this movement formulated by Adotevi and Fanon. It outlined various implications of this movement including the emancipation of black people, the right to be different, and the determination to overthrow Western hegemony. Opposing Fanon's perception of violence as a liberating process, the chapter noted the efficiency of the negritude strategy of endorsement and called for dialogue between cultures and peoples all over the world as a way of promoting the identity of each as well as offering another possible way to live together; that is, being different and equal.

Notes

1 See also Hountondji (2004, 533–535).
2 For more on the approaches of ethnophilosophy, see Lajul (2013, 33–39); English and Kibujjo (1996, 11–17).
3 Thoraval (1994), for example, takes up this interpretation and makes use of the concept of ethnophilosophy to refer to various trends of Chinese philosophy.
4 This way of thinking seems closer to the ideas of the Latin American philosophy of liberation as developed by Dussel (1996, 2002).
5 www.tidiane.net/culture/afrique-negritude.htm. For a synthesis and critical presentation of both the genesis and development of negritude, see Ahluwalia (2001).
6 www.tidiane.net/culture/afrique-negritude.htm
7 See also Kelman (2005).
8 I owe the expression "moving the centre" to Ngugi wa Thiong'o (1993).
9 For a comparative approach to the two thinkers, see Ahluwalia (2001, 23–29).

5

THE PAN-AFRICAN MOVEMENT

From race-based solidarity to political unity and beyond[1]

Introduction

Pan-Africanism originated in African diasporas in the late nineteenth century, and it spread to Africa in the middle of the twentieth century. Originally, this movement relied on the idea that black people all over the world constitute a single nation and that they have a common destiny. Therefore, they must unite to fight the discrimination and exploitation that they endure from white people (Outlaw 1996, 88). This thought developed through various theories, and it dominated the debate on black people's destiny for almost a century. The awareness of new configurations and interdependencies[2] taking shape in the world calls for a new consideration of pan-Africanist discourses. This call has become even more urgent due to the emergence of new and proliferating self-representations of black people through movements and theories such as Afropolitanism, cosmopolitanism, postcolonial theories, and globalization theories. Most critiques denounce the institutionalization and the ossification of traditional pan-Africanist discourse, which is viewed by some as disconnected from black people's reality and aspirations.

This chapter argues that pan-Africanism is neither outdated nor incongruous concerning contemporary black people's realities because its fundamental purpose is not reducible to the defence of black people and black identity as an end in itself. This movement aims at supporting the struggle for human dignity and freedom which was embodied in categories of race and black people's identity. Both these categories are strongly questioned today, as already mentioned, while the issue of human dignity is more than ever a burning debate that calls for the achievement of global justice and human rights. Therefore, this chapter suggests going beyond all kinds of Afrocentrism to instead define black people's solidarity as part of the struggle against social inequalities and exclusion affecting human dignity regardless of African emancipation.

64 The pan-African movement

This chapter is divided into four sections, and it is written in part as a survey to map the many histories and trajectories of the ideas of pan-Africanism. The first section concentrates on the meaning and the genesis of pan-Africanism. It evokes Edward W. Blyden and his call for black people's solidarity, and it examines different constellations of pan-Africanism all over the world. The second section introduces some pan-Africanist founding fathers and their respective theories, including Booker T. Washington (1856–1915) and his idea of black people's accommodation; Anna Julia Cooper (1858–1964) and the issue of value; Marcus Garvey (1887–1940) and his call for "Africa for Africans"; W. E. Du Bois (1868–1963) and his defence of the integration and the achievement of black people's rights. The issue of race and the rehabilitation of African cultural legacy constitute the prevailing topics for this generation of pan-Africanist thinkers and activists.

The third section focuses on the appropriation and subsequent transformation of pan-Africanism by its African heirs. The first generation of African heirs of pan-Africanism concentrated on the political emancipation of Africa so that the struggle against colonization eclipsed the issue of race. The idea of emancipation constitutes the background on which the debate on African solidarity is rooted. People such as Nkrumah, Fanon, and Gaddafi count among important leaders of the movement. Nkrumah is considered as a freedom fighter and standard-bearer of pan-Africanism. Concepts such as "the African personality" and "consciencism" are part of his philosophical legacy. Fanon is viewed as a major activist for African decolonization. He sustained the idea of inseparability between anti-colonial national struggle and the fight for African emancipation. Apart from that, his written work denounces and reverses the colonial paradigm of the relationship between colonizer and colonized, which he thinks is based on a colonial fallacy. More than that, he deconstructed colonial imaginary and discourses that devaluate and turn into essence black people's reality and cultures. Gaddafi is perceived as a *sui generis* pan-Africanist militant and founding personality of pan-Africanism. Summing up, concepts such as African unity, African emancipation, African decolonization, and African sovereignty constituted the war cry for this generation of African thinkers and activists.

The last section examines new perspectives on and directions for pan-Africanism. It takes into consideration new configurations and interdependencies taking shape in the world as well as the self-representations of black people themselves to sustain an alternative approach to concepts such as African identity and sovereignty, concepts that are crucial to pan-Africanist thought. The chapter keeps its distance from fundamentalist and etherealising approaches to African identity that, somehow, lead to what I regard as the current sclerosis and impasse of pan-Africanist thought. On the contrary, it takes into consideration categories such as "exile" and "exodus" (Nouss 2005) and *"la circulation des mondes"* – inward and outward flows – (Mbembe 2005) and their subsequent imbrications in order to sustain a broader view of African identity that is inclusive of the multiplicity of people and cultures shaping Africa. This approach puts forward the claim for human dignity, regardless of skin colour.

To conclude, the chapter argues that global justice and human rights provide a crucial and unavoidable background for solidarity that goes beyond conservative approaches to pan-Africanism and whose perspectives are limited to issues such as skin colour and geographic territory. It also denounces theories that approach the issue of race as an irreducible antagonism between categories such as inside and outside, indigenous and alien, for example, in favour of inclusive approaches and new configurations of identity (Appiah 1992, 56; Mbembe 2005; Nouss 2005, 93–113).

5.1 The idea of pan-Africanism

5.1.1 Edward W. Blyden: A call for African revival

Blyden is viewed as the forefather of African nationalism and pan-Africanism. He believed that black people all over the world constitute a single nation, and they share a common destiny. Therefore, they must unite to fight both the discrimination and the humiliation that they endure from white people. His idea of African revival developed according to three orientations: religious distance between Christianity, paganism and Islamic religion; cultural antagonism between civilized and savage; and racial opposition between white people and black people (Mudimbe 1998, 117).

The issue of race is among Blyden's preoccupations due to his own experience and the intellectual context of his time. He claimed the existence of multiple races, but he rejected their hierarchic classification. He didn't believe in the alleged inferiority of black people. For him, every race was a natural unit with its own territory and mission. Blyden was proud to be black, and he exhorted his fellow black people to behave in the same way, as the consciousness and the pride in being so are essential to their progress.

Following his abandonment of the Christian abolitionist view, Blyden became critical of the mixing of races and was against the identification of someone having a "drop of black blood"[3] as a black individual. In this respect, he seems close to the theory of racial purity. To put things positively, he developed an anti-racist racism. Kebede (2004, 166) considers this racial background as the fundamental weakness of pan-Africanism. It is my feeling that Kebede's criticism rests on a premise reducing pan-Africanism to one of its multiple articulations, that of race. I think that pan-Africanist struggle is not reducible to a racial phenomenon, because it deals with the global issue of human dignity and freedom. It concerns the question of equality of human beings and the right to be different. As Cooper (2000, 120–121) reminds us: "the cause of freedom is not a cause of a race or a sect, a party or a class – it is the cause of humankind, the very birthright of humanity".

5.1.2 One idea, multiple developments

Two steps characterized the development of pan-Africanism: the original pan-Africanism as conceived by African diasporas and the pan-Africanism developed by its African heirs. The former deals with solidarity between black people outside of Africa, in a context of racial discrimination in areas such as the USA, Latin America and Europe, while the latter focused on solidarity inside Africa in the context of colonial domination and exploitation. Several constellations can be drawn in this respect: Trans-Atlantic pan-Africanism, Trans-Saharan pan-Africanism, Sub-Saharan pan-Africanism, Trans-American pan-Africanism, and Global pan-Africanism (Mazrui 2001, 108).

The first constellation focuses on solidarity between people of Afro-American descent and African autochthonous. Blyden's call originated in this context. This perspective prevailed during the first five Pan-African Congresses. It was on account of this that the leadership of pan-Africanism was transferred to African leaders. This trend of pan-Africanism dealt with the idea of race-based solidarity and the rehabilitation of black culture to promote black people's dignity.

The second constellation refers to relationships between people from Maghreb and those living in the South of the Sahara. It developed in the context of the struggle against colonialism and Western hegemony. Fanon is one of its representative leaders. He claimed a substantial unity between people from both the sides of Sahara, and he viewed African decolonization as a borderless struggle; that is, a struggle that must not be enclosed within any local or and nationalist consideration (Fanon, 1979).

The third trend focuses on the relationship between people from the south of the Sahara themselves. It stands on premises such as cultural unity, linguistic similarities, common economic interests, and political affinities between black African countries. The experience of short-lived regional groupings such as the Ghana-Guinea-Mali Union, the Organization of States Bordering the River Senegal (OERS), and the East African Community and Common Market (EACM) can be considered as illustrative of this approach to pan-Africanism (Mbuyi 1993, 104–109).

The fourth constellation concentrates on black consciousness amongst people of African descent in North America, the Caribbean, and Latin America. Its main concern remains the visibility and recognition of people of African origin. Consequently, it involves the claim for their social, economic, and political rights. If this struggle developed in the USA a long time before, it is only in the late twentieth century that this consciousness arose in various Latin American countries. More and more scholars and activists are making claims for the rights of people of African descent in countries such as Mexico, Venezuela, Colombia, Costa Rica, Dominican Republic, among others (Martinez Montiel 1995a, 1995b).[4] This revival of interest in African roots and identity implies also the discovery of philosophies and cultural and political achievements of people of African descent (Outlaw 1996, 75–95; Pittman 1997; Fornet-Betancourt 2011; Gordon 2008).

The last trend widens the commitment of black people from all over the world as a marginalized and oppressed population. Besides the traditional black diaspora, it includes the Arab world, Australian aborigines, people of New Guinea and Papua, and black diaspora of Europe (Mazrui 2001, 108–109). This configuration deals essentially with issues of global solidarity and human rights.

5.2 The theories of founding fathers

The call for solidarity among black people was launched and carried out by Afro-American activists and Caribbean intellectuals such as Blyden, Washington, Garvey, Du Bois and Cooper, to name a few. Each one offered a specific insight to this movement, and this section aims at outlining those contributions and their relevance for today's Africa.

5.2.1 Booker T. Washington: The theory of black people's accommodation

Washington was a major leader of the black American community between 1890 and 1915. His mother was a slave and his father a slaveholder. He was himself victim of injustice due to his origins. He studied at Hampton Normal and Agricultural Institute, which was for the instruction of emancipated slaves. He completed his instructor training at Wayland Seminary (Washington 2012).

In 1881, Washington was appointed responsible for Tuskegee Normal and Industrial Institute in Alabama. This vocational training institution was intended for black students. Washington ruled it with authority and pragmatism for almost three decades. He believed in the redeeming virtue of education for black people, and he considered their education as the starting point of their emancipation and solidarity. Washington joined the pan-Africanist struggle also through his membership of the "African Association" and his relationship with people such as Benito Sylvain and Henry Sylvester Williams, who launched pan-African meetings (Smet 1980, 41). It was on Washington's invitation that Garvey moved to the USA (Gordon 2008, 163).

As Outlaw observes, the core of Washington's theory of black people's accommodation is that

> the economic and political *hegemony of white folks was not to be challenged directly, but was to be finessed by subtle strategies of seeming accommodation* while black folks prepared themselves for economic self-reliance and eventual full political citizenship "earned" by forming and exercising good character and responsibility through education for and the practice of honest work.
>
> *(1996, 69–70, emphasis added)*

Washington believed in the coexistence of and the collaboration between races. Thus, he supported the Compromise of Atlanta (1895) aiming at an agreement of cohabitation and collaboration between white people and black people wherein black people should give up their claims for social and civil rights to benefit from the support of white people concerning training, employment, and funding for their charity works. Washington considered the economic autonomy and respectability of black people as prior to their claim for social and political rights. In this way, he supported the principle of a "give-and-take policy" between white and black people. He conceived social organization as a separate development for which he used the following metaphor:

> Dans toutes les choses purement sociales nous pouvons être aussi séparés que les doigts, mais unis comme la main pour tout ce qui est essentiel au progrès mutual.
>
> *(Quoted in Smet 1980, 37)*

(In all the purely social things, we can be as separate as fingers but as united as the hand concerning our mutual progress.)

Many scholars including Cooper and Du Bois denounced Washington's theory of black people's accommodation and his support of the Compromise of Atlanta. They rejected the idea of restricting the education of black students to a vocational horizon, and they criticized the implicit racism and paternalism underlying this compromise (Gordon 2008, 70). This criticism reveals that pan-Africanism is not a homogenous trend of thought relying on the unanimity of its members. It involves multiple opinions and tendencies. This raises the question of what should be the right process for black people's solidarity. Washington supported the strategy of ruse through his philosophy of accommodation of black people, while people such as Cooper and Du Bois defended the strict achievement of rights of black people. Fanon (1979) thought of violence as a response to colonial domination, while leaders such as Nkrumah (1963) preferred Ghandi's strategy of non-violence. This debate is ongoing as today's struggle for African unity and emancipation involves new configurations and multiple challenges.

5.2.2 Anna Julia Cooper: A defence of higher education for black people and the issue of worth

Cooper was born a slave; her father, G. W. Hayward, was a slave-owner, and her mother, Hannah Stanley Hayward, was Hayward's slave. She married George Cooper, who passed away within a short period of marriage. She never remarried, and she dedicated the rest of her life to education. According to Gordon (2008, 70), "after achieving her bachelor's and master of arts degree from Oberlin College in 1887, she taught at the M Street High School, which became the Laurence Dunbar School for Negroes and Native Americans".

Cooper held a PhD in comparative literature from the Sorbonne University through completion of a dissertation entitled: *L'attitude de la France à l'égard de l'esclavage pendant la révolution*.[5] Gordon (2008, 71) considers that

> Cooper did not make much of her activist work, but she is perhaps most known in that arena as one of the organizers of the first Pan-African Congress ..., and for her feminist writing and her work in education. She is without question the most sophisticated thinker on what is known today as

black feminist thought from the late nineteenth century into the early twentieth century.

Her support of black people's solidarity is noticeable in her commitment to the pursuit of higher education for black students and her theoretical work including her "theory of worth" and the promotion of black women's emancipation. Concerning the education of black people, for example, she opposed the philosophy underlying the Compromise of Atlanta. As Gordon observes,

> *She defied convention* ... by providing the students with an education in the humanities and sciences, which prepared them to go on for liberal arts degrees at some of the nation's most competitive colleges and universities. ... *[I]t soon led to her being attacked by the infamous "Tuskegee machine" of Washington supporters.* ... The result was her being fired (non-renewal of her contract) from her post of principal of the school in 1906.
>
> *(2008, 70, emphasis added)*

Against the racist reasoning according to which the lack of black people's contribution to civilization means that humankind could perform well without them, Cooper developed her "theory of worth", which she applied to the relationship between black people and white people and to the situation of black women. For her, worth is related to what an individual produces in comparison to how much was invested in him or in her. Much more has been invested in white people than in black men and black women, and even less in the latter, she points out. According to Cooper's view, black people contributed more than white people to building America; this is also the case concerning the condition of black women in comparison to black men. Resting on this premise, she exhorts black women to become agents of their own development. This theory received a positive review within contemporary black feminist movements. Cooper is considered as the most sophisticated thinker and pioneer of black feminism (Gordon 2008, 71–72).

5.2.3 Marcus M. Garvey: The back-to-Africa theory

Garvey was confronted with racial segregation since his youth in Jamaica, where he was born in 1887. He moved to the USA in 1916 thanks to an invitation from Booker T. Washington. Unfortunately, Garvey did not have the honour of meeting Washington as the latter passed away shortly before the former reached the USA (Gordon 2008, 163).

As fervent activist and charismatic leader, Garvey created an association for the improvement of black people's condition, known as the Universal Negro Improvement Association and African Communities League (UNIA). He also launched *The Negro World*, a magazine aimed at making known the activities of the UNIA and spreading word of the struggle for emancipation of black people. The slogan of this association was: "One God, One Aim, One Destiny". It expresses the philosophy and the objectives of the UNIA that were based on black people's unity and nationalism.

Garvey believed that black people should live in their own land of origin to be themselves. He linked the emancipation of Afro-Americans with the decolonization of Africa. His political philosophy relied on the principle of self-esteem of black people in order that they can claim independent states, which should develop under the leadership of the African-American diaspora (Gordon 2008, 164). Garvey can be considered close to the racist movement "Back to Africa", as he supported the move of black people and people of African American descent to Africa. By the way, it is worth remembering that this movement is also known by names such as "colonization movement" or "black Zionism". It arose in the nineteenth century in the USA in the exaltation that followed the abolition of slavery. As already noted, this movement was committed to the return of Afro-Americans to Africa.

If Garvey's claim for African independent states is praiseworthy, his idea to put those states under Afro-American leadership seems hardly defensible. Garvey's attitude seems to draw from a Christian and abolitionist scheme, already denounced by Blyden, according to which African salvation must come from outside, particularly from America. In this way of thinking, African indigenous people are not capable of managing and ruling a modern state, as they are still entangled in ethnic conflicts and stagnation. This approach reveals one of the cleavages characterizing the relationship between African indigenous and Afro-American descendants in countries such as Liberia.

Garvey is viewed as the main inspirer of the mystic and religious nebula of Rastafarianism and as the new Moses of black people. In this respect, Gordon (2008, 163–164) observes that

> Garvey set the framework for a form of Black Nationalism of a prophetic and philosophical kind. The prophetic side came from his political argument that black liberation rested upon the liberation of the African continent from colonialism. Prophesying the emergence of a royal liberator in Ethiopia, Garvey became the major prophetic figure for what became the Rastafari in Jamaica. That movement came into being at the crowning of Emperor Tafari Makonen in 1930, the avowed 111th emperor in the succession from King Solomon in Ancient Judea. ... [A]nd some of the followers of Garvey in Jamaica regarded those series of events to be the fulfilment of prophecy in the Hebrew Bible of the coming of the Messiah.

Garvey's concept of emancipation has been considered as racist and separatist by a range of thinkers and Africanists. Relying on Nguyen van Chien's comment, Smet for example, observes that Garvey

> Était un noir de pur sang, ce qui influa à la fois sur ses rapports avec les autres leaders noirs de sang mêlé et sur la politique du mouvement qu'il fonda ....

> Garvey était arrivé aux Etats-Unis, en 1916, *emportant de la Jamaïque, une haine à la fois contre les Blancs et les mulâtres. L'idée de bâtir une solide et puissante nation nègre lui était arrivée dès sa jeunesse.*
>
> *(1980, 38, emphasis added)*
>
> (Was a pure black man, which influenced both his relationship with other black leaders of mixed origins and the politics of the movement he founded. ... Garvey arrived in the USA in 1916, taking from Jamaica the aversion for both white people and mulattos. Since his youth, he had the idea to build a strong and powerful black people's nation.)

His view of emancipation asserts the existence of multiple races on the one hand, and it claims the autonomy and separation of the black race on the other hand. Garvey developed a race-based nationalism that clashed with the integrationist view of Du Bois (Smet 1980, 40). The relationship between Garvey and Du Bois was characterized by great divergences. At first, Du Bois supported Garvey's idea of launching a shipping company (The Black Star Line) to facilitate exchanges between the African diaspora and Africa. He broke with him once he realized that Garvey's project was separatist and thus opposite to the integrationist purpose of his own movement, the National Association for the Advancement of Coloured People (NAACP). Du Bois did not agree with Garvey's view that Africa should be ruled by African-American leaders. In addition, it is worth noting that through the UNIA, Garvey was appointed provisionally as the president of Africa (Smet 1980, 38). As Gordon (2008, 164) observes, Du Bois totally disagreed with Garvey's argument that "African states had to be founded on the black nation (racially understood), which ... was diasporic".

5.2.4 W.E.B. Du Bois: The theory of pluralist integration and pan-Africanism

Du Bois is recognized as a great Afro-American scholar of the twentieth century. He was born in Massachusetts, and after his studies at Harvard University, he taught sociology, history, and economics at the University of Atlanta. He took part in the creation in 1905 of the Niagara Movement. In 1909 he launched the NAACP. He also participated in the first Pan-African Congress, and he edited *Crisis* magazine (Gordon 2008, 73–74).

Du Bois considered the struggle against racism as the concern of his life, so that he could describe his own life as an "autobiography of the concept of race" (Appiah 1992, 28). In *The Souls of Black Folk* (1903), he brings to the fore the question of black people as those for whom both human dignity and status were denied. Substantially, he considered "being black" as human a mode of being as "being white". Seeing that society presumed black people to live outside of the framework of peoplehood, he thought that the study of those people required breaking through the veil imposed on their humanity (Gordon 2008, 75). He denounced lynching,[6] Jim Crow laws,[7] and discrimination in employment and the education of black people. His criticism of the above-mentioned Compromise of Atlanta is illustrative of his intransigence on the issue. Contrary to Washington's theory of accommodation of black people, Du Bois claimed the full achievement of their civil rights. Like Cooper, he supported the idea of an educational project including the possibility for black students to have access to higher education.

Du Bois opposed Garvey's separatist project, which had African-Americans returning to Africa to be free and happy. As Outlaw observes, he was committed

> to achieving *a society that is integrated socially, politically, and economically though made up of a plurality of racial and ethnic groups* which maintain and perpetuate their racial and ethnic distinctiveness to the extent that doing so does not threaten the integration of the social whole.
>
> *(1996, 70, emphasis added)*

In this respect, he can be included among the precursors of contemporary debates on multiculturalism, intercultural dialogue, and cultural crossing (Outlaw 1996, 151–152). Proponents of these issues maintain the existence of multiple cultures of humankind, their right to be recognized as such, and their capacity for dialogue and cultural crossing (Appiah 1992, 2007; Bell 2002; Nouss 2005). This attitude involves a repositioning concerning the question of African identity, as previously discussed, and subsequently the pan-Africanism issue.

In *The Conservation of Races* (2012), Du Bois illustrates his search for integration and also his rejection of denial of all kinds of difference (Outlaw 1996, 151–157). He denounces the prevailing discourses of his time on race because, according to him, they sustain a restrictive view of race, putting emphasis on physical traits such as the colour of skin, the type of hair, or the shape of face. He argues for an approach to race that emphasizes the influence of psychological, spiritual, social, and historical strengths in the configuration of human beings. As he notes himself,

> What then is a race? It is a vast *family of human beings*, generally *of common blood and language, always of common history, traditions and impulses*, who are both voluntarily and involuntarily striving together for the accomplishment of certain more or less vividly conceived ideals of life.
>
> *(Quoted in Bell 2002, 51, emphasis added)*

This concept of race is a source of multiple debates concerning, for example, its utilization in the context of pan-Africanist debate. Many people think that this concept is obsolete and inappropriate for human beings. Appiah, for example, (1992, 45) considers that

> there are no races. … Talk of "race" is particularly distressing for those of us who take culture seriously. For, where race works … it works as an attempt at

metonym for culture, and it does so only at the price of biologizing what is culture, ideology.

For Outlaw (1996, 154), the reconsideration of this notion by Du Bois is part of a "*political* project aimed at prescribing norms for the social construction of reality and identity, or self-appropriation and world making". In addition, Outlaw views Du Bois as believing in the plurality of races and therefore rejecting all kinds of race-based discrimination. Through exploration of the notion of race, he wanted to create a framework of values for the rehabilitation of cultural achievements of people of African descent and other ethnic groups (Outlaw 1996, 157).

Du Bois influenced many resolutions of the second Pan-African Congress in 1921, concerning, for example, racial equality and the governance of Africa by autochthonous instead of Afro-American leaders, even with the consent of the former, as expressed by the first Pan-African Congress. He shaped both the philosophical and practical foundations of pan-Africanism. Therefore, he is viewed as the craftsman and the architect of this movement (Appiah 1992, 40–45; Gordon 2008, 73–74).

The organization of the Pan-African Congresses draws on the initiative of Sylvester Williams, who convened, in 1900, an African conference to denounce the exploitation and despoilment of African lands for the benefit of the Crown. After Williams's death, Du Bois took control of the movement for several decades. The balance sheet of these meetings was rather modest, as their declarations and petitions were given very little attention by the world's ruling countries and systems. Nevertheless, these conferences were a forum for black people to denounce the atrocities of which they were victims. They contributed to awakening African consciousness for dignity and freedom (Smet 1980, 41).

5.3 The era of the African heirs of pan-Africanism

5.3.1 The Pan-African Congress of Manchester: A fundamental turn for pan-Africanism

The Congress of Manchester (15–21 October 1945) represents a fundamental turn for pan-Africanism. It was on this occasion that this movement was Africanized; that is, the torch of the struggle for dignity and the rights of black people that was launched by Afro-descendant leaders was transferred to African leaders (Martin 2012, 58). This Congress took a stand against colonialism, as expressed through its slogan: "Africa for Africans".[8] For Nkrumah,

> Pan-Africanism and African nationalism really took concrete expression when the Fifth Pan-African Congress met in Manchester. ... Instead of a rather nebulous movement concerned vaguely with black nationalism, *the Pan-African movement had become an expression of African nationalism.*
>
> *(1963, 134–135, emphasis added)*

The Fifth Pan-African Congress was organized by Padmore (1903–1959), assisted by Nkrumah, Kenyatta, and Peter Abrahams (1919–2017).[9] For Nkrumah (1963, 135), "unlike the first four Congresses which have been supported by middle class intellectuals and bourgeois reformists, the Fifth Pan-African Congress was attended by workers, trade-unions movements, farmers and students most of whom came from Africa", including some future political leaders such as Banda, Awolowo, Kenyatta, and Nkrumah himself.

For this generation of African heirs of pan-Africanism, the programme of action, methods, and fundamental purpose of the movement were agreed upon by the Pan-African Congress of Manchester. The programme focused on the demand for constitutional changes, the provision of universal suffrage; and the method to be employed was based on Ghandi's theory of non-violence with the purpose of achieving national independence leading to African unity (Nkrumah 1963, 135). The achievement of this project was full of challenges, as I will outline below.

5.3.2 Towards African political unity

African unity represented a fundamental challenge for the first generation of African heirs of pan-Africanism. Nkrumah viewed this unity as the key to African liberation. For him, "it is only when full political unity has been achieved that we will be able to declare the triumphant end of the Pan-Africanism struggle and the African liberation movement" (Nkrumah 1963, 53). But what does the idea of unity mean for the African heirs of pan-Africanism? For many of them, this idea deals more with the "African one-ness" or the "African personality" (Nkrumah 1963, 132) than with the question of the colour of a person's skin. The political achievement of this project followed two main orientations: the maximalist and the minimalist approaches to African unity.

5.3.2.1 Maximalist approach to African unity

Political unity constituted the war cry of defenders of the maximalist view of African unity. In this respect, Nkrumah (1963, 217) declares that "unless Africa is politically united under an All-African Union Government, there can be no solution to our political and economic problems ... our best interests can only be served by uniting within an African Community".

This approach rejects the configuration of African countries inherited from the Conference of Berlin (1884–1885) and supports the creation of a supranational entity named "United States of Africa", conceived of as the political platform to the integration of African economies and the organization of a common African army (Nkrumah 1963, 140).

The maximalist approach to African unity came up against multiple obstacles including, for example, the resistance of former colonial powers who saw in this project a threat for their own interests. Many African leaders also rejected this view of their national sovereignty and privileges. Apart from that, there was and still is a huge gap between African people's expectations and politicians' ambitions. Nkrumah outlines through *Africa Must Unite* (1963) and *Consciencism* (1970) the need to make up this deficit, but he received a very weak response. In addition, his own attitude as political leader has been in contradiction with this proclaimed ideal (Appiah 1992, 158, 161).

5.3.2.2 Minimalist approach to African unity

For defenders of this view, the creation of an African supranational state is purely utopian. They saw African unity as starting gradually and matching the basic needs of African people by providing a better system of transport and communication, better health care and education, and carrying out programmes for development. They supported the intangibility of borders and the sovereignty of African states stemming from the Berlin Act.

This approach to African unity also came up against various obstacles including the want of both political will and financial resources as well as the lack of efficient structure and mechanisms to bring their proposals to reality (Mbuyi 1993, 57). The creation of the Organization for African Unity (OAU) on 25 May, 1963, allowed them to overcome the antagonism between the two approaches, as this organization stood on principles of reciprocal cooperation, respect for the national sovereignty of member states, non-intervention, and the promotion of an African common market (Martin 2012, 56). In June 2001, the OAU formally ended in favour of of the African Union (AU) (Martin 2012, 61).

5.4 Some African heirs of pan-Africanism

5.4.1 Kwame Nkrumah: Consciousness and the African personality

Nkrumah is viewed as the standard-bearer and *primus inter pares* of African pan-Africanist heirs. Most of his thought and political action have already been the object of excellent studies and criticisms by authors including Appiah (1992, 158–172) and Hountondji (1983, 131–155), among others. Nevertheless, in the context of this analysis, let's roughly summarize some of his main ideas.

Nkrumah studied at Lincoln and Pennsylvania universities, USA, between 1935 and 1945. He gained knowledge of the struggle of Afro-Americans for their rights, and he also grew close to leaders such as Garvey and Du Bois. The struggle of these leaders in defence of black people shaped his own commitment to African emancipation. His idea to create an African supranational state echoes to some extent the pan-Africanist dream of Garvey, whereas his concern for African humanism puts him close to Du Bois's concern for Negro-African solidarity.

Concepts such as consciencism and the African personality are part of his philosophical and political legacy. For him, African emancipation concerns "the emancipation of man", or a "social revolution" (Nkrumah 1970, 78), for which a specific philosophy is required; that is, consciencism. This philosophy aims at the rehabilitation of egalitarianism in human society and the mobilization of required resources to attain this purpose. In this respect, he viewed social equality, morality, liberation from colonization, and imperialism as fundamental issues. Standing on the Kantian moral imperative, he considered the cardinal ethical principle of consciencism to be the idea "to treat every man as an end in himself and not merely as a means" (Nkrumah 1970, 95). For Nkrumah, consciencism is also viewed as "the map ... of forces which will enable African society to digest the Western and the Islamic and the Euro-Christian elements in Africa, and develop them in such a way that they fit into the African personality".

In other words, this personality is itself defined by the cluster of humanist principles which underline traditional African societies. The idea of positive action[10] is also important to Nkrumah's theory of consciencism, as it represents the sum of forces seeking social justice in terms of the destruction of oligarchic exploitation and oppression. It is contrary to forces tending to prolong colonial subjugation and exploitation (Nkrumah 1970, 99).

Criticism of Nkrumah points, first, to the gap between his political theory and political action. If he were successfully to become a "philosopher king", his practice as "king philosopher" raises up various criticisms concerning, for example, the development of democracy, the institutionalization of one-party rule, and his international policy, which he developed almost to the detriment of the interests of his own country (Appiah 1992, 159–163).

A second criticism observes that Nkrumah's theory of African unity rests on a hasty generalization of local realities – the experience of Ghana – to the whole of Africa. This attitude relies on an essentialist view (and that is the second postulate) that asserts the cultural unity of Africa and, consequently, ignores the very diversity of this continent concerning traditions, political experience, and social organizations (Hountondji 1983, 138–140). As it will be further outlined, this attitude represents one of the causes of the sclerosis of today's pan-Africanist thought.

5.4.2 Fanon: Deconstructing the colonial paradigm

Fanon's interest in pan-Africanism developed in the framework of the struggle against colonialism. He travelled to sub-Saharan Africa for the first time in 1958 as a member of the Algerian delegation to the First Conference of the Union of African people, convened by Nkrumah in Accra to lay the foundations for pan-African policy (Cherki 2000, 211). On this occasion, Fanon supported African solidarity, postulating that it is important not to isolate national struggles from the larger African struggle for emancipation. From this perspective, he considers that, in Africa, national awareness comes along with African consciousness; and construction of a nation comes along with the discovery and the promotion of universal values (Fanon 1979, 174–175). For him, every African must feel committed in a definite way and must be able to act according to the appeals of such and such African territory. The struggle for national emancipation would be meaningless if it ignores the suffering that neighbour countries undergo on behalf of the colonizer (Fanon 1979).

The core of Fanon's support for pan-Africanism is noticeable through his written works, particularly through books such as *Peau noire, masques blancs* (1975, originally published in 1952) and *Les damnés de la terre* (1979, originally published in 1961). Following the recent development of postcolonial theory for which he is considered one of the main precursors (Mbembe 2005, 123), it can be observed that Fanon has been the subject of multiple studies, covering various domains as they aim at different purposes. Scholars such as Bhabha (2007), for example, emphasize some of Fanon's core premises that, I think, represent a crucial contribution to pan-Africanism. At first, these premises denounce the fallacy underlying the conventional paradigm regulating the relationship between colonizer and colonized. This paradigm was based on permanent opposition between white people (the colonizers) and black people (the colonized), superior and subaltern, developed and underdeveloped, benefactor and assisted, and so on. For Fanon, this approach relies on a fallacy because the relationship between colonizer and colonized was essentially marked by the predation, spoliation, and destruction of the latter by the former. It seems necessary to outline the light and shade that structures this paradigm and subsequent social and political practices.

Second, for Fanon, it is important to go beyond antagonism and deconstruct colonial imaginary and discourse which, being hegemonic, devalue non-Western cultures, which it transforms into things (*réifier*) and for which it makes permanent use of ethereal categories. In doing so, this paradigm ignores the diversity and interlacing that characterizes colonized people. In other words, colonized people are the holders of a hybrid identity (Bhabha 2007, 57–93) that includes the powerless, outcasts, rural and urban masses, all of whom are committed to radical change in order to improve their own situation (Gordon 2008, 222–223). As I shall explain below, neglecting or rather forgetting this reality characterizes some trends of pan-Africanism.

5.4.3 Gaddafi: From Arab nationalism to pan-Africanism

After taking power in 1969, Gaddafi wanted to be a political leader *sui generis* for his country, the Arab world, and the African continent. To achieve such a purpose, he reorganized Libyan institutions by revising the constitution and setting up a new political system called "direct democracy". This system refused any legitimacy to political parties and to their system of indirect representation. On the contrary, this regime pretended to favour "the government of the people by the people", transforming Libya into a *Jamahiriya*, which means a "State of masses". Gaddafi imposed such a rule on his country until his fall in October 2011. He used the financial resources of his country to develop its infrastructure and education and health systems, while restricting political liberties.

On the international scene, Gaddafi appears as a Third World anti-imperialist activist. He put his political skills and Libya's financial resources at the service of his international political ambitions. Many people considered him as an extravagant and shady personality. In this perspective, he was suspected of supporting terrorist organizations and rebellions in Africa as well as all around the world. His implication in the Lockerbie bombing (1988) and in projects of destabilization of Libya's neighbour countries, such as the Republic of Chad, can be viewed as emblematic failures of his international policy.

Through his commitment for both the identity and unity of Arab world, Gaddafi took as his model the Egyptian president Abdel Gamal Nasser. He built his policy of pan-Arabism through the creation of various unions with Arab countries including Sudan and Egypt (1969), Syria and Egypt (1971), Tunisia (1974), Morocco (1984), and Sudan (1990). All these initiatives failed because most of Arab leaders were reluctant to give up their sovereignty for the benefit of any supranational entity. In addition, they didn't support Gaddafi's proposal of what he termed the "Third way", an alternative to both capitalism and scientific socialism. They were also suspicious of Gaddafi's political project exposed in his manifesto, *The Green Book of the Libyan Revolution*.

The majority of Arab leaders refused to support Gaddafi when he was banished from the international community by the United Nations and Western countries because of his implication in attacks against a Pan American Airways Boeing 747 (1988) and a UTA DC-10 (1989). This denial of solidarity from his Arab peers precipitated his disappointment, and consequently it inspired him to bring important support to pan-Africanism, to struggle for African unity and solidarity for the benefit of black African countries. "I fell asleep with 4 million Libyans and I woke up with 700 million Africans", he declared in September 1999 during the summit of the OUA in Syrte where the creation of the AU in substitution of the OAU was approved.

This transfer from Arab world to black African community is important, as it reveals and confirms Gaddafi's desire for both recognition and leadership. It also highlights the potential for solidarity between the two worlds: black Africa and Arab Africa. Ngoma-Binda (2013) notes that solidarity between black Africa and Arab Africa came across multiple difficulties. It can be noted that when black Africans and heirs of pan-Africanism speak of this movement, they put emphasis on black Africa (Ngoma-Binda 2013, ebook, 592). On the other hand, with the creation of the Arab League in 1945, Arab African countries such as Tunisia, Morocco, Egypt, and Libya were keen on sustaining Arab culture, identity, and emancipation (Ngoma-Binda 2013, ebook, 604). Thinkers such as Fanon tried to soften this paradox through commitment to the Algerian struggle for emancipation (Cherki 2000, 202–205).

Within both the OAU and the AU, Gaddafi played the roles of fireman and pyromaniac at the same time, instigating conflicts on one side and playing "good offices" on the other side. His generosity and aptitude for mobilizing financial resources in support of projects of development in various African countries, the creation of banks, and the construction of hotel complexes of high standing were largely recognized. This political and economic activism was in line with Gaddafi's strategy: to be pragmatic in the search for African unity and to show to the rest of the world how financial autonomy can make people free to think of and achieve by themselves their own projects and development. Like Nkrumah, Gaddafi considered the creation of a pan-African government with its own army and financial organization. Like Nkrumah at the creation of the OAU (1961), Gaddafi's dream was blocked with the creation of the AU at the Summit of Syrte (1999).

In October 2011, Gaddafi was killed by insurgents with the support of the international community, including European Union countries. His death marks the end of one of the longest African political reigns – 42 years – with its multiple trips both at national and international levels. Gaddafi has been a controversial personality within the OAU and AU concerning his view on African unity and solidarity. Despite his propensity to authoritarianism, he was financially generous towards many black African countries as well as pragmatic on the issue of development. He embodied both the freedom of speech and courage to challenge Western countries and international funding institutions concerning financial support for African development projects. These two aspects constitute the Achilles heel of pan-Africanism, which, for lack of charismatic leadership, fails to play fully its role throughout the continent.

Although flickering because of lack of stability and due to repeated assaults from neo-liberal policies, the flame of African unity remains alive. The issue of how to bring it into reality is more than ever a burning debate for both African activists and scholars.

5.5 Beyond pan-Africanism

Events that occurred in the last three decades of the last century, including the collapse of communism, globalization trends, and the awakening of a new social, cultural, and political awareness in black communities, contributed to the emergence of a critical reassessment of pan-Africanism. This criticism denounced the institutionalization and the ossification of conventional pan-Africanist thought. It called for an urgent reconsideration of the philosophy underlying pan-Africanist discourse concerning African identity and African sovereignty, as both these concepts are crucial to the call for black people's solidarity.

5.5.1 The issue of black people's identity

First, it should be remembered that the rehabilitation of black people because of misdeeds of slavery and colonization constituted the original principle and the mobilizing ideal of pan-Africanism. For the founders of this movement as well as for their intellectual and political heirs, there is an intimate relationship between black people and Africa. For them, Africa is the natural fatherland of black people. This idea is so deeply engrained that for many of these thinkers, to talk about Africa or about "someone who is African" automatically means "someone who is black"; that is, "someone who is not white", to draw on Mbembe's (2005, 1) formulation. From this perspective, African identity refers to the fact of being black. The emphasis is particularly on the racial dimension; that is, on the ratio of melanin present in the individual in question. Many people think of this ratio as the fundamental basis of a person's identity, regardless of their social, cultural, political, or economic trajectory (Kelman, 2005, 106–139).

This approach to African identity is problematic because of this basic premise which presupposes that African populations include exclusively black people. In addition, as victims of slavery and colonization, these people are the exclusive beneficiaries of a pan-Africanist struggle. My argument aims at questioning this premise because it ignores the impact of current configurations and interdependencies that shape Africa and African diasporas around the world. This view fails to take into consideration the effects of the principle of *la circulation des mondes* as sketched out by Mbembe (2005, 1). This failure contributed to ignorance of the diversity shaping African identity in favour of a fundamentalist or essentialist analysis focusing on biological inheritance, or the perceptible level of melanin of concerned individuals (Kelman 2005, 159–173). For decades, this approach both governed and ossified pan-Africanist discourse (Mbembe 2005). Protagonists of this approach to African identity promoted a biased interpretation of African identity as well as of expected and actual solidarity.

The idea of "*circulation des mondes*" opposes the nativist view underlying the original pan-Africanist discourse (Appiah 1992, 47–72; Nouss 2005). It emphasizes two perspectives that this discourse does not make enough use of. First, there is the fact that Africa can be considered as a *destination* that has attracted people from different countries and cultures. People from Europe, Asia, or the Arab world, for various reasons, have for decades emigrated to and settled in Africa. Such is the case, for example, of Afrikaners and people of Indian origin that are disseminated in Southern Africa. It's the same concerning Lebanese, Greek, and Portuguese populations and other groups scattered across the continent. Depending on how deeply they feel their relationship to Africa is, these people can somehow claim African citizenship.[11] In doing so, they may also claim to be part of African identities, the shaping of which they are contributing to. This postulate questions theories that base African identity exclusively on biological or racial heritage, reserving this privilege to only black people.

To put things positively, this type of initiative takes into consideration the responsibility of individuals in the choice and configuration of their own identity as well as their contribution to local and collective identities, including African ones. This attitude highlights the impact of the overlap between "indigenous and immigrant", "here and elsewhere", "inside and outside", "ourselves and others". Therefore, it softens claims about original features of identity because it supposes that identity formation is an ongoing process that implies various configurations and all kinds of elements including, for example, financial resources, education, individual and collective actors, as well as social and cultural self-representations (Maalouf 1998).

The second perspective relates to Africa as a *departure area*. These departures can be grouped into two categories based on their original motivations. The first category involves migration caused by both the slave trade and slavery. These migrations are marked by pain, victimization, and resignation. Deported people bear the mark of humiliation, self-contempt, and alienation instilled in them by the dominant system. The awareness of this situation explains the struggle for self-esteem and rehabilitation of black people launched by the founding fathers of pan-Africanism, as I previously demonstrated. Unfortunately, this struggle has been confined to racial and Afrocentric discourses whose limits and anachronisms are constantly denounced (Lévi-Strauss 2007; Kelman 2005, 159–161; Nouss 2005).

The second category includes recent migrations due to a variety of motivations including, for example, job offers, studies, exile, or simply individual choice in search of better living conditions. These migrants reverse stigma because they refuse to be considered as victims and resigned people. They claim a new way of being in the world dialogue with other people and cultures. This new self-perception is thought to be free from traditional clichés and prejudices about black people. Therefore, they reveal the complexity shaping their identity concerning both their roots and cross-cultural mode of being. In this respect, I can point out two main trends of this way of thinking; Afropolitanism (Selasi 2005; Mbembe 2005) and cosmopolitanism (Appiah 2007).[12]

Defenders of Afropolitanism denounce the ossification of pan-Africanist discourses and subsequent representations of Africa.[13] According to Mbembe, for example, pan-Africanism counts among the major paradigms that dominated African thought along with anti-colonial nationalism and African socialism for almost a century. This paradigm is, like the other two, ossified. The three of them are no longer congruent with African people's current living conditions as well as with their political, social, and cultural configurations. In other words, they seem to be no longer relevant to African reality and debate. In this respect, Mbembe observes that those paradigms have largely become "*institutionalized* and *ossified* to such a degree that, today, *they no longer make it possible to analyse transformations in process with the slightest bit of credibility*" (quoted in Musila 2016, 110, emphasis added).[14]

Afropolitanism is, according to Mbembe,

> *une manière d'être au monde* qui refuse, par principe, toute forme d'identité victimaire … c'est également *une prise de position politique et culturelle* par rapport à la nation, à la race et à la question de la différence en general.
>
> *(2005, 2, emphasis added)*

> (a way to be in the world that refuses, by principle, any form of victimhood identity … it is also a political and cultural attitude related to the nation, race, and the issue of difference in general.)

This mode of being in the world characterizes a specific category of migrants, meaning a group of highly educated people, qualified professionals and scholars, who can be viewed as socially integrated, "who can express themselves in more than one language (and) not measure up against the village next door, but the world at large" (Membe quoted in Musila 2016, 110).

This mode of being in the world requires a broad-minded attitude concerning inward and outward flows of people, the overlap between "indigenous and immigrant", "inside and outside", "ourselves and others". Resuming Mbembe's description, Musila (2016, 110) sees this mode of being in the world as "a form of broadmindedness, anchored in African histories of flows, both outwards and inwards". Mbembe considers Johannesburg to be the place in Africa where Afropolitan spirit is best expressed. According to him, this city is

> en train de developer *une figure inédite de modernité africaine.* ... *Elle se nourrit à la source de multiples héritages raciaux, d'une économie vibrante, d'une démocratie libérale, d'une culture de la consommation qui participe directement des flux de la globalisation.* Ici est en train de *se créer une éthique de la tolerance* susceptible de réanimer la créativité esthétique et culturelle africaine.
>
> *(Mbembe 2005, 2, emphasis added)*

> (developing an unprecedented figure of African modernity. ... It makes use of multiple racial legacies, developing economy, liberal democracy, and a culture of consumption that directly involves globalization's flows. Here is in process an ethic of tolerance that can revive African aesthetic and cultural creativity.)

Based on this description, it is my feeling that the issue at stake is the epiphany about the multiple faces of humankind. The multiplicity of human beings constitutes a real stumbling block for African nationalist discourse – including a certain approach to pan-Africanism which distinguished itself by its capacity to turn identities into essence or ethereal categories in the name of racial unity and national sovereignty. In order words, African discourse on identity developed as an ideology in support of the African state, which has itself become a predator as well as a persecutor of political pluralism and ethnic and cultural diversity. Based on this observation, Mbembe believes that the racial solidarity advocated by pan-Africanism is also victim of the confiscation and the transformation of black people's identities into essence. Therefore, he denounces the current impasse of pan-Africanism and notes that

> A partir du moment où l'Afrique contemporaine s'éveille aux figures du multiple (y compris le multiple racial) qui sont constitutives de ses identités, decliner le continent sur le seul mode de la solidarité nègre devient intenable.
>
> *(Mbembe 2005, 2)*

> (Since contemporary Africa is becoming aware of the multiple figures [including racial multiplicity] that are part of its identities, it becomes difficult to speak of this continent referring only to black people's solidarity.)

Indeed, Mbembe does not establish any equivalence between pan-Africanism and Afropolitanism. For him, both the paradigms are different: "Afropolitanism is not the same thing as Pan-Africanism or Negritude" (Mbembe 2005, 2). The rapprochement between these two terms relies on their common concern to forge the discourse of African identity. From an Afropolitanist view, this identity is not reducible to the colour of the skin, neither it is limited to the geographic origin and alleged cultural roots of individuals. African identity is shaped through cultural crossings and diversity based on inward and outward flows of people. It is my feeling that according to this perception, African identity is much more an issue of individual paths than an exclusive concern with biological inheritance and cultural roots. Contrary to this approach, the conventional pan-Africanist view relies on the antagonism between inside and outside, indigenous and alien, traditional and Western, local and universal. This approach puts emphasis on both the homogeneity and unity of black identity, and subsequently it etherealizes this identity.

It is my feeling that this distinction highlights both the dilemma and the sclerosis of the conventional pan-Africanist rhetoric that, despite ongoing changes, seems to be fixed and supportive of an essentialist interpretation of black people's realities. I would like to emphasize that any identity, including African identity, is not made up of a simple set of data given once and for all. On the contrary, identity involves constant reconfigurations that include various elements; for example, social and cultural representations, social and political ratios of force, individual and collective choices. In short, no identity is a mere effect of a political nor a metaphysical decision (Kelman 2005, 173). Rather it results from interdependencies between individual and collective history, local and global factors, ourselves and others.

5.5.2 Human dignity and global justice

In addition to ideas of human diversity and cultural multiplicity, it is worth exploring one of the unspoken thoughts, as noted by Mbembe, of Afropolitanism. To be precise, I would like to highlight the issue of people who are not included in the Afropolitan discourse, those who are eclipsed as they don't have outstanding language skills, a high level of education, enough financial resources to travel all over the world, or access to the society of consumption and the flows of globalization. For Musila (2016, 110),

> while (Mbembe's discourse) paints a rosy picture of connectivity, heterogeneous blends of cultures and an ethos of tolerance, the unasked question remains: what about those excluded from these circuits of consumption and access, as is the case for majority of Johannesburg's residents?

This question highlights one of the limits of Afropolitan thought; that is, the ignorance of, or rather the omission of, the other, the other figure of humankind that is embodied by the most disadvantaged in black community and elsewhere. In this respect, Musila (2016, 109–113) and Dabiri (2015, 104–108) have already denounced the risk of Afropolitan discourse being viewed as a defence and eulogy of the current mainstream system of world rule, which appears to remain fundamentally based on social exclusion.

Relying on this observation, I can insist on both the originality and the relevance of pan-Africanism today. I want to suggest that for proponents of pan-Africanism, the defence of black people and culture is not an end in itself. Rather, this movement aims at delegitimizing and even dismantling a social, political, and economic order based on the negation of the multiple figures of humankind. Despite the ups and downs of pan-Africanism, this objective remains intact and still relevant nowadays since this movement aims at supporting everyone's right to human dignity and humanizing life. In this respect, I come back to the above-mentioned thought from Cooper (2000, 120–121), for whom "the cause of freedom is not a cause of a race or a sect, a party or a class – it is the cause of humankind, the very birthright of humanity".

In addition to that, I can also observe that Cooper's struggle for black people's right of access to higher education and for black women's emancipation is echoed through today's African challenges to pan-Africanism. The same observation is still valid concerning Du Bois's commitment to full achievement of black people's rights as well as for Garvey's call of "Africa for Africans" that, despite the impulse given by people such as Nkrumah, Fanon, and many others, remain part of contemporary Africa's challenges. Pan-Africanism cannot be viewed as an outdated movement or idealistic form of thinking enclosed in the search for the exhumation of a black African past. Again, referring to Musila's insight (2016, 110), I can note that for today's pan-Africanism, the key challenge remains the problem of social inequality that has historically been mapped onto a racial grid and blackness. This remains a major crisis, both globally and in Africa, as blackness continues to coincide with multiple marginalities and heavily discounted futures for millions of black people and, more broadly, people of colour across the world.

5.5.3 African state sovereignty

"Africa for Africans!" Such was the repeated war cry of pan-Africanist leaders and African freedom fighters. For them, this slogan refers essentially to African emancipation and black people's sovereignty. Therefore, they struggled for African political unity that they thought to be a fundamental and unavoidable step without which nothing is possible (Nkrumah 1963). The creation of the OAU, recently replaced by the AU, fairly illustrates this preoccupation.

Following the collapse of communism, neo-liberalism has become the ruling perspective globally. This new context raises the question of the sovereignty of African states because, as Gordon (2008, 223) observes, "the general goals of neoliberalism are to expand the hegemony of the market economy or capitalism [and] dwindle away the role of the state in human affairs as much as possible, especially the economy".

Indeed, to achieve this purpose, institutions such as the World Bank and the IMF make use of all their strength to keep African countries under control. Appiah notes that under the coordinated instrumentalities of the IMF and the World Bank, *programs of so-called structural adjustment have forced elites to accept reduced involvement in the economy as the price of the financial (and technical) resources of international capital. The price of shoring up the state is a frank acknowledgement of its limits: a reining in of the symbolic, material, and coercive resources of the state.*

(1992, 167, emphasis added)

Based on these premises, I can observe that African states are weakened and dramatically bound to world ruling structures. They are "emasculated" by the neo-liberal policy developed by international institutions and world ruling powers. In this respect, the situation of the African intelligentsia and political leaders can be viewed as weak and paradoxical. It is barely understandable how they can accept being deprived of a large part of their fundamental prerogatives while at the same time continuing to claim their own legitimacy and sovereignty. As an illustration, it can be observed that those states cannot develop on their own any important initiative or policy for the benefit of their people without first checking for the green light from their godfathers and funding institutions. This attitude makes people think that the original dream for African sovereignty is totally compromised or has become a nightmare (Traoré 1999).

In addition, the fact that African states are also tied to Western institutions because of their so-called national debt is relevant (Traoré 1999; Gélinas 1994). In the name of refunding this debt, they oblige their own people to live in all kind of want and misery. This attitude turned them into ferocious defenders and obstinate protectors of foreign interests to the detriment of the well-being of their own people. They behave as predators as well as being ignorant of human rights and democratic principles. The majority of African leaders seem to be tied to ensuring their individual political and financial survival, particularly through their submissiveness towards their creditors and godfathers (Taiwo 2014). As already mentioned, this attitude compromises pan-Africanist objectives of African unity and sovereignty.

It is a shared feeling that, in the name of neo-liberal philosophy and strategies, African people suffer from drastic budget cuts in areas such as health, education, and social security (Traoré 1999). Subsequently, a large majority of African people have been excluded from the flows and benefits of globalization because they cannot afford the cost of living and do not have access to schooling, medical care, and a range of social services. Contrary to the Afropolitan portrait sketched by Mbembe (2005), this category of African people can be considered as the "wretched of the system" because they are the manifestation of its structuring logic. The human figure that they represent is viewed as not carrying weight in terms of financial benefit and capitalist development. In sum, it is my feeling that the current ruling order can be viewed as discriminative and excluding of the powerless and most disadvantaged people, regardless of the colour of their skin.

Based on these observations, I think that it is urgent to develop alternative thinking on pan-Africanism, putting more emphasis on people's empowerment, global justice, and the struggle for human rights than on the power of African states that are, as already demonstrated, tied and bound to foreign institutions and godfathers. The key challenge here remains the problem of the power relationship that has also been mapped onto a racial grid and blackness, as already demonstrated by Memmi (1985). To tackle this challenge, it seems important to develop a critical attitude towards nativist philosophies shaping the conventional pan-Africanist world view. It is also important to be constantly aware of new configurations and interdependencies at work today in Africa as well as in the world. African sovereignty doesn't mean national self-sufficiency. Every country depends on others for its own development.

5.6 Conclusion

Pan-Africanism is a powerful utopia that has mobilised black communities all over the world for decades. This movement benefited from a range of theories, and it deeply marked political and philosophical thinking on black people's destiny. The emergence of new configurations in the world, and consequently the consciousness of new self-representations of black people themselves, have shone a light on the sclerosis of conventional pan-African discourse, particularly concerning approaches to African identity and sovereignty.

This change of context creates new conditions for fresh paradigms of solidarity based on the search for global justice and support for the struggle for human rights to delegitimize behaviours as well as social and political systems that are predators and persecutors of human dignity and the diversity of humankind.

To match the challenges of black people today, pan-Africanist discourse must go beyond all kinds of Afrocentrism and nativist theories on race and political emancipation and, consequently, give critical consideration to new configurations and interdependencies at work in the current and globalized world.

Notes

1 This chapter is based on the following article: Kasanda, Albert, 2016, "Exploring Pan-Africanism's Theories: From Race-Based Solidarity to Political Unity and Beyond", *Journal of African Cultural Studies*, Vol. 28, No. 2, pp. 179–195. Copyright © Journal of African Cultural Studies reprinted by permission of Taylor & Francis Ltd, www.tandfonline.com on behalf of Journal of African Cultural Studies.
2 I owe the concepts of configuration and interdependency to Norbert Elias (1985).
3 According to this principle, once an individual has a black ascendant, he/she is classified as black regardless of the colour of their skin. This postulate served to rationalize racial classification in the USA. See Semprini (1997, 8–11); Lott (1997, 176–180).
4 Compared to many Latin American countries, Cuba can be viewed as a pioneer in this respect. Soon after the Cuban revolution in 1959 Fidel Castro made racial justice one of his priorities because he considered that black people constituted the great majority of poor and disadavantaged people in Cuba. See Gordon (2008, 169).
5 Cooper's dissertation was edited and translated by Frances Richardson Keller in 2006: *Slavery and the French and Haitian Revolutionists*. Lanham, MD: Rowman & Littlefield.
6 The extrajudicial mob action was common in the USA from the late eighteenth century to the middle of the twentieth century. It served a racist purpose in supporting white supremacy by terrifying and killing black people.

7 The Jim Crow laws were based on the segregationist principle of "separate but equal". They mandated the segregation of public schools, public places, and public transportation, restrooms, restaurants, and drinking fountains for whites and blacks.
8 Regarding the origin of this slogan, Smet (1980, 37–38) thinks that this idea was first formulated by P. Otlet as a title of a booklet in 1888: *L'Afrique aux Noirs*. In 1896, the Reverend Booth, a British missionary working in Nyasssaland, also used the expression "Africa for Africans" in defence of black people. African nationalists such as John Chilembwe, Navuma Tembula, and Salomon Kumalo also rely on this idea to inspire the struggle for emancipation of black Africans. Garvey can be viewed as the one who really made this slogan popular.
9 Peter Abrahams was a novelist from South Africa. His works include *Mine Boy* (1946), *The Path of Thunder* (1948), and *The Wild Conquest* (1950). He left his country by the age of 20 to escape from Apartheid rule. He settled first in Britain, and he moved to Jamaica later.
10 Bell (2002, 41) thinks that Nkrumah borrowed this concept from Gandhi to support social and political changes through a non-violent process.
11 The case of Guy Scott, the Zambian white politician who served as the Zambian acting head of state (October 2014–January 2015) as well as being the country's vice president (2011–2014) can be considered as illustrative in this respect.
12 This analysis leaves aside the debate on cosmopolitanism to concentrate on Afropolitanism, paying specific attention to its formulation by Mbembe (2005).
13 A special issue of *Journal of African Cultural Studies* introduces the debate on Afropolitanism. See *Journal of African Cultural Studies*, Vol. 28, No. 1, 2016.
14 See also Mbembe (2005, 1).

6

AFRICAN DEMOCRATIC TURN

Introduction

Democracy is an endless challenge for African countries. It was introduced as a formal mode of governance on the eve of African emancipation by the colonial regime. Very soon after independence, this process underwent many changes, ranging from Western representative democracy to forms of governance including single-party rule, diarchism, and the no-polity system. These changes were based on the anti-colonial nationalism that had dominated African political thinking for almost a century, plunging it into dogmatism and intellectual lethargy.

The emergence of new configurations at the world scale and African people's new self-representations highlight the sclerosis characterizing African nationalist discourse on democracy. Recall, for example, the reductionism inherent in nativist premises underlying this discourse and the universalist illusion of its opponents. This chapter denounces the African nationalist dogma in support of a pluralistic approach to democracy. Relying on new configurations at work, this chapter also highlights new requirements for the achievement of democracy in Africa.

This chapter is divided into three sections. The first section briefly summarizes both the etymology and early development of democracy in ancient Greece and Western society. It outlines notions such as equality between citizens (*isonomia*), citizens' participation in power, and individual rights as constitutive of the original social contract. The second section explores Africa's walk towards democracy. This section examines the reception of Western democracy by African leaders and its substitution by new modes of governance such as single-party rule, diarchism, and no-party rule, all theoretically rooted in the African precolonial legacy. The last section concentrates on the African (re)discovery of multi-partyism. This (re)discovery implies a long debate between defenders of the African precolonial legacy and protagonists of the universalist approach to democracy. This section suggests overcoming both anti-colonial nationalist premises as well as imperialist universalist arguments underlying this debate in favour of a new approach to democracy that is pluralistic and based on human rights.

6.1 The origin of the concept of democracy

From the outset, let us note that the term "democracy" derives from the combination of two Greek words: *demos* (the people) and *kratos* (the power). It was used as such in the fifth century BC to refer to a specific mode of governance of the polis contrasting with traditional paradigms such as monarchy, oligarchy, meritocracy, and aristocracy. This mode of governance was different in that it privileged the principle of *isonomia*; that is, the idea of equality of citizens regardless of their religious beliefs, family and individual merits, wealth, and social position (Held 2006, 11–28).

Thinkers such as Solon, Périclès, and Clisthène contributed much to the development of this mode of governance. Respectively, they granted to people the status of full political agent; they supported political equality of citizens; and they made the agora the centre of political life instead of traditional spaces including cathedrals and *aéropages*. For those thinkers, the equality of citizens and their participation in power constitutes the immovable ground of political life.

The Athenian democracy suffered from the criticism of thinkers such as Plato (*République VIII, III*) and defenders of traditional modes of governance (Held 2006, 23–27). After a long eclipse during the Middle Ages, this concept appears again thanks to modern philosophers and protagonists of social contract theory including Hobbes, Locke, and Rousseau, to name a few. They highlight the crucial role of individuals (human beings) concerning both social and political organization. According to them, the individual is the main agent and source of his own rules for both social and political organizations (Held 2006; Leleux 1997).

Since the nineteenth century, the idea of democracy has referred to more than a political system, as it also indicates a normative paradigm of governance that includes values such as human rights, political participation and freedom, and justice (Kervegan 1996, 127). People all over the world have had different experiences and developed a variety of and interpretations of democracy. In this respect, it is my feeling that this concept does not resonate in the same way in Latin America, the USA, India, and Africa despite their multiple shared values. In other words, the development and interpretation of the concept of democracy depend on dimensions of space and time, social and political configurations characterizing the human condition. Let's roughly explore the principal trajectories and philosophical background of this word in relation to the experience of African people.

6.2 African trajectories toward democracy

6.2.1 Experience of representative democracy

It is worth keeping in mind that contemporary African states did not emerge *ex nihilo*. They proceeded from the Berlin Conference (1884–1885), their current borders resulting from the Berlin Act, whose main effect was both the sharing and colonization of the continent (Wesseling 1996). From this perspective, it can be outlined that it was the colonizer who, under the pressure of African people and freedom fighters, supervised the process of emancipation, organizing elections and setting up the first modern state institutions, such as the parliament and government, in most of the African countries (M'Bokolo 1985; Iliffe 1998). As might be expected, this process took as its background and model the Western political philosophy and mode of organization, including the paradigm of representative democracy. This mode of governance was thought to transcend cleavages characterizing these African countries, as all of them were a real mosaic of cultures, languages, and ethnic groups (Appiah 1992, 161). A large majority of African leaders adhered to this pattern, and thus began the postcolonial African state under the dominance of both Western political philosophy and godfatherism (Taiwo 2014; ebook 1907, 2076).

A range of African activists and scholars including Fanon (1979), Appiah (1992), Gyekye (1997), and Ake (1996) analyzed the strengths and weaknesses of this mode of governance. For Fanon, for example, representative democracy as inherited from colonizers constitutes a pretty illusion because while colonizing powers entrusted the political power to national bourgeoisie, they kept the economic power under their own strict control. In addition, Fanon observes that corruption, lack of capacity, and a low level of motivation on the part of national bourgeoisie to support national development was a real plague for African countries (Fanon 1979, 95–139). In this respect, it is my feeling that the current development of African countries supports Fanon's view. Those countries seem more dependent than ever on Western institutions and financial support (Willame 1996).

Analyzing the early political development of Ghana, Appiah (1992) observes two things: a duplication of ruling institutions and a growing gap between Ghanaian common people and the sphere of their postcolonial rulers. On one hand, people were still attached to their traditional chieftaincies so that the impact of contemporary and postcolonial structures on their daily life seems to have been very weak. On the other hand, despite their popularity and global recognition, new leaders such as Nkrumah, for example, were often viewed as a kind of artefact, a "foreign-made personality" whose duty is to protect foreign interests which are unknown to the majority of Ghanaian people (Appiah 1992, 161). This observation can also be viewed as valid for most African countries.

Appiah's observation raises a range of questions. First, it evokes the issue of African sovereignty, particularly concerning both the election and designation of African political leaders. Apparently, things occur as if African people had only one role to play in this process: to be the sounding board for a procedure conceived and set up by foreign powers. That calls for the second observation: the permanent divorce between African people and their rulers. Both these spheres appear antagonistic; for example, when people cry poverty, hunger, and lack of health care and education, ruling authorities loudly proclaim the progress achieved in refunding national debt and achieving macroeconomic balance (Traoré 1999). Those two questions call attention to the fact that Africa cannot evolve outside of the global system of rule; subsequently, this requires power, balanced relationships, and global justice (Odera 1997; Kasanda 2013b; Taiwo 2014).

Ake (1996) considers that Western democracy is a deceipt, particularly concerning the participation of people in power and the management of the polis. Ake relies on the Greek etymology of the word democracy (*demos* and *kratos*) to show that the idea of representative democracy is both an obstacle and a mirage concerning the participation of people in power. He thinks that political theories inherited from Western bourgeoisie and those coming from the USA distort the very nature of democracy. For him, those theories enacted a real change of the centre of gravity of democracy by substituting the community of citizens as well as its participative dynamic with the pre-eminence of the individual and the defence of his rights. Therefore, he notes that this form of democracy "Replaces *government by the people* with *government by the consent of the people*. Instead of *sovereignty of the people* it offers the *sovereignty of the law*" (Ake quoted in Martin 2012, 136, emphasis added).

He also insisted that this paradigm restricts the idea of democracy because it gives more power to government to the detriment of the people. Therefore, he writes that

> the classical theory of liberal democracy is less an expression of democracy than its restriction. It does away entirely with the idea of popular power and it replaces the idea of self-government with that of the consent of the governed. Even so the consent of the governed is largely an abstraction which is not operationalized, especially by universal suffrage. It is not about the involvement in government but about minimizing government and its nuisance value.
>
> *(Quoted in Martin 2012, 137)*

The political crises that plagued African countries shortly after their emancipation served as a pretext for most African leaders to abandon the ideal of representative democracy in favour of other modes of organization, as will be developed further.

6.2.2 Searching for direct democracy

6.2.2.1 One-party rule

The idea of one-party rule relies on the premise that there is no incompatibility between democratic thought and the one-party ruling system. As already mentioned, this idea emerged and flourished soon after African emancipation as an alternative to representative democracy. Proponents of this paradigm think that a country should be ruled according to one political party's ideology and principles. They evoke several arguments in support of this mode of governance including, for example, fighting against ethnic antagonism, sustaining the country's stability, and promoting national development. Leaders such as Nkrumah, for example, viewed one-party rule as a necessary tool in the achievement of his political project and the best way to match people's expectations. Therefore, he writes that

> it is necessary for positive action to be backed by a mass party. ... A people's parliamentary democracy with a one-party system is better able to express and satisfy the common aspirations of a nation as a whole than a multiple-party parliamentary system.
>
> (Nkrumah 1970, 100–101)

The majority of African leaders opted for one-party rule regardless of their ideological leanings. Most of them considered that political pluralism is by no means a guarantee of democracy. Such was the case of leaders such as Nyerere, Ben Bella, Sekou Touré, Mobutu, Eyadema, Banda, and Kenyatta, among others. In support of this option, they all evoked the imperatives of consolidation of national unity, political stabilization, modernization, and development of their respective countries (Lajul 2013, 161).

The option of one-party rule rests on the principle of oneness. African leaders preferred the idea of "one" (*monos*) over the concept of "multiple", to make a reference to an ancient philosophical debate opposing Heraclitus and Parmenides (Hersch 1993, 14–22). In the African political context, the idea of oneness is used in support of political mono-partyism; that is, the suppression of political pluralism and, subsequently, the assertion of the absolute dominance of one political leader. Power becomes concentrated in the hands of one individual leader who considers himself as the nation's founding father and benefactor. Regimes such as Kamuzu Banda (Malawi), Eyadema (Togo), Mobutu (Democratic Republic of Congo/Zaïre), to quote a few, illustrate this propensity. They used various metaphors, popular refrains, and slogans to spread and make popular this form of power. Recall expressions such as "One nation, one leader"; "one family, one father"; "one party, one country"; "one country, one people". These slogans were the object of widespread incantatory use.

It is my belief that those slogans relied on a fallacy, a mirage suggesting that mono-partyism was the impregnable shield of peace and prosperity, while accusing multi-partyism of promoting wars, dividing nations and causing stagnation. Defenders of this mode of governance consider that it is in the interest of the people to support and remain loyal to the central figure of the nation, its founding father, the supreme and providential guide (Englund 1996, 119).

As already mentioned, the one-party rule stands against ideas both of otherness and political pluralism. It does not allow checks and balances of power because the single and ruling party operates without any constraint or obligation to act in alignment with people's expectations in order to win more adherents and support. In this respect, it is my feeling that scholars such as Wiredu (1997, 308) and Appiah (1992, 158) are right in noting that the instauration of one-party rule was a hard blow to democracy, and subsequently its disappearance cannot be lamented.

It can also be observed that contrary to the democratic principle of *isonomia*, for example, one-party rule established the worship of hierarchy, particularly concerning the leader and party founding father. Not only was the authority of those leaders personalized, but it was also viewed as proceeding straight from God. As a matter of fact, they concentrated all the power (executive, judicial, and legislative) in their own hands. To some extent, they ensured that they would be considered as special beings by resorting to a variety of characters including, for example, the saviour, the supreme guide, the father of the nation, the "*Vieux/Mzee*", the "*Mwalimu*", and so on.

The worship of African leaders led to their deification, and they could not conceive any authority above them, let alone a competitor. For want of being identified with the divinity, some of them viewed themselves as just a little lesser than God. The idea that they came from an outstanding ancestry was also part of their common claim. Kamuzu Banda, the former Malawian leader, for example, can be considered as an emblematic personage in this respect. In his chapter "Between God and Kamuzu", Englund (1996) gives an illuminating description of Kamuzu Banda's attitudes towards power and the exactions of his regime. Englund observes that Banda's leadership relied on the African gerontocratic tradition in which elders are the main reference concerning authority and respect. He promoted himself in this social and political sphere. Consequently, he claimed the presidency for life. Englund notes that

> Playing upon his seniority and Western education, *Banda became one of the numerous charismatic and patriarchal leaders among the first-generation heads of independent African states*. ... Banda, like Kwame Nkrumah, Julius Nyerere, Kenneth Kaunda, Jomo Kenyatta, Ahmed Sekou Touré, Félix Houphouet-Boigny, among others, embodied the nation building in his person. ... *Banda's life-presidency and style of government carried allusions to paramountcy and, on occasion, to divine kingship*.
>
> (Englund 1996, 108, emphasis added)

The imaginative capacity of Banda's supporters was, according to Englund (1996, 116–117), bordering on proselytism, and they exacted payments from and forced obligations on Malawian people and Mozambique refugees. They concentrated on the purchase of the political membership card, but they also obliged people to attend the meetings of the ruling political party as well as controlling the everyday life of villagers. Englund writes that

> The everyday forms of coercion and oppression to which all villagers were subjected during Banda's regime included the purchase of Malawi Congress

Party membership cards, attendance at political meetings and rallies and, for men, the payment of taxes. Those who did not possess valid membership cards were routinely refused entry to buses and markets. Every "Malawian", including infants and Mozambiquan refugees, was obliged to have one. ... At rallies, village headmen were often asked by party officials to stand up with their villagers to show their numbers. If too few persons had turned up from a particular village, its headman was publicly humiliated by party officials. ... The rallies where Kamuzu Banda appeared were ... the most important of all. (Party officials) obliged villagers to attend, and women and schoolchildren had to find time to rehearse, beforehand, songs and dances praising him.[1]

In sum, it is my feeling that through one-party rule, democracy was deflected from the principles of equality and common participation in a country's politics, and instead all kinds of absolutism took over. Under such a rule, power is no longer, as Arendt asserts, in the capacity of acting together, but becomes a kind of private property whose owner is no longer the people, but the head of state and the party's founding father. From this perspective, both the people and institutions of the republic were robbed of their security, turned into objects of mockery, as well as being exploited according to the interests of the ruling authorities and their allies.

6.2.2.2 The diarchic rule or political cohabitation

The concept of diarchy derives from the combination of two Greek words: *duo* (two) and *arkhein* (power). The protagonists of this paradigm of governance maintain that the state's power can be performed by two actors at the same time. Known also under the name of "political cohabitation", this mode of governance relies much more on the consensus between contenders for power than on the people's will, as it aims at reconciling the holders of power and their rivals. In other words, diarchism can be viewed as a strategic attitude aiming at political compromise between contenders for power.

The recent political history of Africa is full of illustrations. By the 1990s, in the Democratic Republic of Congo (formerly Zaïre), for example, due to the pressure of the international community and Congolese civil society for democratization, president Mobutu agreed to share power with the opposition's political parties led by Etienne Tshisekedi. The same situation happened in Zimbabwe in 2009 between president Mugabe and Morgan Tsvangirai, the leader of the opposition political parties.

This search for compromise can be explained by two postulates: the obstinacy of the holders of power to remain in place endlessly and the requirement of political alternation defended by the opposition parties and the people. But there are also cases of political instability due, for example, to the military putsches that were viewed as a common way to gain access to power in Africa.

Regardless of arguments in support of diarchism, it is important to denounce the logic structuring this mode of governance. It is my feeling that this approach to power intends putting together two opposite forces: the defenders of the status quo on one side and the protagonists of a change of regime on the other. A common saying runs as follows: "don't place two roosters in the same manure". This desperate search for political balance at all cost seems to me a way to accommodate and to prolong the survival of a regime detested by the population as well as the suffering of the latter. Despite its seductive dimensions of peace and non-violence, this attitude can be viewed as not respecting democracy and the constitutional principles governing African countries. In this regard, the emergence of civic movements for the strict observance of fundamental laws in different African countries testifies to both the new consciousness of the people about their participation in power and, subsequently, new perspectives for democracy in Africa.

The idea of involving the military in government to prevent them from enacting a coup is both a mirage and a fallacy at the same time. First, military putsches are already illegal. The people who behave illegally cannot be rewarded no matter what the pretext is. Second, it is my feeling that this way of thinking is far from realistic. First, even if they are part of government, there is no constraint that can impede the military from perpetrating a putsch. The case of Sankara and Compaoré, both military, friends and allies, in Burkina Faso, can be viewed as illuminating in this respect. Second, to think in this way means relying on an incorrect premise that presents political stability as the only problem of African nations and the participation of military in power as the universal panacea. In this respect, it must be observed that the absence of military takeover is not a guarantee of democracy and progress. Countries such as the Democratic Republic of Congo (Zaïre), Togo, and Cameroon, for example, have been stable for decades, but they have not exhibited any political improvement. Their social and economic development is very slow, if not non-existent. On the contrary, the permanence of corrupted regimes has restrained people's development and distorted the principles of democracy, human rights, and social justice. In this respect, Lajul (2013, 160), observes that "Political stability is not a guarantee of political progress, and it causes years of serious political problems, problems that were suppressed and which never resulted in military takeovers".

It is my belief that the intrusion of military in politics is a paradox echoing, in the international context, for example, the cold war and protection of foreign interests, a euphemism standing for both the domination and the exploitation of African countries. This attitude also relies on individual ambitions for power. Takeovers cannot be viewed as a legal and democratic way to access power. As it is not worth putting two roosters in the same manure, so diarchism can hardly be a successful mode of governance in Africa.

6.2.2.3 No-party political system

Proponents of the no-party political system stand for the idea that there is no necessary connection between democracy and the multiparty system. According to them, various precolonial African systems of politics offered examples of democracy without a multiparty mechanism (Wiredu 1997; Wamala 2004; Gyekye 1997). They think that this mode of governance based on competition between political parties is hardly appropriate for the African political reality. Two kinds of arguments are often evoked in this respect. First, the African precolonial legacy which was characterized by concern for consensus and inclusion. Second, the desire to avoid people's suffering due to political pluralism and its subsequent competition. For the advocates of this paradigm, permanent antagonism characterizing majoritarian democracies produces disunity between people. It also creates the permanent exclusion of the minority as it rests on the idea that the winner takes it all. Two figures can be mentioned as contemporary standard-bearers of this mode of governance: Wiredu (1997) and Yoweri K. Museveni, the current Ugandan President.

In 1997, Wiredu published a paper on democracy and consensus in Africa in which he introduced his approach to the non-party polity system: "Democracy and Consensus in African Traditional Politics: A Plea for a Non-Party Polity". In this paper, Wiredu makes a distinction between majoritarian democracies and consensual democracies. The former are viewed as anchored in the Western tradition, while the latter are thought to rely on the African precolonial legacy, particularly on the idea of consensus. The paradigm of majoritarian democracy stands on the majority principle according to which "the party that wins the majority of seats or the greatest proportion of the votes, if the system in force is one of proportional representation, is invested with governmental power" (Wiredu 1997, 308).

For this paradigm, the concept of party refers to political organizations of people sharing similar tendencies and aspirations and aiming to gain power for the implementation of their policies. This idea is crucial as the government relies on the consent of political parties – without consensus – which to some extent eclipses minority groups and keeps them far from power as well as raising all kinds of antagonism and confrontation.

Consensual democracy model considers consensus to be the watchword of social and political organization. For Wiredu,

> the reliance on consensus is not a peculiarly political phenomenon. Where consensus characterizes political decision making in Africa, it is the manifestation of an immanent approach to social interaction. Generally, in interpersonal relations among adults, consensus as a basis of joint action was taken as axiomatic.
>
> *(1997, 303, emphasis added)*

In support of his argument, Wiredu evokes the Ashanti political system, which, for him, was a consensual democracy. According to him, this system was such because the "government was *by the consent*, and *subject to the control of the people* as expressed through their representatives. It was *consensual* because, at least as a rule, ... *the consent was negotiated on the principle of consensus*" (Wiredu 1997, 308, emphasis added).

For this mode of governance, the concept of political party is diluted in entities such as lineages and youth organizations, for example. In this respect, Wiredu notes that

> The Ashanti system ... was not a *party* system in the sense of the word "party" ... which is basic to majoritarian democracy. *But in a broad lexical sense there were parties. The lineages were parties to the project of good government.* Moreover, in every Ashanti town *the youth constituted themselves into an organized party* under a recognized leader who was entitled to make representation directly ... *to the relevant council on all matters of public interest.*
>
> *(1997, 308, emphasis added)*

Contrary to majoritarian democracies, the Ashanti mode of governance did not feature parties in the sense of organized groups aiming to gain power in a way which entailed others not being in power or, worse, being out of it. In other words, this system aimed at consensual inclusion of everyone in the process of power as it privileged the common interest. For Wiredu, awareness of such an interest makes conflicts around power irrational. It is in this respect, he evokes the metaphor of a crocodile having two heads and only one stomach (Wiredu 1997, 306, as described in Chapter 3).

Wiredu seems to be right in rejecting violence and lack of coherence characterizing the development of political systems in Africa, because they are neither representative of democratic spirit nor respectful of human dignity and fundamental rights. Nevertheless, I am somewhat sceptical about the relevance of his proposed alternative to majoritarian democracies, particularly the Ashanti no-party rule paradigm. Based on current configurations taking place in Africa and around the world, this mode of governance not only seems anachronistic, but also includes a variety of theoretical and practical limitations (Eze 1997, 313–323). As an illustration, consider the notion of "lineage" in replacement of the political party system. In this respect, Wiredu writes that

> the lineage is the basic political unit among the Ashanti [and] consists of all the people in a town or village having *a common ... ancestor*. ... Every such unit has a head, and every such head is automatically a member of the council governing the town or the village. Qualification for lineage headship are seniority in age, wisdom, sense of civic responsibility and logical persuasiveness ... *this office was for life.*
>
> *(Wiredu 1997, 305, emphasis added)*

This notion seems to rely on the illusion that African societies are self-sufficient entities that are fixed and evolve out of the reach of changes occurring in today's globalized world. It is my feeling that due to the increasing inward and outward flows of African populations, the growth of African cities, and the permanent mixture of cultures at work in Africa, the concept of lineage seems less and less reliable as a political category leading to political consensus. In addition, this concept refers to natural antecedent or biological legacy as it puts emphasis on the fact of having a common ancestor. This reference is, according to my own view, contrary to one of the fundamental premises of democracy: the idea of *isonomia*, the principle of equality between citizens that goes beyond considerations regarding the origin, social classe, religion, and family heritage of every citizen (Held 2006). More than that, this mode of governance can be also considered as opposed to democratic principles because it suggests a kind of mandate for life. As already mentioned, democracy has rested from its beginning on the idea of taking turns in the management of the city. This idea implies a temporary political mandate for everyone. As a matter of fact, one of the biggest challenges to African policy today is the limitation of the rulers' mandate as presidency for life. Experience reveals that like one-party rule, endless presidential mandates hardly bring something good for the people.

It is also my feeling that to prevent violence, confrontations, and subsequent exclusion attributed to the majoritarian mode of governance, Wiredu intends a mitigating framework for both political dialogue and inclusion. He may be right in this respect. But the question remains as to whether today's most important challenge to both African leaders and people is either the need for political guiding frameworks for their own actions or the need to develop a real political culture that includes both the commitment to and the permanent search for the common good, respect of laws, and strict achievement of fundamental human rights. Likely, my personal feeling is that it is the latter that constitutes the greatest challenge to Africa.

Ugandan President Yoweri K. Museveni's support for the no-party political system is less theoretical than that of Wiredu. His view relies on political pragmatism and consideration of the ups and downs of the Ugandan postcolonial experience. His thinking on the issue is articulated through the project of the National Resistance Movement (NRM), whose basic arguments can be summed up in three categories: national unity and consensus, Ugandan precolonial legacy, and equal sharing of resources.

For the protagonists of the NRM, Uganda underwent a conflict-prone and turbulent history because of competition between political parties. In other words, multi-partyism is viewed as the cause of Ugandan wars and sufferings. In this respect, the country needs to heal old wounds and bring about national unity, peace, and development. Therefore, it is imperative to promote a paradigm of governance aiming at consensus and reconciliation instead of political confrontation. Where to find such a paradigm? The NRM points to – and this is its second articulation – the African precolonial legacy as the matrix of such a project. This option relies on the idea that precolonial traditions included democratic values such as dialogue, consensus, and people's participation in the decision-making process. In addition, those traditions were inclusive and peace-loving. They were supportive of equity in sharing common resources and bringing support to the most disadvantaged.

This approach focused on disunity as the main Ugandan or African political problem. It also denounced confrontational policy characterizing the multiparty system as the source of this scourge. The defenders of this point of view are right that permanent antagonism and division occurring in Africa contribute to African stagnation. But it is my feeling that their argument fails because it turns multi-partyism into the scapegoat for all failures of postcolonial African regimes. This way of thinking fails to consider that one of the most brutal and blood-thirsty African postcolonial regimes, the rule of Idi Amin Dada, had nothing to do with multi-partyism. On the contrary, this regime was characterized by lack of political pluralism and abuses of the power directed against the individual. The proponents of this mode of governance also ignore many other actors and factors that, in different ways, determine the evolution of African politics. This is the case, for example, concerning the impacts of injunctions by international financial institutions on African leaders to provide for the interests of world ruling powers to the detriment of the wellbeing of the African people. This also remains true for sovereignty of African states. In this respect, following many other studies, Willame (1996) finds out how far the change of policy and conception on development by institutions such as the World Bank and IMF forced political reforms in Africa in the last two decades of the twentieth century. Analyzing political changes that occurred in Africa by the end of the twentieth century, he observes:

> Comment assurer ... un renouveau politique en Afrique, comment édifier une capacité locale si le context n'est pas favorable? La Banque mondiale plaide pour l'instauration d'un doube consensus. D'abord un consensus entre les donateurs qui s'organiserait autour de quelques grands axes: réformes profonde de l'assistance technique, reduction de la charge de la dette ... Ensuite, un consensus à l'intérieur de l'Afrique elle-même par le biais d'un débat large et rigoureux qui n'a pas été autorisé jusqu'ici ... la concretization de ce consensus ... est le fait d'une diaspora de technocrates de haut niveau qui constitue la pépinière, le think-thank de la Banque mondiale.
> *(Willame 1996, 12)*

(How to ensure ... a political renewal in Africa, how to build local capacity if the context is not favorable? The World Bank argues for the introduction of a double consensus. First, a consensus among donors that would be organized around several axes: deep reform of technical assistance, reduction of the debt. ... [t]hen a consensus within Africa itself through a broad and rigourous debate that has not been approved up to date ... the realization of this agreement ... is the duty of high-level diaspora of technocrats which constitutes the think-thank of the World Bank).

In his analysis of African states, Bayart (1989) demonstrates the complexity of the relationships between African rulers and their ruled. From another perspective, Amselle and M'Bokolo (1999) outline the effects of ethnicity on African societies and its manipulation on behalf of both political leaders and activists. Based on those observations, I can state that the lack of unity in African countries is not due only to multi-partyism. To focus only on multi-partyism as explanation of failures of African regimes seems to be a truncated approach, a kind of intellectual and political myopia. The African political arena is a site where multiple factors (internal as well as external) come together and compete against one another. The already mentioned studies of Wiredu (1997), Gyekye (1997), Wamala (2004), Appiah (2007), Bayart (1989), and Amselle and M'Bokolo (1999) can be considered, despite their respective limits, as a stimulating starting point concerning the search for an appropriate democratic framework for African countries.

6.3 The return to a multiparty system

The African political landscape is a changing reality in which the idea and practice of democracy has undergone several changes and received multiple interpretations, as already discussed. In the two last decades of the twentieth century, for instance, African people stood up to express their aspiration for political change. Their yearning for democracy was expressed through criticism and rejection of single-party rule. They denounced both its lack of coherence and sophism concerning, for example, the usage of African traditions as a basis for social and political organization. They also criticized the inability of one-party rule to make good on its own promises on development, national unity, and struggle against ethnic antagonism.

A new African political consciousness emerged through the experience of national debates known as National Sovereign Conferences (NSCs), which were being held in various African countries by the end of 1980s and beginning of 1990s. The NSCs represented unprecedented events in contemporary African political history. They consisted of convening a *"koinonia"* where African people, defying fear and intimidation from dictatorships, denounced misdeeds and failures of African postcolonial regimes. They also expressed their dreams and expectations about another possible political future based on democracy, justice, and development (Eboussi-Boulaga 1993; Traoré 1999). Those meetings laid the basis for a new social and political contract between African people and their leaders. Unlike the transition from colonial rule to emancipation, African people took their destiny into their own hands and spoke themselves of their future and fundamental expectations through NSCs. Through this process, they also faced the "invisible hand" of the world ruling system, including institutions such as the already mentioned World Bank and IMF, as they experienced the real capacity of these organizations to prejudice African people's interests (Willame 1996, 9–14).

The failure of single-party rule to bring about its own promises in reality (Appiah 1992, 158–172) encouraged the majority of African people to view liberal democracy as an alternative despite the fact that, as already mentioned, soon after their emancipation, a wide range of African countries had rejected this mode of governance for the benefit of single-party rule. In this respect, I think it is important to explore the reasons for such a change and this return to multi-partyism. Does this return include new values that can be viewed as favourable for better living conditions and development of Africans? What do African leaders understand by democracy? How do they see its fulfilment? These questions instigated a long debate among African scholars, which took two main routes: the universalistic trend and the particularistic interpretation of democracy.

A range of African social and political philosophers think of multiparty democracy to as an appropriate answer to contemporary African political problems. Their belief relies on various considerations. First, they think that multi-partyism implies recognition of and respect for the Universal Declaration of Human Rights, which stipulates individual freedom of association, assembly, and dissent. Those freedoms are viewed as normative values for today's democracy. They cannot be given or denied by any state or even by any people because they are essential to every human being. These rights and freedoms are thought to be a fundamental part of our human condition.

Second, those thinkers consider political parties to play an important role in educating and sensitizing people on issues such as democracy, political accountability, and human rights. They criticize but also provide ideological alternatives to the ruling party. In doing so, and this is the third reason in favour of them, they put pressure on the incumbent government to make it accountable and responsive to people's interests and expectations. In other words, political parties put pressure on the ruling authorities, and thus they ensure the search for human excellence and common good. Relying on those observations, I think that the multiparty system constitutes a stimulating ingredient for democracy in Africa. The reduction of its purpose to political confrontation, national disunity, and backwardness can be viewed as a hasty and prejudicial judgment.

6.3.1 Universalistic approach to democracy

The universalistic approach to democracy is, for the time being, widely favoured among African thinkers and Africanists. It borrows its main framework from the Western paradigm of democracy, as it puts emphasis on human rights, civil society, freedom of speech and freedom of association, freedom of religion, free vote, separation of powers, and multiparty rule. This approach rests on the premise that democracy is a sacred and untouchable principle that is valuable for everybody regardless of time and social and historical contexts. For proponents of this approach, any potential dysfunction would not be attributable to the ruling institutions as such, but rather to individuals, local cultures, and traditions. Following this way of thinking, many studies on African social and political processes both generalize and condemn African cultures as not being compatible with basic requirements of democracy. It can be noted that this attitude underlies the accusations of corruption, tribalism, and egocentrism often raised against African political leaders (Willame 1996; Smith 2003).

It is my feeling that the universalistic approach to democracy suffers from an inherent gap between the ideal of democracy and its multiple manifestations in reality. As already suggested, democracy is more than ethereal theories since it deals with people's daily lives through issues such as freedom, cultures, and traditions. It is a permanent struggle against egocentricity and obscurantism of political leaders.

The escapades of African leaders regarding endless rule illustrates the extent to which the concern for principles for their own sake can be a piece of bluff for democracy. Taiwo (2014) denounces the excessive attention (and the lack of criticism) paid to procedural democracy as one of the main germs of corruption concerning democratic thought in Africa. The propensity of African leaders to attempt to deviate from the fundamental law of their people in order to stay endlessly in power is symptomatic of such a lack of democratic culture.

6.3.2 Particularistic approach to democracy

The particularistic approach to democracy rejects the imperialist view of democracy promoted by the ruling system. Defenders of this approach denounce the relevance of the Western style of democracy for African people. They think of the current drive toward liberal democracy as being due to Western pressure to adopt the multiparty mode of governance (Wiredu 1998). They wonder, as Ramose (1999, 135) observes, whether this system can be viewed as a necessary and sufficient condition for the political emancipation of Africa.

For these thinkers, the premise according to which the Western paradigm of democracy would be the appropriate solution to the need for efficient political organization of contemporary Africa is flawed. Thus, they evoke two main categories of argument to explain this failure: its philosophical background and the lack of interest in the African precolonial legacy.

Ramose (1999, 135), for example, considers that the pretention to universalistic democracy is erroneous because it doesn't take into consideration the contingency of existence. This pretention ignores fundamental conditions of time and space characterizing every human being, society, and culture. He thinks that the universalistic approach to democracy rests on an unrealistic premise considering Western political paradigm to be valuable and applicable forever to every people and culture all over the world. In sum, the emergence of universalistic democracy can be viewed as the updated expression of Western cultural and political hegemony, one of the main characteristics of which consists of ignoring subaltern voices and cultures (Bhabha 2007).

The defenders of the particularistic view of democracy also consider Western democracy as offering an inauthentic expression of African political culture because it leaves aside the precolonial African legacy in favour of the Western view (Gyekye 1997). Ramose, for example, thinks that the Western paradigm of democracy is a political monologue leading a solipsistic life in a context where African indigenous political cultures are sentenced to silence and disappearance (Ramose 1999, 135). Consequently, such a paradigm cannot be emancipatory. It cannot be an authentic expression of contemporary African political culture.

Wamba-dia-Wamba (1992) shares the same line of thought. In 1992, he published an article entitled "Beyond Elite Politics of Democracy in Africa". In this paper, he analyzes the process of political transition in African during the course of the 1990s as well as at postulating an emancipatory mode of politics for Africa.

According to him, conventional modes of politics, including multiparty parliamentary democracy and the Third international (Stalinist) mode, failed in promoting emancipatory policy in Africa. Concerning the multiparty parliamentary paradigm, for example, he notes that this model did not promote African emancipation at all. The reasons for the failure are the following: first, this model makes political parties dependent on the state consensus and turns them into state organizations competing for the distribution of state positions as opposed to being entities working toward reconstruction of the state by and for the people. Second, this paradigm reduces politics to a matter of numbers so that the winning of more votes constitutes the foundation of legality and legitimacy (Wamba-dia-Wamba 1992, 30–31). In sum, for Wamba-dia-Wamba, as developed in Africa, the multiparty parliamentary model confines the emergence of democracy to claims such as the development of a market economy, privatization of state enterprises, and laissez-faire government, to mention a few. To overcome this failure, Wamba-dia-Wamba suggests the abandonment of the dominant modes of politics for the sake of new political paths. He thinks that it is crucial to create necessary conditions for the emergence of emancipatory politics in Africa. He insists that in Africa, "We must, therefore, move away from the process of *moving away from* traditional society *and* internalizing *the colonial state*" (Wamba-dia-Wamba 1992, 32).

The return to African political legacy implies, according to Wamba-dia-Wamba, the rediscovery of traditional modes of politics, such as *Mbongi* (the lineage assembly), as well as their specific modus operandi, such as the palaver. For Wamba-dia-Wamba, traditional modes of politics include salutary virtues for both African people and the development of democracy in Africa. They can be viewed as adequate grounds for emancipatory African policy (Hallen 2002, 88–89).

I agree with the criticisms of both Ramose and Wamba-dia-Wamba concerning the erroneous idea of universalism underlying the Western approach to democracy. I also share their postulates concerning the failure of this paradigm to emancipate African people. Nevertheless, it is my feeling that the alternatives they suggest are affected by the same weaknesses that they denounce in other approaches. First, there is their propensity to generalize; that is, to apply a specific experience to the whole African continent. The experience of Mbongi might well be efficient and successful in its original context, but there is no guarantee that its approach will work for other African ethnic groups and cultural contexts. In other words, Ramose and Wamba-dia-Wamba ignore the diversity of African cultures and the multiplicity of political contexts and traditions. Second, it seems important to outline the risk of anachronism underlying their proposals. Both thinkers, like many proponents of the African precolonial legacy,[2] pay very little attention to permanent changes that Africa and African people are undergoing by virtue of globalization and new configurations taking place in the world. Ramose denounces the fact that the universalistic approach to democracy doesn't take into consideration the "contingency of being", but his own proposal for an emancipatory approach to democracy ignores the power relationship ruling the world. It also seems blind to changes that are happening in Africa today. The same observation is valid concerning Wamba-dia-Wamba's call for the recovery of new political paths that seem totally out of tune with the current African political context. They both give the impression of thinking that African societies are homogeneous and impermeable to and out of reach of any change.

It is my feeling that, as has been the case across the world, Africa has undergone deep social and political change. Reliance on both the African past and its peculiarity is important, but this should not constitute an obstacle to political change and development. I believe that change constitutes a permanent condition of every human being, country, and culture. Individual commitment and democratic culture are required for change to be achieved. In terms of the requirement for democratic culture, I stress the urgency of the duty to provide education about such a culture not only to the African people, but also (and probably with much more emphasis than ever) to African leaders, who, since African emancipation, have given the impression of undermining standard political rules concerning the respect of one's word or the fundamental law and constitution of their own countries as well as lacking concern for common good and justice. Democracy relies not only on the evocation of cultural paradigms regardless of their origin, but mainly on a state of mind, a culture, and a subsequent attitude. These seem to me to be the unavoidable rules of the game. To violate these rules is to limit the very idea of democracy.

6.4 Conclusion

This chapter discussed the issue of democracy in Africa. It stated that the majority of contemporary African countries inherited their first paradigm of modern governance from their respective colonizers. This mode of governance was based on Western political philosophy and practice articulated through the idea of representative democracy. Shortly after their emancipation, African leaders abandoned this paradigm in favour of African nationalism and addressing people's expectations. Subsequently, they relied on the African precolonial legacy to promote paradigms such as one-party rule, diarchy, or no-party rule (democracy without political parties).

The changes that occurred in the late twentieth century gave African people the opportunity for a new democratic turn. Through the NSCs, they developed new political consciousness and achieved, in many cases, the move to a multiparty system to the detriment of one-party rule. Once again, they recovered neo-liberal democracy, recycled through the globalization process.

The return to representative democracy raises burning debates about the relevance of this paradigm for today's Africa. Proponents of the universalistic approach to democracy think that Africa, for its own development and stability, should follow the predominant ruling paradigm globally; that is, neoliberalism. For defenders of the particularistic approach, it is important to take into consideration the African precolonial legacy to be consistent with the actual African way of life. Both those approaches developed in a context of antagonism between the local and the universal, the native and foreign. The chapter calls for going beyond this antagonism in reconciling both universal values and the African traditional legacy, since they both are required to establish excellence in human existence.

Notes

1 The same is still true for countries such as the Democratic Republic of Congo (the former Zaïre), particularly during the 32 years of Mobutu's rule. See Kalulambi (1997, 180–204).
2 See also Wamala (2004); Teffo (2004); Lajul (2013).

7

APPROACHING AFRICAN CIVIL SOCIETY

Paradigms and philosophical backgrounds

Introduction

A range of analysts consider that awareness with regard to civil society resurfaced in Africa in the last two decades of the twentieth century. According to them, it concentrated on the struggle against postcolonial regimes that were viewed as authoritarian and undemocratic. This chapter focuses on identifying African civil society. It also aims at exploring its theoretical background and its articulations through African history.

This chapter is divided into four sections. The first section analyzes the debate concerning application of the concept of civil society to African social and political reality. It outlines two opposing trends: antagonists of the application of the notion of civil society to African social and political reality and protagonists of such an application. The former group relies on the Western origin of the concept of civil society to reject its application to Africa, while the latter argues for the universalist nature of the notion of civil society, its essential link with democracy, to support such an application. This section goes beyond this antagonism and asserts the relevance of using the concept in relation to African social and political reality by virtue of its multiple interpretations and the variety of experiences of African people.

The second section focuses on social and political contexts shaping the emergence of African civil society. For many analysts, African civil society emerged as an effect of decisions and strategies of the Post-Washington Consensus institutions in support of neo-liberal policy, imposing a range of measures and strategies to African countries. This way of thinking presents African civil society as both a foreign product and a tool for expansion of neo-liberalism. Contrary to this perspective, a number of thinkers and activists consider African civil society as the expression of African people's desire to reject undemocratic regimes and all kinds of system that exploit and impoverish them. From this perspective, African civil society is viewed as a platform from which to tackle neo-liberalism and to promote alternative social and political thinking. This section insists that the analysis of African civil society take into consideration the current process of globalization and its inherent new configurations without neglecting the awareness and struggle of African people for a better social and political life.

The third section rests on the premise that the concept of civil society benefits from multiple interpretations. This section explores some of its articulations through Africa's history. In the precolonial period, civil society was viewed as integrated into the ruling social and political system. During colonial rule, in spite of the disintegration of precolonial heritage, civil society developed according to two paradigms: on the one hand, it was considered as the expression of the "civilized world" as opposed to "uncivilized and traditional" African societies. On the other hand, it was expanded as a tool of resistance against colonial rule. In this respect, it was viewed as the ferment of African nationalism. During the postcolonial period, African civil society also developed as resistance against undemocratic postcolonial regimes. This propelled it as the spearhead of African democratization and new agency for the development of Africa.

The fourth section approaches current challenges of African civil society, particularly in light of the globalization process. It focuses on the relationship between African civil society and the state. Rejecting the antagonism between them as set out by defenders of neo-liberalism, this section sustains the idea of mutual support and complementarity between African state and civil society.

7.1 Addressing the concept of African civil society

The idea of civil society counts amongst the successful global concepts of our time. This concept became popular in Africa in the context of criticism concerning the African postcolonial state and the subsequent democratic turn that took place in the last quarter of the twentieth century. Despite its popularity, this idea does not refer to a single definition that can reconcile African social and political thinkers, because all of them provide varied interpretations. Based on the evolution of the notion of civil society in Europe, for example, Bratton observes that

> Not only did the concept evolve in distinctively European historical and cultural milieux, but *its usage by political philosophers has changed dramatically over time. ... As a result, its contents for purposes of comparative political analysis in the late twentieth century is highly contestable.* Analysts who have tried to apply the concept to non-Western politics have found it "unwieldy" and "complex".
>
> *(1994, 52, emphasis added)*

This background has given rise to a vast debate on the nature, role, and effectiveness of African civil society (Harbeson 1994). Two main tendencies characterize this debate: on the one hand, critics of the application of the concept of civil society to African social and political realities and, on the other hand, protagonists of such an application.

7.1.1 Critics of the idea of African civil society

Critics of African civil society argue that it is inappropriate to apply the concept of civil society to African social and political realities. They rely on premises such as the Western roots of this concept, the ambiguity of the relationship between African state and African societies, and the weakness of African market as a mode of economic regulation. Scholars such as Chabal and Daloz (1999) and Haubert and Rey (2000) represent this way of thinking. Chabal and Daloz (1999), for example, think that the idea of civil society is a legacy of Western social and political philosophy. As such, this idea has developed according to a Western world view that promotes individual rights and a sharp distinction between state and society. Therefore, they think that it is difficult and inappropriate to apply this concept to non-Western cultures and contexts, particularly to sub-Saharan Africa. In this respect, they observe that

> *the emergence of a properly institutionalized civil society*, led by politically independent citizens, separate from governmental structures, *is only possible where there is strong and strongly differentiated state*. Only then is it meaningful to speak of a "counter-hegemonic" civil society. Historically, however, the only instances of the development of civil societies of this type have occurred in Europe – where their formation was fortuitous, or rather unplanned and unpredictable. *The situation in contemporary Africa is, at this stage, historically so different that it is hard to see how it could evolve in the same direction* – at least in the foreseeable future.
> (Chabal and Daloz 1999, 21, emphasis added)

For these scholars, the lack of sharp distinction between state and society constitutes a stumbling block for the emergence and development of a properly institutionalized civil society in Africa. According to them, the supposed dichotomy between state and civil society is an overhang, and it doesn't reflect the reality of sub-Saharan countries. To try and put emphasis on this distinction can create the illusion that African political systems are similar to their Western counterparts. In reality, for those scholars, there is no sharp disconnection between a structurally differentiated state and a civil society composed of organized and politically distinct interest groups in Africa. On the contrary, Chabal and Daloz (1999, 17) insist that there is a "constant interpenetration, or straddling, of the one by the other". Such a context makes difficult and unlikely the use of the concept of civil society with regard to African social and political reality.

It is my feeling that Chabal and Daloz (1999) rely on their own interpretation of modes of governance in vogue in postcolonial Africa – in practice, state authoritarianism – and the prevalence of cultural traditions to make such a statement. Following a range of Africanists and political theorists, Chabal and Daloz (1999, 19) view the African postcolonial state as an authoritarian state that relies on African cultural traditions to impose one-party and authoritarian rule. This mode of governance stifles all stray impulses of civil society through its hegemonic structures.

Bayart (1989, 270–280) thinks that it is commonplace for the African state to get involved with family kinship, social ties, and all kind, of strategic alliances. This attitude allows the African state to keep its own balance and legitimacy. He thinks of the African state as "*Etat rhizome*"; that is, a state which is deeply involved in a complex net of social and political relationships for its own survival and expansion. Therefore, Bayart uses an organic metaphor to describe African postcolonial state development. He observes that

> *l'Etat postcolonial vit comme un rhizome*, plutôt que comme un ensemble radiculaire. Pour être doté d'une historicité propre, il ne se déploie pas sur une seule dimension, à partir d'un tronc génétique, tel un chêne majestueux qui plongerait ses racines dans l'humus fondamental de l'histoire. *Il est une multiplicité protéiforme de réseaux dont les tiges souterraines relient des points épars dans la société.* Sa compréhension exige que l'on dépasse l'examen de ses parties aériennes … pour celui des racines adventives, pour l'analyse des bulbes et des tubercules dont il se nourrit en secret et dont il extrait sa vivacité.
>
> *(1989, 272, emphasis added)*

(the postcolonial state lives like a rhizome rather than a radicle root. As it is endowed with its own historicity, it does not deploy a single dimension, from a genetic trunk, like a majestic oak tree whose roots go deep into the fundamental humus of history. It has multiple networks that connect, like stems, at the underground level. The understanding of its development requires going beyond the analysis of its visible parts … for the benefit of adventitious roots as well as the analysis of bulbs and tubers from which this state secretly feeds itself and extracts its vivacity.)

This model of state was common in postcolonial Africa. Leaders such as Nkrumah, Houphouet-Boigny, Ahidjo, Mobutu, to name a few, essentially relied on this paradigm of governance, whose effect was the strangulation of civil society's dynamic and all political alternatives to the benefit of authoritarian rule. In such a context, every social and kinship interstice was considered as an opportunity for both African postcolonial state and elite. The former aimed at expanding its dominance, while the latter intended to keep their financial and political privileges (Bayart 1989, 272–274).

Antagonists of the idea of African civil society also argue the weak influence of the market as an economic mode of regulation in Africa. For them, the proliferation of informal mechanisms excludes African economy from ruling standards of the market, and, subsequently, this process contributes to the marginalization of this continent. This singularity impedes the establishment of a balanced relationship between state, market, and society. It also makes complex the use of the concept of civil society since economic standards are not clearly identified and matched (Pirotte 2007).

The resort to the Western origin of the concept of civil society to deny its application to the African context relies on an unspoken prejudice and politically mistaken reasoning. Antagonists of the application of the concept of civil society to African social and political reality rely on an ethnocentric premise for which Europe is the fixed centre of gravity of humankind's thought and development. Outside Europe, there cannot be any salvation for non-Western people and cultures. All hopes for democacy and development on behalf of these people and cultures has to follow the Western path and paradigm in order to be successful. It can be noted that this way of thinking not only includes an ethnocentric approach to foreign people and cultures, but it also implies a linear view of human evolution by pointing toward European thought as providing the exclusive and mandatory paradigm of the social and political development of humankind. Scholars such as Lévi-Strauss (2007), Mudimbe (1988), and Mbembe (2013), among others, have brilliantly denounced the limits of this ethnocentric attitude. Subsequently, there is no need here to excavate this criticism. On the contrary, it seems relevant in pointing out the deceipt that underlies the denial of the concept of civil society in African social and political reality.

First, it can be observed that critics of the application of the concept of civil society to African reality ignore the premise that cultures all over the world develop on account of encounter, exchange, and loan from each other. Not a single culture evolves *en vase clos*, in autarchy or a self-sufficiency mode. It is worth remembering here that Western civilization itself is not free from foreign loans. It owes quite enough to Arab civlization, for example, for the development of Mathematics (Algeber), not to mention the (re)discovery of ancient thinkers such as Aristotle through Aquinas. Moreover, the influence of African art in works of Western artists such as Picasso is widely recognized, though it seems useless to insist on an African contribution to the development of cubism.

Second, it can be observed that the idea of civil society is not the only concept relevant to the encounter between Western and non-Western people. Ideas such as democracy, human rights, constitutionalism, equality, liberty, and good governance, to name a few, which also have roots in Western culture and philosophy are equally relevant. Despite of their Western origin, these concepts have been adopted and adapted by various peoples and cultures all over the world. The idea of democracy, for example, is even viewed as one of the world's leading political and normative principles, regardless of its Greek origin and regardless of the mixed experiences of people willing to rely on it as their normative and political reference. Kervegan notes in this respect that

> [la] démocratie ne désigne plus un régime parmi d'autres, mais semble être *l'horizon de tout ordre politique légitime*. L'accession de la démocratie au statut de l'idéalité normative se traduit par le fait que *cette notion recouvre désormais plus que les institutions définies, un ensemble des valeurs: les droits de l'homme.*
>
> *(1996, 127, emphasis added)*

(democracy no longer refers to a political regime among others, but it seems to be the horizon of any legitimate political order. The fact that democracy achieved normative status can be explained by the fact this notion now includes more than defined institutions, but also refers to a set of values: human rights.)

Third, antagonists of the application of the concept of civil society to African realities focus on a narrow interpretation of this concept. They reduce it to only one view that consists of opposition by civil society to the state; civil society is exclusively viewed as "counter-hegemonic society" (Chabal and Daloz 1999, 21). Contrary to such reductionism, it seems worth emphasizing the many other traits characterizing civil society. Bratton (1994, 64–71), for example, outlines factors such as the material dimension of civil society and its organizational capacity as well as its underlying ideological dimensions. Along the same lines, the emergence of new configurations calling for new modes of management of social issues as well as the failure of both the state and the market can be considered relevant (Pirotte 2007, 42).

7.1.2 Proponents of African civil society

Defenders of the idea of African civil society consider this society as the compound of African people's social and political experiences, which evolved at the mercy of African history. To make use of the concept of civil society to express these experiences will not transform African reality merely into a pale copy of Western social and political process. It is my feeling that for the defenders of the idea, concepts are extendable tools that can be adjusted to approach and express reality that is always multiple, complex, and changing. The point at stake seems to be the contradiction between two epistemological backgrounds: from one side, the essentialist view and, from the other side, the constructivist approach. For the former, identities and systems of values and organization – including civil society – are part of social reality. As such, their existence as well as their internal homogeneity and specificity can be viewed as fixed and distant from any change. In this respect, ethnic communities and their inherent organization, for example, are considered as fixed pieces of the social mosaic. On the contrary, in the latter view, identities and social systems of values and organization are an effect of social evolution, political and economic choices, and social interaction between people (Semprini 1997, 64–65).

In support of their thesis, protagonists of the idea of African civil society also postulate the universality of civil society, its intrinsic link with democracy, and its multiple theorizations. According to them, the notion of civil society embodies universal beliefs that are to be shared by every society regardless of its cultural, social, and political singularity. These beliefs include, for example, principles and practices concerning human rights, democracy, legitimacy, and control of power. On account of this postulate, it can be observed that protagonists of the idea of African civil society consider civil society as a common and universal legacy transcending both cultural and political particularism (Harbeson 1994; Young 1994).

The resort to universalism to justify the application of the concept civil society to African social and political reality begs some caution and criticism. It is important to keep clearly in mind the significance and philosophical background given to this idea. In other words, does the idea of universality refer to totalitarian expansion of a model of civilization? (Mudimbe 1988; Fornet-Bentacourt 2011, 194); or to put it another way, does this refer to an endless expansion of Western cultural and political imperialism? Protagonists of the application of this concept to African social and political reality look less favourably on this interpretation. On the contrary, their approach to universality implies pluralism, recognition of the other, and dialogue. Despite its Western origin, for them, the idea of civil society has already been adopted and adapted by African people to express their daily social and political struggles.

In support of their premise, proponents of the idea of African civil society also evoke the existence of an intrinsic link between democracy and civil society. For them, democracy and civil society are intimately tied, so they can be considered as revealing one another. Democracy presupposes the existence of (strong) civil society, and inversely, civil society constitutes an indicator of the achievement of democracy. Exploring the role of civil society in recent African transition processes, Larry Diamond observes that

> *The mobilization of civil society for democracy has perhaps been most striking in Africa.* ... Since the early 1980s, it has become increasingly apparent that the impetus for political renewal and resistance to authoritarian domination in Africa has come from students, the churches, professional associations, women's groups, trade unions, human rights organizations, producer groups, intellectuals and informal networks that are either autonomous from the state or struggling to break free from its control. *Thus, it is now virtually beyond dispute that to fully comprehend democratic change in Africa and [the] developing world, one must study civil society.*
>
> (Quoted in Sithole 1998, 27–28, emphasis added)

Going from this premise, African civil society can be viewed as essential to African democracy. In the same way, thinkers such as Bratton (1994) and Sithole (1998) also consider civil society as a crucial reference point for the recent political changes taking place in Africa. For them, without civil society, democracy is simply a meaningless reality. In this respect, Pirotte observes that

> Il n'y a *pas de démocratie sans société civile* où que ce soit. ... [L]a société civile [est] à la fois *un élément actif du processus de démocratisation et un indicateur du degré d'avancement de ce processus.*
>
> (2007, 87, emphasis added)

(There is no democracy without civil society wherever it might be .... [C]ivil society [is] at the same time an active factor in the process of democratization as well as an indicator of progress achieved in this process.)

Defenders of the idea of African civil society also rely on the plurality of meanings given to the concept of civil society in claiming its applicability to African social and political analysis. As already suggested, Bratton (1994) goes beyond the conventional approach defining civil society only on account of its relationship (counter-hegemonic factor) with the state, and he highlights other traits defining civil society including, for example, the capacity of people to organize themselves and material independence as well as principal ideologies underlying the discourse on civil society. Pirotte also notes that

> il conviendrait d'intégrer à l'analyse de ces nouvelles sociétés civiles les dimensions constitutives autres que le simple fait associatif en tenant compte de la production idéologique, *des représentations de ses acteurs et des dynamiques en cours* dans des espaces publics dont l'existence même est souvent perçue comme problématique.
>
> *(2010, emphasis added)*

> (It should be convenient to integrate into the analysis of new civil societies constitutive dimensions other than mere associative aptitude, and take into consideration the ideological production, performances of its actors, and ongoing dynamics in public spaces, whose existence is often perceived as problematic.)

It is my feeling that this broadening of the concept of civil society contributes to the inclusion of a variety of contexts and cultures when considering its application, particularly concerning African countries. Focusing on a single interpretation of civil society means promoting a unilateral and truncated vision of a reality that is rich and complex. Considering the complexity inherent in human experience, I think it is appropriate to rely on a flexible and critical reading for a balanced interpretation.

7.2 Theoretical background

Is the current burgeoning of civil society in Africa due to external agency or is it a genuine expression of African people's desire? In other words, is the African civil society an imported project or can it be considered as an African and locally rooted phenomenon? This question is important because it calls for a clarification of the theoretical background to the debate on African civil society. This debate divides Africanists and analysts into two blocks: defenders of the foreign origin of the idea of African civil society and protagonists of its African genesis and roots. It also reveals philosophical backgrounds shaping this concept, including a neo-liberal approach and critical thinking.

Those who argue the origins of African civil society are foreign maintain that it is the effect of external dynamics including, principally, the Post-Washington Consensus policies. They rely on the criticism of international and financial institutions that consider the African postcolonial state as both authoritarian and failing with regard to both the people's welfare and growth. Therefore, these institutions try and reduce the prevalence of such states in their international cooperation and development aid policies. As an alternative, they think of civil society as spearheading new values including democracy, political pluralism, good governance, and accountability, to name a few. Their leitmotiv can be summed up in terms of *moins d'état, plus de société civile.*

The foreign origin of African civil society is noticeable, according to defenders of this position, in the massive support that global ruling institutions and funders of development gave to emerging NGOs in Africa during the last two decades of the twentieth century. Pirotte (2010) outlines how this support was achieved through modalities such as financial support toward NGOs from both Europe and Africa; professionalization of actors in emerging African NGOs; capacity building of these associations; and their inclusion in partnerships between Europe and Africa.

> *Les politiques impulsées par des acteurs dominants du complexe développeur international ont facilité ... la prolifération de pratiques associatives qui semblaient incarner ce « réveil de la société civile ».* Une nouvelle légitimité de la société civile et de ses acteurs s'est peu à peu élaborée sur la base de quelques éléments majeurs: les stratégies de soutien des grands bailleurs de fonds multilatéraux ou bilatéraux aux organisations non gouvernementales du Nord puis du Sud, l'insertion de celles-ci dans des organes consultatifs ou comme partenaires de projets financés par ces institutions ou encore des réformes visant l'interventionnisme étatique en matière économique et sociale et l'intérêt renouvelé pour les dynamiques associatives à la base pour faciliter la prise en charge de certains secteurs sociaux par exemple.
>
> *(Pirotte 2010, emphasis added)*

(The policies promoted by the international ruling and development agencies allowed ... the proliferation of associative practices that seemed to embody this "awakening of civil society". A new legitimacy of civil society and its actors gradually developed on account of some major elements: the support of major multilateral or bilateral donors to both the northern and southern Nongovernmental organizations, the inclusion of these NGOS in consultative bodies or as partners of projects financed by these institutions, or even more the reforms concerning the state's intervention in the economic and social fields, as well as the renewed interest in associative dynamics at the grass-roots level to facilitate support for certain social sectors, for example.)

It can be observed that in order to consolidate the emerging civil society, Western and development funding institutions contributed also to professionalization in a range of local NGOs as well as to improving capacity building for their leaders. In this respect, Pirotte writes that

[Ces] stratégies ne se sont pas réduites à des flux financiers Nord/Sud (ou Ouest/Est) pour soutenir la vitalité de nouveaux tissus associatifs. *Les bailleurs occidentaux ... se lancèrent dans des stratégies de professionnalisation sélective de certains acteurs de la société civile* et principalement les nouvelles ONG locales. ... [L]e soutien à ces ONG ... se traduisit ainsi par une politique de modernisation, dite de capacity building, *qui prit également les traits d'une stratégie de formatage et de mise en clientèle sélective de ces nouveaux courtiers locaux du développement.*

(2010, emphasis added)

([These] strategies were not confined to North/South (or West/East) financial flows to support the vitality of new associative tissues. Western donors ... also promoted strategies of selective professionalization of certain actors of civil society and mainly new local NGOs. ... [T]he support for these NGOs ... was articulated through a policy of modernization, called capacity building, which also took the form of a strategy of formatting and selecting these new local development agencies.)

On account of these observations, it can be noted that African civil society has developed as a subcontractor for neo-liberal development policy. This paradigm of civil society seems to be essentially formatted according to the neo-liberal world view with the core values of market, consumerism, individualism, and profit. Houtart describes this hold of the neo-liberal vision on civil society in the following way:

En effet la place que prend le système économique [dominant] dans les sociétés du Nord et du Sud, devient telle que ce dernier se transforme progressivement en référence et critère de toute l'action collective, ce qui indirectement affecte le contenu du terme société civile ... *Le marché apparaît comme la seule forme économique, modèle de l'ensemble des rapports sociaux et configuration du champ culturel (la privatisation).* ... *[L]e marché ... soumet également la société civile à ses normes.* ... La société civile se dépolitise, ce qui permet de mieux l'instrumentaliser. *La politique devient La politique devient virtuelle face au marché qui a le champ libre.*

(1998, 11, emphasis added)

(Indeed, the role of the [ruling] economic system in industrialized countries as well as in developing countries becomes so important that this system gradually transforms itself into the reference and criterion of all collective action, which indirectly affects the content of the term civil society. ... The market appears to be the only economic form, a model of the whole of social relations and the configuration of the cultural field. ... [T]he market ... also subjects civil society to its standards. ... Civil society depoliticizes itself and this allows its instrumentalization. Politics becomes virtual in the face of the free market.)

For defenders of the African roots of African civil society, its emergence relies on African people's social consciousness and desire for real political change. African people became aware of the exploitation that they suffered from colonial times up to postcolonial rule. Subsequently, they rejected oppressive structures and world views supportive of exclusion and poverty. Therefore, they commited themselves through civil organizations to achieving their aspirations for human dignity and better living conditions. Here, civil society is approached as critical agency toward ruling structures. It is viewed as a platform from which people denounce the failures of the African state as well as neo-liberal fallacies. In this respect, Traoré observes that

> Désabusées par trois décennies d'essai de «développement», d'erreurs et d'échecs, *les populations africaines ont fini par se ressaisir ... et par revendiquer haut et fort le droit de vivre autrement.* Cotonou, Nairobi, Abidjan, Niamey, ... sont autant de noms de villes qui résonnèrent alors des cris de colère et de douleur des victimes du « développement » et de la repression.
>
> *(1999, 17, emphasis added)*

(Disillusioned by three decades of trying development, as well as by errors and failures, the African populations have finally regained their consciousness ... and they loudly claim the right to live differently. Cotonou, Nairobi, Abidjan, Niamey ... are names of cities where the victims of "development" and repression expressed their cries of anger and pain.)[1]

It is my feeling that this approach to African civil society relies on African people's capacity to unmask the fallacies and imbalances that characterize the power relationships structuring African societies. This paradigm of civil society relies on the idea of resistance not only to the African postcolonial and authoritarian state, but also against the neo-liberal ruling system and philosophy. One of the main duties of this model of civil society is to denounce the existing mix between neo-liberal economic reforms and the expectations of African citizens. It is my feeling that both foreign agency and the awareness of African people are important this respect. It is worth keeping in mind the people's hopes concerning political change, which doesn't refer only to electoral processes and political alternation but, fundamentally, also includes the improvement of their living conditions as human beings and members of the polis (citizens). In addition, this paradigm of civil society stands against the misdeeds of dominant neo-liberal policy.

The debate concerning the very origin of African civil society contributes to the unmasking of ideological forces behind African enthusiasm for political change. It is too narrow a view to think of African countries as developing self-sufficiently, free from the global market and international networks. African people are more and more aware of the interconnections at work in the world, and they have adopted and adapted various strategies from foreign cultures. Thus they are not a simple sounding board for the world's dominant countries; they have agency when it comes to their own future. Their capacity for creating new relationships and taking advantage of new social and political configurations can be viewed as guaranteeing a promising future.

7.3 Typologies of African civil society

Relying on the premise that the concept of civil society has multiple meanings and various articulations, I would like to roughly outline a few typologies expressing its manifestation in African history. This analysis is in four parts corresponding to the chronology of contemporary African history: the precolonial model, the paradigm of colonial rule, the model of the postcolonial African state, and neo-liberal era typologies.

7.3.1 Precolonial African civil society

A range of African scholars and political leaders maintain the existence of precolonial African social and political organization, including civil society (Wiredu 1998; Gyekye 1997; Appiah 1992). For them, the concept of civil society refers to structures aiming at balancing traditional authority and promoting social peace. Unfortunately, these structures were victim to a colonial system which destroyed them. Wiredu (1998) considers that regardless of the lack of an effective theoretical background, the duties of civil society were enacted in precolonial African societies through integration. The advent of colonial rule broke down this mode of regulation. In this respect, he notes that

> One way in which colonialism injured Africa was through *the rupture it caused in the integration of the civil with political aspect of her social life.* That integration was one of the strong points of traditional society. Indeed, *in traditional life the distinction between the state and civil society was largely inoperative.*
> *(Wiredu 1998, 241, emphasis added)*

Wiredu (1998) thinks that precolonial African communities were organized according to the principle of continuity between African state and civil sphere. According to him,

> in traditional milieu the state itself can be seen as a special organization for the pursuit of mutual aid; and its underlying principle bears the same analogy to moral principles as those of the civil institutions and practices of traditional communalism.
> *(Wiredu 1998, 243)*

From this perspective, Wiredu considers that every extended kinship linkage plays an important role in social relationships. He observes that "the smallest kinship setup to which any young adult belongs with a lively sense of belonging is already a significant society" (Wiredu 1998, 241).

According to him, in precolonial societies, the "sense of obligations and rights and of reciprocity is developed on the basis of natural feelings of sympathy and solidarity" (Wiredu 1998, 242). The idea of continuity between state and civil society relies, for Wiredu, on the upstream principle of adjustment of the interests of both the individual and the community. This principle aims at promoting solidarity between community members and avoiding irrationality and conflicts. To illustrate his postulate, Wiredu makes use of a metaphor of a crocodile having two heads and only one stomach (Wiredu 1997, 306, as described in Chapter 3).

It is my feeling that Wiredu's argument ignores the reality of antagonism, rivalry, and conflict that structured power relationships in African precolonial societies. This omission relies on Wiredu's preoccupation with making African precolonial values, particularly concerning civil society, the cornerstone of an alternative mode of governance, which he thinks should be based on consensus and no-party rule. For him, this paradigm of civil society "can offer to the state extremely important models, or at least illustration of the possibility, of non-party government and, in some cases, of government by consensus" (Wiredu 1998, 252).

A range of African thinkers including Gyekye (1997), Wamala (2004), and Teffo (2004) share Wiredu's opinion on excavating and rehabilitating African precolonial values and traditions. Beyond all consideration of African legacy, it is important to keep in mind the question concerning the relevance of traditional paradigms with regard to current African political and social challenges. It is my feeling that to be coherent, such a project must apply a permanent and critical vigilance, which means an endless hermeneutical process or, in other words, a constant interpretation of African heritage in accordance with social and political configurations in process in Africa.

7.4 African civil society in the colonial era

7.4.1 African civil society as a mode of resistance against colonial rule

The colonial state placed African communities under its tutelage, and subsequently it established a relationship with them based on domination and destruction. Young observes that during colonial rule

> much of the social space within which a society might become civil was blocked. By *legal concept*, the colonized was a "subject" with highly circumscribed civil and political rights. *Economically*, the colonial subject was a unit of labor. ... In *religious terms*, the African was a *fetishiste* awaiting redemption by Christian conversion (unless a secondary zone of salvation through Islam blocked the path). *Culturally*, the African domain required sorting and labeling through an often alien classificatory schema. *The radical reordering of political space* imposed by the colonial partition deconstructed potential civil societies.
>
> *(1994, 38, emphasis added)*

In this context, African civil society developed through interstices and multiple forms of colonial rule. Sometimes it appears as a mirror of the pattern of dominance of African people; sometimes it reveals itself as a tool for African resistance and rebellion against colonial rule and undemocratic regimes (Breytenbach 1998).

Mamdani (1996) explores the evolution of African civil society in his seminal book *Citizen and Subject: Contemporary Africa and the Legacy of Late Colonialism*. This book deals with the controversial issue of postcolonial African state's failure to address its chronic crisis, conflict, and search for democratization process. For Mamdani, the failure of the African postcolonial state had its roots in the African colonial past rather than in any substantial lack of ability on the part of African people when it comes to ruling themselves. The source of the crisis of the African postcolonial state is the mode of governance inherited from colonization. For Mamdani, the logic that governed the South African apartheid regime, for example, was the same one deployed through colonial rule all over the African continent. This logic was based on Lugard's (1858–1945) view that black people are like children. They should be ruled and not treated as if they are equal to white people. In this respect, Gordon reminds us that for Lugard,

> *indigenous Africans are more like children. They should be governed or ruled, and the failure to understand that leads to the misguided notion of having political relations with them. Such relations, designed for mature people known as "citizens", would require equality between colonizers and colonized*, between, since we are referring to highly racialized situation, whites and the varieties of color all the way down to blacks.
>
> *(2008, 224, emphasis added)*

Colonial rule implies dualism and disconnection between urban and rural areas, modern and traditional rules, civilized and uncivilized peoples. In these binaries, those associated with the former were treated as citizens and ruled according to modern law. They were part of civil society. The latter were governed through indirect rule with emphasis on traditional authority and customs. They were not viewed as part of civil society. In other words, Lugard's distinction was used in support of a racist and oppressive system as well as to deny African people's capacity for both democracy and organization of civil society. Gordon sums up Mamdani's argument as follows:

> States have citizens, who collectively rule either by parliamentary representation or some other form of representative means, for whom there is equality before the law. Civil society enables these relations to emerge as the sets of customs, mores, or way of life that are conducive to social order. [Colonial thinking] leads to the thesis that *blacks cannot properly have a "civil" society because they are by definition not civilized.*
>
> *(2008, 225, emphasis added)*

It can be noted that for different reasons and making use of different arguments, Mamdani reaches a conclusion similar to the one advanced by the above-mentioned thinkers who deny the application of the concept of civil society to African realities. For him, civil society didn't exist in Africa, and current use of this concept is, as concerning the idea of the African state, for example, based on mistaken and unrealistic premises. In this respect, I personally agree with Breytenbach (1998, 40) who, contrary to Mamdani's view, notes that "the roots of civil society go back far in history, and [it] is not alien to Africa". Based on this premise, he denounces the silence of African historiography on this issue, particularly with regard to the pre-independence era. For him, this silence constitutes a "curious omission" whose effect is to ignore all kinds of African resistance to colonial policies as well as emergent forms of civil society. He points out that

> In African history one looks in vain for references to the role of civil society during the era of the pre-independence social movements [this silence is] a "curious omission". But equally curious is the omission of assessment of the various forms of so-called secondary resistance against colonial policies ... as forms of emergent civil society.
>
> (Breytenbach 1998, 39)

Breytenbach argues that there have been multiple forms of resistance in African history. Such is the case, for example, concerning "the Sierra Leone hut tax revolt, Samori Touri's uprising against [the] French, the Herero-Nama and Maji-Maji resistance against the Germans, and the Bambatha rebellion, Chilembwe and Harry Thuku protests against the British" (Breytenbach 1998, 39).

These forms of resistance may not be properly considered as expressing African civil society. But considering that they have been displayed as instances of collective action aiming at redressing colonial grievances and interacting with the colonial state, they could be viewed at least as "proto-civil society" (Breytenbach 1998, 40). Breytenbach's claim relies on an upstream postulate according to which there are two distinct historical epochs that deal with the role of civil society in Africa: the African protest against colonial policies and the anti-authoritarian resistance against undemocratic regimes in independent Africa (Breytenbach 1998, 39).

The idea of African civil society as protest against colonial rule expanded from the beginning of colonization up to nationalist struggles for emancipation that started soon after the Second World War. This epoch "witnessed the rise of voluntary associations that were mainly *grievance-driven and aimed at reforms rather than the destruction of colonialism*" (Breytenbach 1998, 39, emphasis added). These associations relied on collective action, and they were organized through a relatively permanent associational base and in interaction with the colonial state.

It is my feeling that for this period of time, civil society chimes with civilization. It is equated with the mainstream thinking that saw Europe as both the unique and exclusive reference for human civilization. It was in such a context that Belgian colonizers in the Democratic Republic of Congo created the well-known social category of *Evolués*, those who could justify through their education, social and civic behaviour, and standard of living that they were capable of benefiting from civil rights and better consideration from colonizers. They were viewed as "civilized" – thus, members of civil society – as opposed to their fellow countrymen who did not match Western colonial standards. Due to their permanent assimilation, this category of people somehow constituted a kind of mirror to the prevailing ruling system, unlike local communities which were viewed in the realm of conservatism and obscurantism and, subsequently, as lacking civil society.

Local elite who joined this form of civil association quickly became disenchanted because the ruling authority paid hardly any attention to their expectations for reform, or to be treated as equal to white people. On account of this disillusion, they changed their view. They became aware of both their own dignity and the relevance of their struggle for emancipation. This period is known as the rise of African nationalist self-assertion. It developed by the end of the Second World War, and it was clearly independence driven. As Young observes,

> In the final years of the colonial state – after World War II in most of Africa – a swiftly intensifying voice of protest emerged. *At the time the rise of nationalist self-assertion appeared to herald the birth of civil society, even if that term was not employed.* A proliferating web of associational life knit society together in ways that supplied the structuration indispensable for the impending nationalist challenge. ... *If one defines civil society by its organizational life, one might suggest that the decolonization era was its golden age.*
>
> (1994, 38, emphasis added)

In sum, it can be noted that nationalist self-assertion relied on a philosophy of resistance against colonial rule which included two main trends: on one hand, the claim for human dignity and, on the other hand, the criticism of failures and lack of coherence on the part of both colonial rule and Western civilization. Two thinkers can be viewed as spearheading this resistance: Fanon and Césaire,

7.4.2 Civil society in postcolonial Africa

African civil society also expanded as a form of criticism of the African postcolonial state, which stood, for decades, as an integral state. The concept of an integral state comes from Gramsci, who uses it to refer to the whole machinery of rule and hegemony of the ruling class. Young thinks that this concept refers to

> A design of *perfect hegemony, whereby the state seeks to achieve unrestricted domination over civil society.* ... The integral state requires not only the autonomy from civil society achieved through comprehensive instruments of political control but also suzerainty, if not monopoly, extending over social and economic vectors of accumulation.
>
> (1994, 39, emphasis added)

This state paradigm dominated Africa from the early 1960s up to the last two decades of the twentieth century. African leaders who assumed political power upon the demise of colonial rule evoked varied pretexts in support of this mode of governance. Focusing on the preoccupation with national unity and development, for example, they promoted hegemonic mechanisms leading to the stultification of the emergence of political pluralism and associational life. In doing so, they quelled the growth of strong and self-supportive civil society. In this regard Appiah (1992), for example, denounces the violence with which African leaders such as Nkrumah annihilated the emerging Ghanaian democracy, suppressed political pluralism, and persecuted or sent into jail political rivals and opposition leaders. Remembering his father's prosecution by Nkrumah, he notes the following:

> I grew up also believing in constitutional democracy, or to speak more precisely, believing that what those words stood for was important. When my father and his friends were locked up by Kwame Nkrumah in the early sixties, I was too young to think of it as anything more than a family tragedy. By the time they came out, I knew that *the abolition of the legal opposition in 1960 had been a blow against democracy, that it had led naturally to imprisoning those who disagreed with our president* and what my father called the "gaping sycophants" who surrounded him, that *all this evil began when multiparty electoral democracy ended.*
> (Appiah 1992, 158, emphasis added)

Nkrumah was not alone in putting an end to electoral democracy in Africa. Many other African countries including Cameroon, Togo, Chad, Zaïre (Democratic Republic of Congo), Malawi, Zambia, and Zimbabwe, among others, underwent the same process under the supervision of their respective leaders. On account of the above-mentioned pretexts of unity and development, African leaders launched authoritarian regimes aiming at annihilating diversity and political pluralism. Contrary to Young's statement that the decolonization period was the golden age of African civil society (Young 1994, 38), I have the feeling that the postcolonial era was a time of coercion, muzzling, and the extinction of any attempt at this kind of society. Sithole (1998, 27) observes in this respect that the

> subordination to nationalist movement intensified after independence when one-party rule was introduced. The hegemony and imposition of the one-party state in most African countries stultified the growth and independence of associational life, thus preventing the growth of a strong self-supportive civil society.

In the face of authoritarianism in the African state, a range of people relied on passive resistance, while active resistant social forces developed within spheres such as churches, university campuses, and to some extent through trade unions (Sithole 1998, 27). They spearheaded anti-authoritarian resistance and awakening of African civil society. Their agenda can be approached according to two perspectives: the struggle against undemocratic regimes and the consolidation of democracy in African countries (Eboussi-Boulaga 1993, 61–68; Perret 1994, 127).

Resistance to authoritarian regimes took place in the late 19980s and early 1990s. It expanded through claims concerning corruption, accountability policy, and the abomination of the one-party rule. Its manifestations were similar in most African countries, as the desire and determination of African people were clearly the same: to put an end to undemocratic regimes once and for all. It is worth noting that it was in this context that the National Sovereign Conferences took place in various African countries (Young 1994, 43). As discussed previously, these conferences represent the most important political activity ever carried out by African people as they consisted of a national debate among representatives of the people (from all social and political groups) in order to lay the foundations for a new political contract. As an effect of this process, new political prospects emerged in Africa. In this respect, Breytenbach (1998, 41–42) observes that

> The rise of constitutionalism, the flourish of civil society, and the comeback of parliaments ... new political parties were formed; former social movements were rejuvenated; apolitical groups also adopted political agendas; new leaderships arose in many parts of Africa; the public agendas were broadened to include socio-economic issues.

The consolidation of democracy in Africa addresses the challenge of putting an end to authoritarian regimes, particularly concerning ways and means to prevent the return of these denounced regimes. In this respect, a range of NGOs integrating African civil society concentrate on issues that are essential to the improvement of democracy in Africa, such as human rights, public accountability, capacity building, gender equity, and people's participation in decision-making spheres, to mention a few (Tripp, Casimiro, Kwesiga, and Mungwa, 2009; Kabarhuza et al. 2003).

The exploration of these specific issues leads to a key debate concerning NGOs interpretation of the concept of democracy and how far they manage to sustain it. Does this term refer exclusively to a procedural requirement (regular elections, for example), or does it imply the balance of social forces? How far can African civil society resist African leaders' attempts to rule endlessly in their respective countries? As already observed, the paradigm of liberal democracy dominated the African democratic turn that took place in last decades of the twentieth century. It is my feeling that such a paradigm is hardly sustainable, because elections don't constitute sufficient evidence of democracy, particularly in Africa where such a procedure is often marked by great distortions and massive irregularities.

In addition, democracy relates to the social sphere in terms of the development of social networks aiming for the balance of social forces that, translated into strong organizations, can, for example, successfully oppose the attempts of African leaders to ensure an endless presidential mandate. In this respect, it is worth recalling the struggle of African youth movements such as Y en a marre, Balai citoyen, Filimbi, and LUCHA. Those groups are made up principally of young people who, regardless of their religious belief, educational level, ethnic origin, and gender, stand for democracy and political alternation in Africa. They stand for strict respect of the nation's fundamental law and the full achievement of human rights. They are persuaded that Africa is the place where they must be, their real homeland. So, they feel committed to fight to make it a better place to live. They rely essentially on non-violence, and they make use of strategies such as theatre, arts, music, and citizen capacity building, to mention a few means at their disposal, to promote social and political change. In other words, the emergence of those youth movements attests to the renewal of African civil society through a new and civic consciousness. It is my belief that those movements reflect a renewed African nationalism in accordance with current challenges facing the African continent. As an illustration, let's roughly sketch the philosophy and some of the associated actions of those youth movements.

The Y en a marre was launched as a citizen movement in Senegal in 2011 by a group of Senegalese rappers and journalists. This movement can be viewed as the Senegalese sentinel of democracy. It aims at promoting a society shaped by civic values such as citizen participation, respect for law and the constitution of the republic, and the fight against corruption and impunity. Relying on a range of citizen initiatives, this dynamic overcame the carelessness and nepotism of President Wade's regime. Thus, it contributed to the emergence of the "Senegalese spring". This movement contributed actively to consolidating the achievements of the "spring" as well as to the citizen control of the public action.

The concept of "Balai citoyen" is a metaphor for the freeing of the Burkinabe society from political corruption. It also calls for citizens to take control of their political and social destiny. In other words, this expression refers to the emergence of a new civic consciousness centred on justice, democracy, and the commitment of everyone to a better society. The social dynamics known under this name existed in Burkina Faso in 2013, and it stands on the political legacy of Thomas Sankara (1949–1987). This movement played a central role in the fall of President Blaise Compaoré in 2014, notably through the political sensitization of young people and several protest actions and civic resistance. The leaders of this movement do not envisage transforming it into a political party or for it to be a kind of springboard for the conquest of the political power. On the contrary, they wish to remain as a critical conscience regarding the evolution of democracy and the respect of human rights. Through music, empowerment sessions, and various other events, they work to awaken the consciousness of younger generations.

The word *filimbi* comes from Swahili and means "whistle". It is used as a metaphor inspired by the world of sport, expressing the will of the defenders of this movement to whistle the end of the game concerning corruption, authoritarianism, and lack of respect for fundamental laws, particularly concerning the duration of the presidential term and political alternation. Filimbi is a platform for movements that see themselves as "deliverers of democracy" (*accoucheur*). They prefer non-violence against the disproportionate violence of the state. They are aware that this commitment requires determination, patience, and perseverance. For Filimbi activists, the emblematic figure of Nelson Mandela is a role model.

The movement Struggle for Change – Lutte pour le Changement (LUCHA) – emerged in 2012 as one of the platforms for Congolese civil society. It mostly brings together young people dreaming of a new and prosperous Democratic Republic of Congo, where democracy and peace reign. The protagonists of LUCHA put very little faith in the capacity of international institutions and foreign NGOs to reverse the course of things in their country. For them, change must come from inside. Despite the repression that they suffer from Congolese authorities, the activists of LUCHA rely on their own sense of sacrifice to bring about long-awaited change. They take as a model for their struggle the figure of Patrice Emery Lumumba, the Congolese national hero. LUCHA's members mainly use non-violent actions such as sit-ins, theatre performances, protest marches, campaigns of sensitization, and civic initiatives such as street sweeping.

In sum, it is my feeling that African civil society is more active than ever. The emergence of the platforms discussed above testifies to this dynamism. New social and political actors, especially young people, are struggling for the emergence of a new Africa where democracy, human rights, and human excellence are a priority for all. Those platforms also highlight the changing political philosophy and paradigms in the continent. Contrary to conventional approaches, young people are taking the lead in social and political change regardless of their educational levels, ethnic origins, or religious beliefs. Through their actions, they challenge modes of governance that have been commonplace in varous African countries, such as authoritarianism and gerontocracy.

7.5 Towards the future

The current dominance of neo-liberal thought, particularly through the globalization process, constitutes an important factor for the agenda and development of civil society in Africa. It is worth noting the many influences on the development of African civil society, such as terrorist attempts, massive migration of African people (internally and externally), ecological disasters, armed conflicts, poverty, tutelage of international funding agencies, and the impact of world ruling powers. In other words, African civil society faces a variety of challenges. This section does not aim to explore all of them. It focuses on one that seems to be central: the relationship between African civil society and the state.

The relationship between state and civil society, as developed in Africa, raises the question of whether African state and civil society will evolve as antagonists or as supplementary to each other. What can be the role of civil society in a context where, due to globalization, the idea of nation state has been transformed and adapted to market requirements? Protagonists of the neo-liberal world view denounce the African postcolonial state as flawed, weak, and ineffective with regard to growth, democracy, and liberalization. Regardless of the varied factors that caused this situation, defenders of neo-liberalism call for the removal of this postcolonial state and search for its replacement. They point to civil society as the alternative to the African state and its role in African development and policy (Pirotte 2007). In so arguing, they relegate the African state to a marginalized position in favour of global market principles (Houtart 1998, 11–12 ; Willame 1996). Now the question is, with regard to Africa's future, can civil society legitimately replace the African state?

First of all, it is worth recognizing that the African state underwent (and is still undergoing) multiple changes due to various configurations at work throughout the world. Despite these transformations, this state remains the established reference for African citizenship in the current world system. Unlike other states, the African state is the only institution habilitated to act with required authority in order to ensure security and peace, order, stability, and equity within a given territory. It is my belief that despite its recognized dynamism, the mission and capacity of African civil society hardly lives up to these kinds of duties (Tripp, Casimiro, Kwesiga, and Mungwa 2009; Kabarhuza et al. 2003). In this respect, the idea of substituting the African state with civil society appears destabilizing and undermining for African countries.

Second, it is important to unmask neo-liberal sophism that pits civil society against African state, turning them into rivals of one another. This perception dominated the African transition era, as it relied on a subtle mirage mixing the "ruling political regime" and the state as the administrative and political structure organizing people's social and political life in a given territory. An effect of this elision was the opposition between civil society and state; consequently, civil society aimed at supporting – or to some extent improving – economic and political liberalization of African countries (Bratton 1994, 63). Actually, as the euphoria for political change slows down in Africa, it seems relevant to rediscover the very role of civil society and its fundamental relationship with the state.

Various social and political thinkers including Hegel, Hobbes, Locke, and Rousseau maintain the existence of an intrinsic link between state and civil society.[2] According to them, both institutions are intertwined and they mutually influence each other. In this respect, Osaghae (1998, 270) observes that the "state is transformed by a changing civil society; civil society is transformed by a changing state. *Thus state and civil society form a fabric of tightly interwoven threads*, even if they have their own independent patterns" (emphasis added).

This existence of common threads does not imply a fundamentally antagonistic development, but a critical and supportive relationship promoting, for the state, the capacity to identify and express the common good and making possible, for civil society's members, the sense of state ownership, participation in decision-making, and accountability. In this respect, African civil society is asked to turn aside from the beaten tracks and to deal with its specific challenges including, for example, the consolidation of democracy through the restriction of presidential mandate, the respect for African countries' fundamental charters, and the achievement of human rights, accountability, and equity. In other words, civil society is called on to tackle all deviation of the state from actions to improve the common good and people's well-being. Instead of opposing the state, it has the duty to rescue and rehabilitate values constitutive of *vivre ensemble* (Touraine 1997).

7.6 Conclusion

This chapter discussed the theoretical background and main paradigms of African civil society. For many thinkers, African civil society emerged during the African democratic turn that took place in the late twentieth century. This society is viewed as the expression of African people's desire to challenge undemocratic regimes and systems of exploitation that they suffered since independence. Contrary to thinkers denying the application of the concept of civil society to African social and political realities, this chapter relied on the existence of multiple interpretations of this concept as well as on its normative value in order to maintain the evoked application.

This chapter also explored different articulations of African civil society according to stages in the conventional history of Africa. First, it pointed out that in precolonial Africa, civil society was conceived of as part of social structures aiming at balancing traditional authority and promoting social peace. Second, it was postulated that during colonial times, African civil society was viewed, on the one hand, as a platform for discrimination between citizens and subjects and, on the other hand, as a way of resistance to colonial domination. Third, African civil society in the postcolonial era was described as a field of social confrontation as well as spearheading the struggle against undemocratic rule. The emergence of African youth platforms contributed to the renewal of African civil society, particularly in denouncing decaying modes of governance such as gerontocracy and authoritarianism as well as emphasizing both respect for and achievement of human rights.

Finally, this chapter examined the debate concerning the ambiguous role of African civil society in the current context of globalization. On one hand, people see African civil society as supportive of neo-liberal policy under the banner of international and financial institutions; on the other hand, protagonists of African nationalism see in this process African people's tool of resistance against the ruling neo-liberal system.

Notes

1 Concerning the debate on the philosophy and practice of development, see, for example, Keita (2011), Latouche (2004), and Njoku (2004).
2 See, for example, Hobbes's *Du citoyen* (1642) and *Le Leviathan* (1651); Locke's *Essai sur un gouvernement civil* (1690); Rousseau's *Du contrat social* (1762); and Hegel's *Principes de la philosophie du droit* (1821).

8

AFRICAN CULTURES AND GLOBALIZATION

Introduction

Many people depict Africa as a continent dominated by one common culture identified as "The African culture". This description fails to mention African cultural diversity, reducing Africa to a kind of metaphysical substance, unique, unchangeable, and free from all external contaminations (Bidima 1995, 3). The advent of globalization gives rise to the question of the relevance of such a premise as in reality no culture, no people live in a nationally self-sufficient way anymore. The world has become a global village where, thanks to new information and communication technologies, people and cultures are in permanent contact. They are constantly exchanging information and influencing one another.

This context raises questions related to the future of both the African culture and the globalization process in Africa. As is the case for societies all over the world, in Africa one set of thinkers wonder whether globalization constitutes a threat to African cultural diversity through a process of homogenization of cultures, while others think of it as a source of cultural pluralism, with its consequent antagonisms. Others perceive this process as an opportunity for African cultures to meet and exchange with other cultures. This chapter examines the relevance of these postulates with reference to the social and political experiences of African people.

The chapter is divided into three sections. The first section analyzes the issue of globalization and homogenization of African cultures. First, it takes the idea that Africa includes a variety of cultures that cannot be reduced to "One (The) African culture". Second, the chapter points out that those cultures have always been in contact with each other. It would be a mistake to deduce the principle of their cultural homogenization from this contact and exchange. All cultures are developed through mutual contact and exchange. Therefore, this section denounces the idea that globalization necessitates the absorption of African cultures by American or Western culture. In the same vein, it criticizes the confusion made between artefacts and cultural traditions that somehow leads to the illusion of homogenization of cultures. This section also outlines the fact that the most dangerous effect of globalization is not the circulation of artefacts as such, but the (neo-liberal) philosophy characterizing the context in which artefacts are used, which is dominated by the alteration of human values of solidarity and gratuitousness, for example, in the name of the profit at all cost.

The second section explores the question of cultural differentialism. It rejects the idea that globalization is the source of clashes between cultures. On the contrary, it unmasks philosophical premises and political manipulations that lead to cultural confrontations throughout the world. The use of categories such as ethnic group and tribe can be viewed, in the African context, as a more dangerous source of discrimination than globalization itself. In addition, the section also addresses the Enlightenment and colonialism as theoretical and political background to differentialism. It outlines the fact that cultures need each other to develop and to become richer. The era of cultural self-sufficiency doesn't exist anymore. Cultures are called to develop mutual recognition and promote rehabilitation of both pluralism and alterity.

The last section concentrated on the debate about African cultural pluralism and the emergence of new ways through which African people define themselves and relate to the world. In essence, it examined the concept of Afropolitanism. After considering the origin of this expression, coined concomitantly by Selasi (2005) and Mbembe (2005), this section explores Mbembe's approach to Afropolitanism. It points out the new consciousness around African identity based on the "circulation of the worlds". It also criticizes the limits of the Afropolitan discourse in that it seems silent on Africa's current social and economic issues such as poverty, exclusion, and gender. This section goes beyond the outputs of Mbembe and Taiye Selasi to outline the necessity for equity and an inclusive approach to African cultures and identities.

8.1 Globalization and homogenization of African cultures

For a range of thinkers, globalization represents a threat to cultural diversity. Defenders of this premise argue that this process leads to increasing sameness throughout the world. Thinkers such as Barber (1996, 1998) consider the cultural and economic reciprocity alleged by protagonists of globalization to be simply a mirage. To illustrate his premise, Barber makes use of the metaphor of a python swallowing up a hare. This means, for him, that the strongest culture gulps down the lesser one. Based on this metaphor, Barber points out the American cultural and economic icons which have spread all over the world – McDonalds, Disneyland, Coca-Cola, CNN, and Nike, among many others – to show how far they ring the knell of other cultures. He considers that instead of so-called cultural and economic reciprocity, the current process – which he qualifies as McWorlding – tends to forge a standardized world which includes a community of consumers and where all cultural singularity is eclipsed for the benefit of market principles (Barber 1996, 1998).

Ritzer (2007) also deals with increasing global homogeneity. He focuses particularly on the concept of McDonaldization. For him, the issue at stake refers to much more than the worldwide consumption of American food products; it is more to do with the transformation of people's thoughts and behaviours. In this respect, he writes that

> McDonaldization is not about the globalization of homogenous food products but rather about the globalization of a set of principles and a system of operations. *More important than the global spread of fast-food chains themselves is the fact that restaurants and restaurant chains … are adopting the principles of McDonaldization and operating on the basis of the same basic system.*
> *(Ritzer 2007, 11, emphasis added)*

The McDonaldization of the world illustrates, according to Ritzer, the propagation of Weber's paradigm of rationalization in different cultures. He thinks that the main principles of Weber's rationalization theory are subjacent to the process in question. Therefore, he points out ideas such as "efficiency, predictability, calculability, and control, … it is these principles, as well as the associated irrationality, that are being [globalized] through the spread of McDonald system" (Ritzer 2007, 24).

Ritzer also explores other forces bringing greater sameness in the world including, for example, the spread of credit cards (Visa and Mastercards) and the expansion of what he calls the "cathedrals of consumption".[1] The former leads many people in the direction of higher levels of debt and lower savings, while the latter encourages them to higher levels of consumption, following the American way of life. At a different scale than McDonaldization, these forces contribute to the Americanization of the rest of the world. The notion of Americanization refers to "the propagation of American ideas, customs, social patterns, industry, and capital around the world" (Ritzer 2007, 28). This process is often viewed as an "inclusive form of American cultural, institutional, political, and economic imperialism" (Ritzer 2007, 28).

I think that the postulates of both Barber and Ritzer denounce all kinds of cultural convergence as they see in cultural encounters a trap for the destruction of the weakest cultures. They both think of the relationship between cultures as based exclusively on antagonism between Western cultures and non-Western cultures. The former are credited with being the strongest, dominating and leading, while the latter are viewed as the weakest, dominated and occulted. Relying on this premise, it can be noted that non-Western cultures – including African cultures – are essentially depicted as victims of globalization as they are in the process of being absorbed by the dominant ones.

It can be pointed out that, concerning African reality, the postulates of both Barber and Ritzer need a bit of contextualization and nuance. There is no single African city where these denounced icons are not present. They penetrate more than ever the everyday lives of Africans. For the time being, it is not possible to renounce modern means of transportation and communication, such as motor vehicles, airplanes, mobile phones, and the Internet, to safeguard African cultural purity. The African people take advantage of the services and comfort offered by these innovations as far as they can financially afford them. To accept the idea of getting rid of these icons in favour of preserving African culture can be viewed as proof of a lack of discernment as well as a denial of African people's aspiration to development (Kasanda 2013b, 228–229).

It is also my feeling that these denounced icons cannot be viewed exclusively as factors of annihilation of African cultures. They can be considered the other way around; that is, as a contribution to the rejuvenation, improvement, and expansion of African cultures because, as already mentioned, cultures develop through contact and exchange with each other. The use of mobile phones instead of traditional instruments of communication can contribute to strengthening relationships between people since they offers a quicker and easier service than traditional tools of communication. But at the same time, as I will explain further, the hidden context in which this technological tool is used should be pointed out: the neo-liberal concern for expansion of the global market and greater profit. This preoccupation turns everything into merchandise and (paying) service, to the detriment of human gratuitousness. As a result – and this must be denounced – the ruling system creates both discrimination and lack of equity for the powerless, the poor who cannot afford the cost of such technologies and their advantages.

The argument about homogenization of cultures can also be contested because of the development of African cities, for example. These cities have been part of the global market since the eve of Western modernity, particularly through slavery and triangular trade (Mbembe 2013). Despite this connection, they already have been, and they remain, spaces where different people and cultures meet, including African ethnic groups themselves and people from all over the world. Studying Congolese music, for example, Stewart (2003), Tchebwa (1996), and White (2008) found that since the end of the nineteenth century, Kinshasa has been a meeting point for cultures and communities. There are, for instance, autochtonous from inside the country, migrants from other African countries, Western African workers, and Europeans (Greeks, Portuguese). Local exceptionality and peculiarity has not been destroyed by this blending of cultures and people. On the contrary, this process contributed to shaping Kinshasa's specificity, as well as to enriching the Congolese rumba. The emerging studies on Afropolitanism raise the question of how Africans perceive themselves and negotiate with the world in the current context of mobility of people and cultures (Mbembe 2005; Selasi 2005).

This mixture of people and cultures contributes to making society and gives African cities their singularity. Despite foreign presence and increasing migration, for example, Kinshasa has not changed its identity, nor has Nairobi become a Western city. Dakar and Lusaka are still the same apart from unavoidable transformations due to factors such as demographic growth, modernization, and the political and economic choices of their leaders. These cities keep their respective *stimmung*, or rhythm and tone. Their identity and culture have not evaporated because of foreign icons. They did not become identical or similar. In this respect, the following comment by Sony Labu Tansi about Kinshasa, and by extension about all African cities is relevant:

> Kinshasa ne sera jamais New York. Tant mieux d'ailleurs. Chaque ville a son âme. Chaque ville a son corps, sa peau, son intelligence, sa bêtise, son côté monstre, sa poétique, sa part de mystère.
>
> *(Quoted in Deboeck and Plissart 2004, 4)*

(Kinshasa will never be New York. It is better like that. Each city has its own soul. Each city has its own body, its own skin, its own intelligence, its own stupidity, its own monster side, its own poetry, its own part of mystery.)

In addition, it can be noted that the concept of culture constitutes a trap for various critics of cultural imperialism because of its multiple definitions. Wieviorka (2005, 18) considers this notion as

> [une] "jungle conceptuelle" ... non seulement la notion est complexe, mais qui plus est, son territoire est en expansion constante.
>
> ([a] "conceptual jungle" ... not only is (this) a complex notion, but in addition to that, its territory is constantly expanding.)

This complexity can be viewed as explaining the lack of nuance and subsequent hasty generalizations by many critics of cultural imperialism. Some of them speak of cultural standardization as if the concept of culture was a univocal and unambiguous word. They view cultures as static and passive entities without any capacity for resistance and initiative. They think of non-Western cultures as permanent and passive victims, as a kind of *tabula rasa* on which dominant (Western) culture can easily and freely make its mark.

I believe that a wide range of critics of cultural imperialism fail to make a distinction between artefacts and cultural traditions, for example. Artefacts result from engineering. They are a product of *Homo faber*, who designs them according to a model and to bring comfort to the human condition (Arendt 1994). Their manufacturing supposes control of nature. They are intended for current use, and they can be reproduced endlessly. Every culture produces its own artefacts to meet the material needs of its members. It is obvious that, nowadays, Western artefacts prevail all over the world. To have electricity, access to tap water, better quality medical care – these are part of the basic standard for viable living conditions. Any deficit in this respect that relies on the idea of protecting the integrity of African cultures from foreign invasion cannot be viewed as a heroic deed nor a virtue to be proud of. On the contrary, this attitude can be considered a sign of obscurantism and backward thinking (Appiah 2007, 101–102).

It is worth remembering that cultural traditions develop thanks to their reciprocal revelations to each other, their mutual recognition and exchange. As such, they include the human desire to making sense of and achieve a common world (Arendt 1994). Cultural traditions can be viewed as the result of patient transmission and laborious apprenticeship. They can be considered as a compass without which members of a society would not know where they are from or how to behave. It is on account of them that everyone can claim to be member of a specific culture, such as Berber, Italian, Amerindian, Massai, Zulu, or Yoruba, and so on (Warnier 1999, 3). As such, those traditions embody the axiology of community. Because they are situated on the axis of time and space, they are submitted to unceasing transformations regardless of their permanence.

For the time being, if the Internet is yet to bed down in many African countries, the mobile phone network is more evident than ever in African cities and villages. As already suggested, nobody would react against this process because this technology constitutes a suitable answer to people's need for an efficient tool of communication. This artefact spread in Africa to the detriment of local methods of communication which perform less well. Regardless of this point, it is worth remembering that the use of new information and communication technologies is based on economic principles marked by the neo-liberal concern for profit at all cost. Their main premise seems to be the idea of *do ut des*, which implies denying all gratuitousness of human behaviour for the benefit of commercial exchange. In other words, this attitude limits and distorts relationships between human beings because it transforms them into merchandise. Based on this logic, social relationships, communication, and care for others are all transformed into services, even paying services for which gratuitousness no longer exists. As a result, this mode of communication can be viewed as prohibitive for poor people because of its higher cost for the majority of Africans. It is my feeling that the concept of *fracture numérique* constitutes an appropriate term for the exclusion of poor people from new information and communication technologies.

In this respect, I can observe that the development of new information and communication technologies in Africa remains a crucial challenge for African leaders and thinkers in relation to policies aiming at the real well-being of their populations and equitable access to those technologies. This challenge calls for a critical approach to ruling neo-liberal principles. It also raises a set of questions about, for example, the global market income for African countries and philosophical premises structuring concepts such as justice and solidarity. In a world dominated by market competition, it is worth considering how far African countries will remain merely as poor consumers. In other words, the challenge at hand concerns setting policy and ensuring the capacity of African peoples to also be competitive in this domain of science and technology (Odera 1997; Wiredu 2000).

8.2 Globalization and African cultural differentialism

The paradigm of cultural differentialism rests on the premise that, at their core, cultures are largely unaffected by globalization or by other forms of relationship between them including, for example, "bi-, inter, multi-, and transcultural" modes (Ritzer 2007, 10). The protagonists of this approach argue that regardless of current rhetoric on cultural change, globalization only occurs on the surface, leaving the deep structure of cultures unaffected. For them, cultures remain what they have always been, and subsequently it seems important to protect the singularity of every community and cultural group.

A controversial work by Huntington (1966), *The Clash of Civilizations and the Remaking of the World Order*, is often evoked as an illustration in this respect. Huntington thinks that theories denouncing American hegemony in the world are unfounded or, rather, they rely on a mirage. The idea that the West enjoys a monopoly on modernity and power is in decline. Western countries are currently threatened by the emerging powers of, for example, China and India. This is also true concerning cultural and religious entities having strong capacity for mobilization, such as Islamic communities. Based on this potential geopolitical change in power relationships between Western countries and emerging powers, Huntington formulates the hypothesis of a confrontation between civilizations. This clash of civilizations will not have economic or financial interests as the main bone of contention, but rather will stand on cultural and religious frictions. Contrary to the defenders of cultural homogenization, Huntington thinks that globalization generates both cultural fragmentation and differentialism. It leads to strengthening poles of antagonism all over the world.

It is my belief that the differentialist approach includes a reductive definition of cultural identity, and it neglects its subjacent philosophical principles. This issue is addressed extensively by a wide range of African scholars including, for example, Mbembe (2000, 2013), Eze (1997), and Mudimbe (1988). For them, in Africa, differentialism takes it roots in the founding premises of Enlightenment (*Aufklärung*). The Enlightenment not only proclaimed the triumph of reason, but also defined human nature in light of generic principles or universal essences from which were deduced common values and shared rights, including individual freedom and autonomy, for example. The Western dynamic of world conquest brought to the fore the question of recognition of non-Western peoples and cultures as fully part of humankind.

But it is also worth keeping in mind that two centuries before the Enlightenment, the Debate of Valladolid (1550–1551) dealt with a similar topic. This debate was convened by Charles Quint, and it aimed at defining whether colonization and slavery of the Amerindian people were legitimate attitudes. In other words, this debate explored the question of whether Amerindian people were worthy of treatment as humans equal to Spanish people. Regardless of antagonism between its main protagonists, Bartolomé de Las Casas (1484–1566) and Juan Ginés de Sepulveda (1494–1573), the Valladolid Debate recognized Amerindian people as equal human beings to Spanish people. Subsequently, they were exonerated from slavery and its degrading treatments. On the contrary, African people did not benefit from the same consideration. Thus, they were submitted to slavery and its inherent obligations. The Valladolid Debate largely contributed to intensifying the slave trade from Africa to the New World (Mbembe 2013).

Thus, it can be noted that differentialism originally spread out in Africa as both a political and a philosophical attitude aiming at excluding the African people from the category of human beings. Its main concerns were alterity and the achievement of a common world. In this respect, Mbembe observes that

> A ces questions, les Lumières apportent [des] réponses aux implications politiques relativement distinctes. Une première constellation de réponses préconise l'enfermement des Africains dans leur *différence* présupposée. Car, dans leur versant obscur, les Lumières considèrent que le *signe africain* aurait quelque chose de distinct, de singulier, qui le séparerait de tous les autres signes humains. Rien ne témoignerait mieux de cette spécificité que le corps du Noir, ses forms et ses couleurs. ... Toujours selon ce versant des Lumières, les Africains auraient développé les conceptions de la société, du monde et du bien fort singulières, qui ne témoigneraient, en rien du pouvoir d'invention et de l'universalité propres à la raison.
>
> *(2000, 22, original emphasis)*

(The Enlightenment provides answers to these questions marked by relatively distinct political implications. The first constellation of responses advocates the confinement of Africans in their presupposed difference. For in their darkness, the Enlightenment considers that the African sign would have something distinct, singular, which would separate Africans from all other human signs. Nothing would testify better to this specificity than the body of the black people, its forms and its colours. ... According to this version of the Enlightenment, Africans would have developed singular conceptions of society, the world and the good that don't bear witness to the power of invention and the universality characterizing reason.)

I think that differentialism is neither an end in itself nor a mere resistance to homogenization. This attitude includes a variety of objectives and expands through different paradigms. Its guiding and philosophical backgrounds can be summed up according to three historical moments: colonial rule, the postcolonial period, and the era of globalization. The colonial time relied on the principle of the Enlightenment that denies alterity, which led to non-Western people being viewed with superiority, and repulsion (Eze 1997, 103–140). The difference is used in support of social and political inequalities. Both apartheid and colonial policies achieved in Africa during the two last centuries can be viewed as illuminating concerning both the philosophy and policy of difference (Mamdani 1996; Memmi, 1985). In this regard, Mbembe observes that

> le principe de la différence et le refus de l'altérité persistent. ... Si l'African est un être *à part*, c'est qu'il a des choses à lui. Il a une identité et celle-ci repose sur la coutume. Il ne s'agit, ni d'abolir, ni de détruire la coutume. Il s'agit, au contraire, d'inscrire la difference dans un ordre institutionnel distinct tout en

contraignant cet ordre distinct à opérer dans un cadre fondamentalement iné-
galitaire et hiérarchisé. ... *La différence n'est reconnue qu'en tant qu'elle justifie
l'inégalité et la discrimination.* ... *[L]'Etat colonial utilisera la coutume, c'est-à-dire le
principe de la différence et le refus de l'altérité, comme mode de gouvernement en soi.*
(2000, 22, emphasis added)

(the principle of difference and the rejection of otherness persist. ... If the African is a being apart, it is because he has things of his own. He has an identity that is based on custom. It is not a question of abolishing or destroying custom. On the contrary, it is a question of inscribing difference in a distinct institutional order while forcing this order to operate in a fundamentally inegalitarian and hierarchical framework. ... Difference is recognized only in so far as it justifies inequality and discrimination. ... [T]he colonial State will make use of custom, that is to say the principle of difference and the rejection of otherness, as a mode of government for itself.)

Mbembe's assertion completes and strengthens Mamdani's idea according to which, colonialism was essentially based on a logic of discrimination. The logic of apartheid that characterized the South African regime for decades was also deployed across the continent. For Mamdani, this logic relied on premises sketched by the already mentioned Lord Frederick John Dealtry Lugard, for whom African indigenous people were more like children. They should be ruled and treated like children. For Lord Dealtry Lugard, it would be a mistake to attempt to develop political relationships, that are basically designed for mature citizens, with black people. This kind of relationship would imply the unacceptable idea of equality between colonizers and colonized. So, colonial rule not only confined the African indigenous people to the status of subject and different, but it also found appropriate strategies to rule and control them. Gordon (2008, 24) notes that "The historical result was the setting up of systems of chiefs who maintained supposedly native rule while organizing citizenship between white settlers".

The African postcolonial period is the time of African self-governance. Most African countries obtained their emancipation and started to be ruled by Africans themselves. This period can be viewed as the golden age of African authoritarianism because, as already mentioned, the majority of these leaders set up undemocratic regimes entirely devoted to the cult of personality. In addition, they made ambiguous use of cultural difference. On one hand, they relied on differentialism to reject colonial rule as well as to mobilize the people for African emancipation; on the other hand, they relied on the principle of difference to set up their own power to the detriment of political pluralism and development. As Mbembe (2000, 37) observes

Au fond, il ne s'agit plus tant de revendiquer le statut *d'alter ego* pour l'Africain dans le monde que d'affirmer désormais haut et fort sa différence. C'est cette différence qu'il faudrait préserver à tout prix.

(Basically, the central claim of the African in the world is no longer the status of alter ego, but the assertion of his singularity. This difference should be preserved at all costs.)

Differentialism also relied on ethnic antagonism that developed soon after African emancipation. Theoretically, protagonists of this view claim factors such as common ancestry, shared language, culture, history, and religion as dividing lines between ethnic groups. This premise has been used to explain most African social and political conflicts. Scholars such as Amselle and M'Bokolo (1999) denounce the reductionism characterizing this way of thinking. For them, the issue of ethnicity is not as simple as many people think. Beyond visible phenomena, there are always invisible forces in various forms: ideological confrontation, individual interests, and search for legitimacy and power, to mention a few. According to Amselle and M'Bokolo (1999), for instance, the use of differentialism in this case relies much more on political manipulation than on real expression of people's desires. The debate on the identity of Ivory Coast and the waves of xenophobic crisis[2] that regularly take place in various African countries can be also viewed as illustration of such manipulation of both the people and the concept itself.

8.3 Globalization and heterogeneity of African cultures

The globalization process implies the need to think differently about the social, political, and cultural reality of Africa in a changing world dominated by the ideal of the global market. Contrary to the premises of homogenization and differentiation of cultures, a range of African scholars and Africanists argue for an approach that takes into consideration the requirements of heterogeneity and otherness. The concern for heterogeneity rests on the hypothesis of original pluralism according to which humankind, like the universe, is made of multiple units, which means that it is the result of the union of numerous elements (Nouss and Laplantine 2001, 289–302). This idea has as a corollary the notion of movement that implies transformative dynamics and otherness. As a result, it calls for going beyond conventional and nativist world views (Appiah 1992, 47–72; Mbembe 2005).

The emergence, in recent decades, of the debates on multiculturalism, interculturalism, cosmopolitanism, and Afropolitanism, for example, illustrate the awakening of a new African consciousness. "We are Africans of the world" – this is the expression used by proponents of Afropolitanism, for example, to identify themselves (Selasi 2005). In this respect, it is worth remembering that ownership of the term Afropolitanism is concomitantly attributed to both Selasi (2005) and Mbembe (2005). Etymologically, this term combines two words: the word "Afro", referring to Africa as geographic entity as well as a cultural and political sphere; and the Greek word "polis" (city), referring to citizenship and its subsequent characteristics. In sum, this neologism refers to the claim for a new perception of African people and realities.

Selasi views Afropolitanism as a cultural hybridization, especially concerning the younger generation of African migrants. In her sociological essay "Bye Bye Babar" (Selasi 2005), she approaches this generation, on one hand, as being marked by multiple social origins and cultural identities and, on the other hand, as embodying the will to produce and display a new African identity, contrary to diffused stereotypes and prejudices about Africans. She writes in this respect that

> What distinguishes this lot and its like (in the West and at home) *is a willingness to complicate Africa* – namely, to engage with, critique, and celebrate the parts of Africa that mean most to them. *Perhaps what most typifies the Afropolitan consciousness is the refusal to oversimplify*; the effort to understand what is ailing in Africa alongside the desire to honor what is wonderful, unique. *Rather than essentializing the geographical entity, we seek to comprehend the cultural complexity*; to honor the intellectual and spiritual legacy; and to sustain our parents' cultures.
>
> (Selasi 2005, emphasis added)

For Selasi, this generation of Africans aim at rehabilitating Africa from a painful colonial past. It also commits itself to exposing the continent to new opportunities occurring in the world. This generation expresses itself through different channels including, for example, literature, art, music, fashion, and language. Selasi herself notes that

> [We] are Afropolitans – *the newest generation of African emigrants*, coming soon or collected already at a law firm/chem lab/jazz lounge near you. *You'll know us by our funny blend of London fashion, New York jargon, African ethics, and academic successes. Some of us are ethnic mixes*, e.g. Ghanaian and Canadian, Nigerian and Swiss; others merely cultural mutts: American accent, European affect, African ethos. *Most of us are multilingual*: in addition to English and a Romantic or two, we understand some indigenous tongue and speak a few urban vernaculars. There is at least one place on The African Continent to which we tie our sense of self: be it a nation-state (Ethiopia), a city (Ibadan), or an auntie's kitchen. Then there's the G8 city or two (or three) that we know like the backs of our hands, and the various institutions that know us for our famed focus. *We are Afropolitans: not citizens, but Africans of the world.*
>
> (2005, emphasis added)

Mbembe conceives Afropolitanism as the expression of a double resistance which aims at denouncing African metaphysics of difference as well as rejecting Afrocentrist paradigms that for over a century dominated and paralyzed the debate on African identity and culture. Therefore, he relies on the idea of "circularity of the worlds" and its subsequent pluralism that implies the emergence of new cultures and identities. For Mbembe (2005), Afropolitanism refers to a way of being in the world, a lifestyle whose starting point is not difference, but rather common humanity. He thinks that the assumption for common humanity constitutes the difference between Afropolitanism and theories such as negritude and pan-Africanism, among others, for which difference represents a fundamental notion.

In the same vein, Mbembe (2000) denounces philosophies based on the search for African singularity and that, by this fact, restrict African identity to a defeatist perspective and victimhood. For him, this new way of being in the world is revealed through indices such as the performances of African elite concerning professional and artistic commitments, their mastery of foreign languages and ability to live with other cultures of the world, facility to travel, and many others details of modern life. In this respect, for Mbembe (2005), South Africa constitutes an illuminating paradigm thanks to mixing of races, cultures, and people.

Indeed, both Selasi's and Mbembe's theories of Afropolitanism have received various criticisms, denouncing, for example, the elitism of this way of thinking and its propensity to pass over the difficult political and social issues of contemporary Africa including immigration, increasing poverty, the decline of education, and the agony of democracy and peace in different regions of the continent (Dabiri 2015). It is my feeling that the criticisms are relevant even though both Mbembe and Selasi are voiceless on these issues. They both give the impression of being satisfied with attractive aspects of globalization, subsequently overshadowing other aspects, because of an unspoken desire to avert from people's memory the sad and painful past of African people, the less successful African stories, and its failures and humiliations. Both Mbembe and Selasi seem to be voluntaristic, idealistic, and less critical concerning the dark side of the current ruling system, known as neo-liberal globalization. From this point of view, despite the relevance of their original intuition for developing a new paradigm of thought on African identity and cultures, it must be pointed out that their approach remains to be perfected. Here starts the complex challenge and long-term duty of contemporary African social and political philosophy.

8.4 Conclusion

This chapter explored the effects of globalization on African cultures and traditions. It denounced the illusion underlying the hypothesis that globalization leads systematically to homogenization of cultures, including African cultures and traditions. It outlined the distinction between artefacts and cultural traditions. The former are universal, and they are made in support of human living conditions, while the latter refer to particular ways of living. It called attention to the risk of transformation of thought based on the use of those artefacts.

The chapter also addressed the debate related to differentialism. The relationship between different cultures is not necessarily based on antagonism and mutual denial. On the contrary, difference is viewed as a source of cultural enrichment. The emergence of discourses such as cosmopolitanism and Afropolitanism reveals the new African consciousness about the cultural pluralism and configurations that are in process.

Finally, the chapter focused on the emergence of new African consciousness through the idea of Afropolitanism. Specific attention was paid to the approaches of Selasi and Mbembe as the originators of this concept. These two thinkers invert conventional stigmas often applied to African people. They claim new African identity based on factors such as the ability to speak several languages, to have a successful careers, to travel all over the world, to enjoy the output of globalization, and so on. This chapter denounced the fact that this new approach to African identity and culture omits the powerless and their daily struggle for a living. The chapter concluded that contacts and exchanges are important for the development of every culture. Globalization should be an opportunity for mutual enrichment, respect, and intercultural dialogue.

Notes

1 This term refers not only to the growing number of shopping centres all over the world, but also to every space where consumption goes beyond the strict fulfilment of basic needs and becomes a way of being. More than a commercial transaction, the act of purchasing is viewed as the expression of both common culture and identity. In her famous book, which became a symbol of resistance to globalization, Klein (2002) denounces the manipulation and the tyranny of brands. Baudrillard's (1970) essay *La société de consummation* is still a relevant critique of the materialist, individualist, and merchantilist world view shaping those cathedrals of consumption.
2 Recurrent waves of xenophobia and violence taking place in South Africa towards black migrants in recent decades can be viewed as symptomatic in this respect.

CONCLUSION

To conclude this volume, it is important to emphasize its key points and their implications for the development of contemporary African social and political philosophy. From the outset, this volume explored the specificity and the sources of this philosophy. It denounced a range of conventional views considering contemporary African social and political philosophy as a nationalist ideology and, in doing so, reduce this philosophy to the thought of single African leaders and professional philosophers. Opposing this attitude, the volume rested on the premise that African social and political philosophy represents an autonomous attempt to think of African people's daily lives, management of power, and paradigms of good governance. It approaches the purpose of African social and political philosophy as including the duty to clarify political concepts in use in African political debate. The search for human excellence constitutes its major and prevailing objective.

The analysis highlighted that contemporary African social and political philosophy doesn't coincide with categories of thought such as ontology and ideology, which have restricted it for decades. It is different because it rests on African people's daily experience, whereas ontology expands on the search for the essence of being. Its relationship to the concept of ideology doesn't imply a strict identity or coincidence. The fact that a political philosophy can include some ideological elements doesn't necessarily imply that, by principle, this philosophy is an ideology, and vice versa.

This volume also denounced the reduction of sources of African social and political philosophy to written texts and works of professional thinkers. Therefore, it explored the legacies of precolonial African societies and the African diaspora. The reference to this double legacy confirmed the permanence of issues such as the search for consensus, dialogue, race, and identity. In addition, this analysis also expands and expresses itself through spheres such as African art, music, religions, and urbanism of African cities, for example.

Identity is one of the most addressed issues in contemporary African social and political philosophy. In this respect, the concern for ethnophilosophy as a discourse of African rehabilitation became central to many African thinkers and Africanists. The concept of ethnophilosophy was first used in African philosophy by Nkrumah to refer to every people's *weltanschauung*. Towa and Hountondji diverted from this interpretation, both applying a pejorative and restrictive meaning in order to denounce the potential confusion between philosophy and ethnology on behalf of various African thinkers and Africanists. Hountondji has altered his view in this respect, and many thinkers all over the world claim for a broader and more positive meaning for this concept. For them, every thought can be ethnophilosophical as far as it refers to cultural peculiarity. In this respect, regardless of their individual frame and origin, thinkers such as Heidegger, Hegel, and Kant, for example, can formulate ethnophilosophical discourse.

This study also explored the negritude movement as part of African discourse on identity. It focused on Senghor's theory of negritude and addressed criticism formulated by thinkers such as Adotevi and Fanon. Both these thinkers denounce the fact that Senghor equated emotion with the quintessence of black people. In this perspective, according to his criticisms, he reproduces the racist clichés of colonialism. They also think that Senghor encloses black people in their past and self-contemplation. For them, by this attitude, Senghor avoids political debate in favour of a romantic approach to culture and identity. In response to those criticisms, Senghor outlined three things: first, he has been misunderstood by these critics; second, he never denied the fact that black people were also rational; and third it out of the question for black people to exist outside of world progress. In addition, this volume also noted the relevance of negritude's method of endorsement and its revolutionary dimension aiming at inverting colonial stigmas to relativize Western discourse. For defenders of negritude, this movement doesn't consider the defence of black people as an end in itself; focusing on black people, protagonists of negritude claim for both the dignity of every person and the right of every human being to be different. Along the same lines, the analysis relied on Gandhi's approach of non-violence to oppose the call for violence supported by thinkers such as Fanon.

Contemporary African social and political philosophy deals with the problem of solidarity between black people all over the world. That gave rise to the concept of pan-Africanism, first launched by Blyden. This Afro-American thinker called for solidarity of black people all over the world to resist the racial discrimination and exploitation that they suffered at the hands of white people. This call spread out all over the world and took different constellations including the trans-Atlantic pan-Africanism, trans-American pan-Africanism, and sub-Saharan pan-Africanism, among others.

The founding fathers of this movement developed a range of theories. Booker T. Washington, for example, promoted the idea of black empowerment through vocational education, work, and the theory of black people's accommodation. Marcus Garvey encouraged the return of black people to Africa. Cooper is known for her "theory of value" as well as her struggle for black students access to higher education. Du Bois, through his life and his work, established himself as the epitome of pan-Africanism.

The Fifth Pan-African Congress of Manchester in 1945 inaugurated a new era for the movement in terms of the transfer of the leadership of the movement to African heirs. The search for emancipation and unity of African countries eclipsed the racial claim that characterized the approach of the movement's founders. The struggle for African unity was driven by two opposing tendencies: supporters of the creation of a supranational state named the "United States of Africa"; and defenders of a progressive achievement of this unity through meeting the needs of the African people. The creation of the Organization for African Unity (OAU) in May 1963 allowed the controversies between these two tendencies to be overcome. The African Union (AU) came into existence in 2002 to replace the OAU. Personalities such as Nkrumah, Fanon, Gaddafi, Nyerere, and many others count amongst important African heirs of pan-Africanism.

Representative democracy can be considered as the original mode of governance of contemporary African states since those states emanated from the Berlin Conference (1884–1885). Paradoxically, it was the colonizer who supervised Africa's first elections and gave legitimacy to new leaders as well as setting up new institutions. Accepted at first by the majority of African countries, this mode of governance was rejected soon after their emancipation in favour of a variety of principles of governance including single-party rule, diarchy, no-party rule, and multi-partyism. Changes that occurred globally during the late twentieth century contributed to the development of a new political consciousness among African people concerning their rights and struggle for a new social and political contract. The experience of the Sovereign National Conferences that took place in various African countries in the two last decades of the twentieth century can be viewed as an illustration of this aspiration.

There were two trends in the (re)discovery of democracy by African people in the late twentieth century: protagonists of the universalistic approach to democracy and defenders of the particularistic view of democracy. For the former, democracy is a universal process, valid and applicable to every people and culture all over the world. For the latter, it is important to focus on the particular values and experiences of every people and culture concerning a better mode of political governance. This debate highlights the dilemma of the African intelligentsia: the choice between the global market paradigm imposed by international funding institutions and proponents of neo-liberal thought and the defence of African values and traditions of governance. To conclude this analysis, I developed a plea for constructive values of humankind from every concerned culture as a way of leading to a possible other common world.

This volume also approached African civil society as a compound of organizations standing apart from the state and economic sphere as well as being committed to the well-being of African people. The analysis addressed the perception amongst Africanists and African thinkers of the concept of civil society. For a range of them, this concept is not adequate to express African social and political reality because of its Western origin and theoretical background, which differ radically from the African context. For others, this word does express African social and political reality by virtue of its universalism and its ability to serve as an indication of progress regarding democracy.

The emergence of the struggle against the postcolonial regime in the two last decades of the twentieth century emphasizes the new consciousness of African people concerning their social and political life as well as their determination for change. African civil society is involved in different areas including democracy, people's empowerment, conflict resolution and peace-building, and improving health care and education. The role of youth movements in claiming for civil rights, justice, employment, and democratic alternation can be viewed as a novating process. Despite its important achievements, African civil society suffers from financial dependence on both the African state and foreign institutions. This brings into the fore the problem of its sovereignty and full achievement of its projects.

This volume also examined the development of African cultures in the era of globalization. From the political perspective of power relationships structuring African societies and the world, it addressed three main debates including the homogenization of cultures, differentialism, and cultural pluralism. The study denounced the illusions of cultural purity and antagonism between cultures underlying the concepts of homogenization and differentialism. On the contrary, it postulated the salvific character of cultural pluralism and exchange between cultures. To be achieved, this project requires standards of mutual recognition and intercultural dialogue.

Concluding this volume, I can reiterate my impression from the beginning that contemporary African social and political philosophy is an immense project that has been little explored up to now. From this perspective, I wanted to attract the interest of African thinkers and Africanists on the issue, but also to invite them to a critical and constructive debate on emerging social and political challenges of today's Africa. The future of Africa depends on this noble and exciting duty.

EPILOGUE

A struggle for the right to live. Mandela, in defence of pluralism and democracy

Concluding this volume, I could not resist the temptation to put into perspective some of the ideas of one of the most important African leaders of the late twentieth century and early twenty-first century: Nelson Mandela. The evocation of Mandela's struggle for the right to live can be viewed as representative of most African people's fight for democracy and well-being. The challenge of the apartheid system can be approached, through Mandela's experience, as concerning all paradigms of discrimination and exclusion from which African people are suffering.

This comment is in three sections. The first section summarizes the political and social background of Mandela's struggle: the South African apartheid regime and its philosophy. The second section analysis Mandela's first steps in politics through the Youth League of the ANC. The final section addresses major articulations of his political credo including democracy, collective action, African nationalism, and diversity.

1 The social and political context of Mandela's struggle

From the outset, it is worth remembering that racial discrimination did not disappear with the abolition of slavery and slave trade. Rather, it took on new codes and structures, such as colonization and apartheid, that characterized Africa for many years. In South Africa, for example, this phenomenon took the form of structural state racism. Since its emancipation in 1910 up to the last decade of the twentieth century, South Africa presented itself as a state in which racial discrimination was recognized and approved by law. A range of laws were published in this respect, such as the Land Act (1913) that, to the benefit of white settlers, deprived black people of 87 per cent of the territory in the land of their birth. The Urban Area Act (1923) created teeming African slums, known as native locations, aiming at providing cheap labour to white industry. The Colour Bar Act of 1926 banned Africans from carrying out skilled trades. The Native Administration Act of 1927 made the British Crown the supreme chief over all African areas (Mandela 2013, 114).

The electoral victory of the Afrikaner National Party in 1948 marked the development of racial segregation as both philosophy and mode of governance. Legal discrimination was practiced concerning, for example, mixed marriages (1949) and sexual relationships between white people and black people (1950). This was also the case concerning use of public transportation, restaurants, parks, and beaches. Academic institutions were not exonerated from racial segregation (More, 2004, 150). A wide range of security measures were deployed to check and limit the presence of black people in areas reserved to the white population. This system of racial oppression governed South Africa for almost half a century and was known under the name of apartheid.

For scholars such as More (2004), associating the genesis of apartheid with the advent to power of the Afrikaner Nationalist Party seems reductive of the issue as well as neglectful of the history of racial discrimination in South Africa. The attitude of the Afrikaner National Party in 1948 was only one episode in a long series of racist phenomena aiming at strengthening the idea of white supremacy. He notes that such an attitude aimed at

> strengthening and perfecting an already existing system of racial discrimination and domination rooted in attitudes and values of the whites ever since they got into contact with the African. So, the Afrikaner Nationalist Party, which first came to power in 1948 and introduced the name "apartheid" established its fortification on grounds already prepared by the first Dutch settlers in the Cape of Good Hope under Jan van Riebeeck in 1652, and later by the British settlers in 1820.
>
> *(More 2004, 151)*

More's observation coincides in several places with the perception that Mandela himself has of apartheid. According to this approach, apartheid is only a new name and a new form of expression standing for a secular system of oppression that attempts to negate otherness, the existence of the other as equal human beings regardless of the colour of their skin. In other words, apartheid constitutes a process of annihilation of the other as human beings, particularly black people. Mandela (2013, 127) expresses this as follows:

> Apartheid was a new term but an old idea. It literally means "apartness", and it represents the codification in one oppressive system of all the laws and regulations that had kept Africans in an inferior position to whites for centuries. What has been more or less *de facto* had to become *de jure*. The often haphazard segregation of the past three hundred years was to be consolidated into a monolithic system that was diabolical in its details, inescapable in its reach and overwhelming in its power.

The proponents of the apartheid system maintain the idea of white people's supremacy. This postulate relies on religious, philosophical, political, and economic premises.[1] The defenders of the religious approach, for example, rely on a controversial interpretation of the biblical story concerning the malediction of Cham to justify the domination and the exploitation of black people. According to this story, Cham is cursed because he mocked his father for getting drunk and sleeping naked (Gen. IX, 20–27). This interpretation of the biblical story raises questions regarding both the hermeneutical methodology and the tools used, because the biblical texts are not a mere description of facts, nor is the Bible itself a book of history. Reading the Bible requires a set of hermeneutical skills to avoid erroneous interpretations, anachronism, and fundamentalism. This interpretation of the story of Cham's malediction can be viewed as illustrative in this respect. Contrary to supporters of Cham's curse to his offspring of black skin, this narrative is silent concerning the skin colour of Noah's sons and their offspring. It is my feeling that the attribution of black skin colour to Cham rests much more on people's imagination and prejudices than any expression in the Bible itself.

Protagonists of racial segregation also undermine democracy because they distort the ideas of otherness and human equality. They classify and prioritize human beings as they proclaim the supremacy of white people over other people. They exclusively confer to white people attributes such as rational capacity, moral authority, intelligence, among others, that they deny to black people, who are, subsequently, considered lesser than human (Memmi 1985). This attitude stands on the postulate that identity is the convergence of the same (A = A). As a result, this view reflects the rejection of all difference and the negation of the other (Kasanda 2013b). It can be considered as contrary to the democratic spirit and the principle of diversity amongst equals. In addition, there is no need to insist that the access to land, the exploitation of natural resources, and the subsequent demand for cheap labour also contributed to strengthening racial prejudice (Mbembe 2013).

Racial discrimination has repeatedly been denounced by international institutions such as the United Nations and the OAU. Black organizations committed to change have done the same, making use of a variety of strategies: civil disobedience, strikes, and boycotts, for example. The riots in Soweto (1976) illustrate the resistance of the South African people as well as the stubbornness and brutality of the ruling authority. The emancipation of former Portuguese colonies in southern Africa, including Angola (1975), Mozambique (1975), and Zimbabwe (1980), created a core of regimes opposed to apartheid. This increased the pressure on the system of apartheid. Changes occurring in the last two decades of the twentieth century, including the change of American policy towards South Africa (Delacampagne 2000, 261), the end of the cold war, and the collapse of the communist system, urged South African authorities to consider deep reform, which led to the dismantling of the apartheid system.

2 Mandela's earlier political commitments

Mandela was born in 1918 in Mvezo, Transkei region. He arrived in Johannesburg at the age of 22 to study. Thanks to the support of Walter Sisulu, he started his law studies. Sisulu was, along with Oliver Tambo, one of the pillars of the African National Congress (ANC). He was the vice president of the ANC, whilst Tambo acted as president and chairman of this political organization.

Mandela took part in the formation of the ANC's Youth League in 1944. He joined the executive committee of the League, whose purpose was close to ANC's constitution of 1912: to support the struggle for freedom of black people. African nationalism constituted the battle cry of the leaders of ANC's Youth League. They all believed in the creation of one nation out of many tribes, the overthrow of white supremacy, and the establishment of a truly democratic form of government. Mandela (2013, 114) recalls their common belief and mission statement as follows: "We believe that the national liberation of Africans will be achieved by Africans themselves ... the Congress Youth League must be the brains-trust and power-station of African nationalism".

The idea of African nationalism includes two interpretative trends. First, it refers to a narrow and radical approach of nationalism based on Garvey's theory that "Africa should be for Africans". Second, this notion evokes a broader view of African nationalism according to which, in addition to the freedom of black people, South Africa should be recognized as a multi-racial country. A range of leaders of the Youth League, including Mandela, were closer to the latter perspective than the former.

The leaders of the Youth League intended to be original and enterprising in tackling various challenges. They kept away from communist analysis considering black people's oppression as the effect of class antagonism and economic struggle. For them, this explanation was not satisfying because their chief concern was the issue of race. They considered that both the creation and empowerment of a strong nationalist movement led by Africans can help get over the experience of white domination. From this perspective, leaders of ANC's Youth League can be viewed as close to Indian protest movements against racial discrimination, as they borrowed from this movement many things including fighting spirit, the principles of non-violence and civil disobedience inspired by Gandhi, and the belief that true emancipation is a result of rigorous organization and an unwavering sense of sacrifice (Mandela 2013, 119).

Leaders of ANC's Youth League also wanted to be more active and enterprising than the conservative wing of the party. They supported candidates open to change at the head of ANC. In doing so, they approved programmes of action including new methods of political struggle, such as "boycotts, strikes, civil disobedience and non-cooperation" (Mandela, 2013, 132). The achievement of the ANC's Youth League's project came up against various obstacles including both the repression and the arrest of ANC leaders such as Sisulu, Mandela, Kathrada, Mbeki, Bernstein, and many others. Let us leave aside these events and focus on Mandela's political thought.

3 Mandela's political action and thought

Mandela's political thought was anchored in the daily struggle of South Africans for their social and political rights. From the outset, this thought was articulated through specific events and documents such as the "Freedom Charter" (FC), "Freedom in our Lifetime" (FL), and the "Rivonia Trial" (RT) and accompanied by the experience of state violence, repression, and the arrest of anti-apartheid activists. Imprisonment, for example, constituted a deep physical and psychological torture due to the loneliness and lack of comfort imposed on the prisoners, as Mandela himself expressed after 27 years of being in an apartheid jail (Mandela 2013). Both his courage his and perseverance and his solidarity on behalf of his comrades and anti-apartheid activists can be viewed as a source of inspiration for all those who, even now, are fighting all over the world for a more equal and just society. Let's briefly explore a few of the principles that guided Mandela's political action and thought.

3.1. Collective action and democracy

Mandela firmly believed in democracy. For him, democracy was not a set of principles defined and organized from a metaphysical pedestal. On the contrary, he viewed this mode of governance as a collective commitment of the people to build a society where everyone can live free with dignity and move towards excellence. According to Mandela, the premise of this social and political project is contained in the FC, which he qualified as "a major political and unprecedented event" in the South African struggle for black people's emancipation (2013, 201). The FC was adopted in 1955 at Kliptown by a Congress of nearly 3,000 delegates including members of civil and political organizations such as the ANC, the South African Indian Congress, the South African Coloured People's Organization, the non-racial South African Congress of Trade Unions (SACTU), and the Congress of Democrats, composed of liberal whites (English and Kalumba 1996, 335).

This diversity of participants in the Congress and their great number in a context of racial discrimination and social repression made a crucial social and political event of the FC. The claims formulated in this document call for a radical social and political change. Thus, this document can be viewed as expressing the aspirations and struggle of South African civil society against racial segregation and social and political exclusion. It is more than a simple list of civil claims because it calls for an upheaval of the current rules of the game. In this respect, Mandela observes that "The Charter is more than a mere list of demands for democratic reforms. It is a revolutionary document precisely because the changes it envisages cannot be won without breaking up the economic and political set-up of present South Africa" (quoted in English and Kalumba 1996, 340).

The FC denounced the country's ruling system as oppressive and dehumanizing. It claimed for political rights including the right to vote, to take part in the decision-making process and management of thte country, the freedom of expression and the right to basic means of subsistence like food, health care, education, and shelter (Mandela 2013, 205). In this regard, it can be noted that the FC looked similar to the socialist project. For Mandela, this perception is just an illusion. The FC is by no means a blueprint of the socialist project, because it doesn't support ideas such as class antagonism and exclusive control by workers and peasants or the suppression of the notion of profit. Mandela himself observes that

> *Whilst the Charter proclaims democratic changes of a far-reaching nature, it is by no means a blueprint for a socialist state but a program for the unification of various classes and groupings amongst the people on a democratic basis.* Under socialism the workers hold state power. They and the peasants own the means of production, the land, the factories, and the mills. All production is for use and not for profit. The Charter does not contemplate such profound economic and political changes. Its declaration "The People Shall Govern" visualizes the transfer of power not to any single social class but to all the people of this country, be they workers, peasants, professional men, or petty bourgeoisie.
>
> (Quoted in English and Kalumba 1996, 340–341, emphasis added)

The FC's political programme doesn't coincide with a socialist political paradigm, for it is indebted to the tenets of modern liberalism, particularly concerning notions such as individual rights to life, liberty, and estate (Mandela 2013, 206). Following English and Kalumba (1996, 335), it can be observed that this approach relies on Locke's political tradition of thought, for which individual rights are sacred.[2]

Mandela thought of the labour movement as spearheading this expected change of political regime. But he quickly adds that this movement cannot by itself reverse the trend, particularly in the South African context, of repression of both social movements and trade unions. Therefore, he called for solidarity and unity of everybody. This solidarity is fundamental to the success of the struggle against the ruling system. He notes that

> The workers are the principal force upon which the democratic movement should rely, but to repel the savage onslaughts of the Nationalist Government and to develop the fight for democratic rights it is necessary that the other classes and groupings be joined. Support and assistance must be sought and secured from the ... African and Coloured mine-workers, ... non-European labours employed on European farms and from the millions of peasants that occupy the so-called Native Reserves of the Union. ... The non-European Traders and businessmen are also potential allies.
>
> (Quoted in English and Kalumba 1996, 341)

3.2. The Rivonia Trial: Pluralistic society and nationalism

Rivonia is a suburb of Johannesburg. It owes its reputation to Liliesleaf farm, which was thought to be the hideout of ANC leaders and activists during the struggle against apartheid. To evade security police, Mandela hid himself in this farm, taking a false identity and pretending to be the cook and gardener at this farm. This can be viewed as part of Mandela's strategic creativity in the context of struggle for life and resistance: the ruse. This issue has received very little attention in African political philosophy[3] despite its importance for the African struggle for emancipation and its presence in African traditional legacy.[4] In this respect, Bidima (1995, 72) recalls that

> *Deux paramètres ont été oubliés dans la réflexion philosophique sur le politique en Afrique: la ruse et la réflexion du point de vue de la deixis.* Sur le plan de la macropolitique internationale, l'Afrique ne fait pas son poids. Il ne s'agit pas de bons sentiments mais d'un rapport de force. Dès lors, quelle est l'arme des faibles? La Ruse (Métis)! … La Ruse, c'est l'intelligence, le détour. A celui dont la droiture et les pleurs ne peuvent être évalués sur le plan international, « l'obliquité » devrait être la règle.
>
> *(1995, 72, emphasis added)*

(two parameters have been forgotten in the philosophical reflection on politics in Africa: the *ruse* and reflection on the *deixis*. Concerning international relationships, Africa doesn't count so much. That is not a question of good will, but the issue at stake is the balance of power. Therefore, what is the weapon of the weak? The Ruse (Métis)! … The Ruse is the capacity of both understanding and deviation. For a man whose uprightness and crying cannot be assessed at the international level, "obliquity" should be the rule.)

Mandela's capacity for political ruse is also illustrated through his shaping of what he himself called the "M-Plan" or simply the "Mandela Plan" (Mandela 2013). This refers to the strategic organization of ANC members and freedom fighters to avoid state interdiction and to continue operating secretly. This plan included social organization and political lectures. Unfortunately, it came across multiple difficulties, and its success was mitigated (Mandela 2013, 168–169).

Various leaders of the ANC were arrested at Rivonia's Liliesleaf farm, where important ANC documents were seized by the police. Though their trial actually took place between October 1963 and June 1964 in Johannesburg, symbolically, the trial kept the name of Rivonia. ANC leaders were charged with preparing a violent revolution and committing acts of sabotage; conspiring to commit these acts and to aid foreign military units when they [hypothetically] invaded the Republic; acting in these ways to achieve the objectives of communism; and soliciting and receiving money for these purposes from sympathizers outside South Africa. Mandela presented a plea from the dock in which he emphasized his political creed and motivations. Through this plea, he differentiated between the ANC's purposes and the political project of the Communist Party (CP). According to him, the allegation that the ANC served the interests of CP was far from the truth (English and Kalumba 1996, 342). For Mandela, the CP project was based on class antagonism and aims at creating a society ruled by the proletariat class, while the ANC was committed to a nationalist project that did not advocate the exclusion of the white man from the country and did not support the idea of a society based on racial, political, or economic domination. In other words, the ANC's project supported the inclusion of all races in a society based on equal rights and equitable redistribution of resources.

> The ideological creed of the ANC is ... the creed of African Nationalism. It is not the concept of African Nationalism expressed in the cry, "drive the white man into the sea." The African Nationalism for which the ANC stands is the concept of freedom and fulfilment for the African people in their own land.
> *(Mandela quoted in English and Kalumba 1996, 342)*

The claims for the redistribution of land and nationalization of the means of production, including banks, mines, and some powerful enterprises, should not lead to viewing this nationalism as the blueprint of either a socialist or a communist project. For Mandela, nationalization is just a means to break the chains of exploitation and to promote social justice and balance. Apart from this, Mandela did recognize some affinities between his political struggle and the concerns of the CP. First, he pointed out the long tradition in the CP of supporting emancipatory struggles all over the world. Such was the case concerning Algeria, Malaya, Indonesia, and so on. This approach appears to have been inspiring to Mandela. Considering the context of South Africa, he thought that it would be a luxury for ANC leaders, including himself, to neglect such support in focusing on their struggle against apartheid. According to him: "We accept the need for some form of socialism to enable our people to catch up with advanced countries and overcome their legacy of extreme poverty. But this doesn't mean we are Marxists" (quoted in English and Kalumba 1996, 344).

It is my feeling that Mandela's attitude towards both the CP and Marxism can be viewed as ambiguous. The debate about his membership of the CP is even murkier as nobody can bring evidence to formally confirm or contradict it. Otherwise, there is a range of indicators of a close collaboration between ANC leaders including Mandela himself and the CP. This attitude can be considered part of Mandela's political ruse and pragmatism, in which efficiency seems to be much more important than the mere question of membership. The bottom line is that results matter more than anything else. This attitude raises a fundamental question related to his perception of violence in the struggle for democracy and the removal of apartheid: does the end justify the means? This is the concern of the following section.

3.3 From violence to negotiation and reconciliation policy

In February 1990, Mandela was freed from the jail where he had spent 27 years, half of his life. Three years later, he was awarded – together with Frederik de Klerk – the Nobel Peace Prize. In 1994, following the first non-segregationist elections of South Africa, he was elected as president. These years can be considered as a period of popular euphoria during which he was perceived as a non-violent man, a missionary of peace and reconciliation. However, this reputation can be viewed as somewhat biased because it fails to take into consideration two things: first, the complexity and the pliability of Mandela's attitude concerning violence, and second the difference between the young Mandela and the more mellowed one. The reference to young Mandela is to his political commitment before his incarceration for life, while the concept of mature Mandela evokes the attitude of the post-Robben Island Mandela. The former seems dominated by the passion and fire of youth, while the latter seems to be mellowed by the experience of struggle and by age. In other words, the former seemed more radical than the latter (More 2004).

The issue of violence has been a source of endless debate amongst African nationalist leaders, thinkers, and Africanists – mostly between Mahatma Gandhi's disciples and Fanon's followers. The former are viewed as supporting the philosophy of non-violence, while the latter are considered proponents of the philosophy of violence. It is my feeling that this antagonism simplifies the debate and eclipses, as already suggested, the complexity of and paradox within Mandela's attitude concerning the resort to violence as a tool for social and political transformation. In this respect, it is worth keeping in mind that Mandela addresses this issue in the general context of the ANC's policy, as he considered himself a loyal and disciplined member of the party despite the divergence of views between himself and some prominent ANC leaders including Luthuli, for example (Mandela 2013, 321–322).

The young Mandela believed that non-violence is not an inviolable principle. For him, the resort to violence or to non-violence to promote social and political change is not a question of philosophical principles. It is a matter of tactics, and subsequently it depends on actual social and political conditions. It is a practical necessity rather than an option. In this respect, the young Mandela seems far from Gandhi's view on non-violence, which was shared by a range of ANC leaders including Luthuli, as already mentioned. Reporting a debate amongst ANC leaders on the issue, Mandela observes that

> We also discussed whether the campaign should follow the Gandhian principles of non-violence. ... Some argued for non-violence on purely ethical grounds, saying it was morally superior to any other method. ... Others said that we should approach this issue not from the point of view of principles but of tactics, and that we should employ the method demanded by the conditions. If a particular method enabled us to defeat the enemy, then it should be used. ... *This made non-violence a practical necessity rather than an option. This was my view, and I saw non-violence on the Gandhian model not as an inviolable principle but as a tactic to be used as the situation demanded.*
>
> (2013, 147, emphasis added)[5]

In addition to that, confronting the increasing state's repression and violence toward both the black community and social organizations, that was illustrated through events such as Sharpeville and Soweto's repressions, for example, Mandela cannot resist the temptation to resort to violence. Rejecting the absolute pacifism, he considered that the state did not give to the people any alternative, and subsequently the violence will arise from the desire of the people to defend themselves. He thinks it would be better for the ANC to anticipate and control such a process. Otherwise, according to him, it would be

> *wrong and immoral to subject [the] people to armed attacks by the state without offering them some kind of alternative.* (…) people on their own had taken up arms. Violence would begin whether we initiate it or not. Would it not be better to guide this violence ourselves, according to principles where we saved lives by attacking symbols of oppression, and not people? If we did not take the lead now …, we would soon be latecomers and followers to a movement we did not control.
>
> (Mandela 2013, 322, emphasis added)

The young Mandela considers that asking those who suffer violence not to use violence themselves in fact means sanctioning the violence of the oppressor and encouraging the oppressed to turn the other cheek (More 2004). In this regard, it can be observed that the young Mandela moved away from Gandhi's pacifist philosophy because he favoured armed struggle, particularly through the armed wing of the ANC, the *Umkonto we Sizwe*. He committed himself to this option, organizing the armed wing of the ANC and planning strategies for the struggle (Mandela 2013, 328–329, 422–425). For him, to be efficient, this resort to violence should respond to a variety of conditions:

> At the beginning of June 1961, after a long and anxious assessment of the South African situation, I and some colleagues came to the conclusion that as violence in this country was inevitable, it would be unrealistic and wrong for African leaders to continue preaching peace and non-violence at a time when the Government met our peaceful demands with force. *This conclusion was not easily arrived at. It was only when all else had failed, when all channels of peaceful protest had been barred to us, that the decision was made to embark on violent forms of political struggle,* and to form *Umkhonto we Sizwe* [the spear of the Nation]. We did so not because we desired such a course, but *solely because the Government had left us no choice.*
>
> (Mandela 2013, 433, emphasis added)

It is worth remembering that the world underwent deep political and geostrategic changes during the last decades of the twentieth century. In addition to the collapse of the communist system and the process of globalization, there was the emancipation of African countries such as Angola (1975), Mozambique (1975), and Zimbabwe (1980), for example, which constituted the anti-apartheid front line. These events contributed to thwarting South African government plans concerning the political stability of the area and the strengthening of apartheid policy. This context weakened the segregationist South African government that, on various occasions, had offered

Mandela the possibility of release under the condition he gave up violence as a political instrument (Mandela 2013, 620). Theoretically, the mellowing Mandela remained intransigent concerning violence while nurturing philosophical alternatives based on the reconciliatory spirit that he displayed and pursued once freed from jail. He articulates his rejection of the government's offer of release as follows:

> I wrote a letter ... rejecting the conditions for my release ... I was keen to do a number of things in this response, because [the government's] offer was an attempt to drive a wedge between me and my colleagues by tempting me to accept a policy that ANC rejected. I wanted to reassure the ANC ... that my loyalty to the organization was beyond question. I also wished to send a message to the government that while I rejected its offer because of conditions attached to it, *I nevertheless thought negotiation, not war, was the path to a solution.*
> (Mandela 2013, 621, emphasis added)[6]

Mandela's alternative behaviour was based on the African philosophy of *Ubuntu*. The concept of *Ubuntu* comes from Nguni languages. The Nguni is a compound of ethnic groups including Zulu, Xhosa, Ndebele, and Swati. More (2004) gives two main interpretations of the concept of *Ubuntu*. First, he thinks that this word can be viewed as a

> Moral or ethical concept ... according to *which moral practices are founded exclusively on consideration and enhancement of human well-being; a preoccupation with human welfare*. It enjoins that what is morally good is what brings dignity, respect, contentment, and prosperity to others, self, and the community at large.
> (More 2004, 157, emphasis added)

Second, More thinks that the idea of *Ubuntu* is a traditional politico-ideological concept, a principle aiming at regulating all forms of social and political relationships. As such, this principle "enjoins and makes for peace and social harmony by encouraging the practice of sharing in all forms of communal existence. ... it expresses an understanding – a societal bond – and forms the basis for consensus" (More 2004, 157, emphasis added).

In sum, this concept highlights a premise that is fundamental to African thinking according to which an individual is not a human being except once he or she is part of a social order. This conception refers to the (individual) self as intrinsically linked to, and forming a part of, the community (More 2004, 157). In such a perspective, the self is viewed as dependent on others and is approached through his relationships to them. Tutu (1999) epitomizes this dependency, contrasting Descartes's premise "*Cogito ergo sum*" with the *Nguni* thinking according to which "*Umuntu ngumuntu ngabantu*", meansing "a person is a person through other persons" or "I am because we are".

South African leaders of the late tweentieth century, including the post-Robben Island Mandela, relied on this philosophical background to exorcize their country from the hatred and violence generated by decades of segregationist policy, as well as the subsequent rancour and thirst for vengeance. The Truth and Reconciliation Commission served this end, as did the fundamental project of the new South African constitution. It is my feeling that the spectre of the post-Robben Island Mandela hangs over the development of all these initiatives. In this respect, Derrida observes that

> Le mot ubuntu ... est celui dont s'est servi le discours officiel, à la fin de l'apartheid, pour traduire la mission même de la Commission Vérité et Réconciliation, pour traduire la « réconciliation » meme [...] [pour] assurer les conditions nécessaires pour dépasser les divisions et les conflits du passé qui avaient engendré de brutales violations des droits de l'homme et laissé « un héritage de haine, de peur, de culpabilité et de vengeance ». Cet héritage doit maintenant être traité à partir « d'un besoin de compréhension et non de vengeance, d'un besoin de réparation et non de représailles, d'un besoin d'*ubuntu* ... et non de victimisation ».
>
> *(2004, 116–117, emphasis added)*

(The word *ubuntu* ... was used in the official discourse at the end of apartheid to translate the very mission of the Truth and Reconciliation Commission, to translate "reconciliation" itself ... [and in order to] guarantee the required conditions to overcome both the divisions and conflicts of the past that engendered brutal violations of human rights and generated "a legacy of hatred, fear, guilt, and vengeance". Now, this inheritance must be treated from "a perspective of understanding and not of revenge, a need for reparation and not the desire of reprisals, a need for *ubuntu* ... and not victimization".)

However, it should be outlined that despite the removal of apartheid and the emergence of the spirit of reconciliation and negotiation, a large majority of South Africans – especially people from black communities – are still victim of economic and social exclusion. The density of the population living in slums such as Alexandra or Soweto, for example, is far from diminishing. The same is true for urban violence. These realities reflect a denial of social and economic justice. Both equality and social peace are deeply threatened. It is my feeling that this situation constitutes a long-term challenge, but it also reveals an unfulfilled dream of Mandela, the achievement of which can be viewed as the duty of current African leaders, thinkers, and Africanists. This is true for South Africa, but it is also the case for the rest of Africa. A true challenge for both African leaders and social and political thinkers.

Notes

1 For a synthetic approach to the genesis and development of racist theories, see Delacampagne (2000).

2 For Comments on Locke's political theory, see, for example, Raynaud (1996); Held (2006, 62–65); Leleux (1997, 101–109).
3 Various other topics also received very little attention; for example, punishment, gender, accountability, and corruption.
4 A lot of African tales outline the role of the ruse in people's daily lives. Metaphorically, they attribute it to some representative animals; for example, stories of the Luba refer to *Kabundi* (fox).
5 See also Mandela (2013, 321–322).
6 Concerning Mandela's full answer to the government, see Mandela (2013, 622–623).

BIBLIOGRAPHY

Acardo, Pierre and Corcuff, Philippe. (eds). 1986. *La sociologie de Pierre Bourdieu. Textes et choisis et commentés*. Paris: Le Masscaret.
Achebe, Chinua. 1987. *Anthills of the Savannah*. London: Heinemann Publisher.
Adotevi, Stanislas, S. 1998. *Négritude et négrologues*. Paris: Castor Astral.
Ahluwalia, Pal. 2001. *Politics and Post-Colonial Theory: Africa Inflections*. London and New York: Routledge.
Ake, Claude. 1996. *Democracy and Development in Africa*. Washington, DC: Brookings Institution.
Amselle, Jean-Loup, and M'Bokolo, Elikia. 1999. *Au cœur de l'ethnie. Ethnies, tribalisme et Etat en Afrique*. Paris: La Découverte.
Appiah, Kwame Anthony. 1992. *In My Father's House: Africa in the Philosophy of Culture*. Oxford: Oxford University Press.
Appiah, Kwame Anthony. 2004. African Philosophy and African Literature. In Wiredu, Kwasi (ed.), *A Companion to African Philosophy*. Oxford: Blackwell Publishing Ltd, pp. 538–548.
Appiah, Kwame Anthony. 2007. *Cosmopolitanism: Ethics in a World of Strangers*. London: Penguin Book.
Arendt, Hannah. 1994. *La condition de l'homme moderne*. Paris: Pocket. Translation by G. Fradier.
Aristotle. 1959. *Politics*. London / and Massachusetts: William Heinemann Ltd / and Harvard University Press.
Barber, Benjamin. 1996. *Djihad versus Mc World. Mondialisation et intégrisme contre la démocratie*. Paris: Hachette. Translation by M. Valois.
Barber, Benjamin. 1998. Culture McWorld contre démocratie. In *Le Monde Diplomatique*, No. 533, pp. 14–15.
Baudrillard, Jean. 1970. *La société de consommation. Ses mythes, ses structures*. Paris: Editions Denoël.
Bayart, Jean-François. 1989. *L'Etat en Afrique. La politique du ventre*. Paris: Fayard. Begin, Luc. 1996. Société. In Canto-Sperber, Monique (ed.), *Dictionnaire d'éthique et de philosophie morale*. Paris: PUF, pp. 1411–1418.

Bell, Richard H. 2002. *Understanding African Philosophy: A Cross-Cultural Approach to Classical and Contemporary Issues*. New York andLondon: Routledge.
Bennett, T., Brems, E., Corradi, G., Nijzink, L. and Schotsmans, M. (eds). 2012. *African Perspectives on Tradition and Justice*. Cambridge, Antwerp, Portland: Intersentia.
Bénot, Yves. 1969. *Idéologies des indépendances africaines*. Paris: Maspéro.
Bhabha, Homi K. 2007. *The Location of Cultures*. London and New York: Routlegde.
Bidima, Jean-Godefroy. 1995. *La philosopphie négro-africaine*. Paris: PUF.
Bidima, Jean-Godefroy. 1997. *L'art négroafricain*. Paris: PUF.
Bidima, Jean-Godefroy. 2004. Philosophy and Literature in Francophone Africa. In Wiredu, Kwasi (ed.), *A Companion to African Philosophy*. Oxford: Blackwell Publishing Ltd., pp. 549–559.
Bodunrin, Peter O. 1991. The Question of African Philosophy. In Serequeberhan, T. (ed), *African Philosophy: The Essential Readings*. Minnesota: Parangon House, pp. 63–86.
Boele Van Hensbroek, Pieter. 1998. *African Political Philosophy, 1860–1995: An Inquiry into Three Families of Discourse*. Groningen: Center for Development Studies, University of Groningen.
Bofane, In Koli Jean. 2008. *Les mathématiques congolaises*. Paris: Actes Sud.
Bourdieu, Pierre. 1994. *Raisons pratiques. Sur la théorie de l'action*. Paris: Seuil.
Bratton, Michael. 1994. Civil Society and Political Transitions in Africa. In Harbeson, John W., Rothchild, Donald and Chazan, Naomi (eds.), *Civil Society and the State in Africa*. Boulder and Covent Garden: Lynne Rienner Publishers, Inc., pp. 51–81.
Breytenbach, Willie. 1998. The Erosion of Civil Society and the Corporatization of Democracy in Africa. *Quest*, Special issue, Etat et société civile en Afrique. Actes du Colloque Internationale Interdisciplinaire, ed. Yacouba Konate. Abidjan (13/18 July). Vol. 12, No. 1, pp. 39–46.
Brink, André. 1979. *A Dry White Season*. London: VH Allen.
Brown, Lee M. (ed.). 2004. *African Philosophy: New and Traditional Perspectives*. Oxford and New York: Oxford University Press.
Calvitt Clark, Joseph. 2011. *Alliance of the Colored Peoples: Ethiopian and Japan Before World War II*. Oxford: James Currey.
Carton, B. and Lahouel, B. (eds). *L'Afrique au futur. Etat contre mondialisation. Pensées de résistance*. Bruxelles: Gresea.
Cerutti Guldberg, Horacio. 1992. *Filosofia de la liberacion latinoamericana*. Mexico: Fondo de Cultura Economica.
Cerutti Guldberg, Horacio. 1997. *Filosofias para la Liberacion. ?Liberacion del Filosofar?* Mexico: UAEM.
Césaire, Aimé. 1976. *Discours sur le colonialisme*. Paris: Présence Africaine.
Cesaire, Aimé. 1987. Discours sur la négritude. www.genius.com/Aime-cesaire-discours-sur-la-negritude-lyrics (accessed 15 November 2016).
Chabal, Patrick and Daloz, Jean-Pascal. 1999. *L'Afrique est partie. Du désordre comme instrument politique*. Paris: Economica.
Cherki, Alice. 2000. *Frantz Fanon. Portrait*. Paris: Seuil.
Clark, Phil. 2010. *The Gacaca Courts, Post-Genocide Justice and Reconciliation in Rwanda. Justice without Lawyers*. Cambridge: Cambridge University Press.
Colas, Dominique. 1996. Marx et le marxisme. In Renaud, P. and Rials, S. (eds), *Dictionnaire de philosophie politique*. Paris: PUF, pp. 380–387.
Cooper, Anna Julia. 2000. *A Voice from the South*. Electronic edition. University of California. Docsouth.unc.edu/church/cooper.html (accessed February 2016).
Cooper, Anna. 2006. *Slavery and the French and Haitian Revolutionists: L'attitude de la France à l'égard de l'esclavage pendant la revolution*. Edited and translated by Frances Richardson Keller. Lanham: Rowman & Littlefield.

Coquery-Vidrovitch, Catherine. 1994. *Les femmes africaines. Histoire des femmes de l'Afrique noire du XIXème siècle*. Paris: Desjonquères.
Crozier, Michel and Friedberg, Erhard. 1997. *L'acteur et le système*. Paris: Editions du Seuil.
Dabiri, Emma. 2015. Why I am (Still) not Afropolitan? *Journal of African Cultural Studies*, Vol. 28, No. 1, pp. 104–108.
De Boeck, Filip and Plissart, Marie-Françoise. 2004. *Kinshasa. Récits de la ville invisible*. Brussels: Renaissance du Livre.
Delacampagne, Christian. 2000. *Une histoire du racisme*. Paris: Librairie Générale Française.
Derrida, J. 2004. Versöhnung, ubuntu, pardon: quel genre? In Cassin, B., Cayla, O., and Salazar, P.-J. (eds), *Vérité, réconciliation, réparation*, Le Genre Humain, No. 83. Paris: Seuil, pp. 111–156.
De Villers, Gauthier. 2005. Trajectoire historique et idéologique d'une société civile: le cas de la RDC. In Houtart, François (ed.), *La société civile socialement engagée en République démocratique du Congo*. Paris: L'Harmattan, pp. 23–37.
Diagne, S. Bachir. 2001. *Islam et société ouverte. La fidélité et le mouvement dans la pensée de Muhammad Iqbal*. Paris: Maisonneuve & Larose.
Diagne, S. Bachir. 2011. *African Art as Philosophy: Senghor, Bergson and the Idea of Negritude*. London, New York, Calcutta: Rosalind C. Morris. Translated by Chike Jeffers.
Diagne, S. Bachir and Kimmerle, Heinz (eds). 1998. *Temps et développement danns la pensée de l'Afrique subsharienne. Time and Development in The Thought of SubSaharan Africa*. Amsterdam and Atlanta: Editions Rodopi B.V.
Diop, Cheikh Anta. 1974. *The African Origin of Civilization. Myth or Reality*. Chicago: Lawrene Hill Books. Edited and translated by Mercer Cook.
Diop, Cheik Anta. 1979. *Nations nègres et culture. De l'antiquité nègre égyptienne aux problèmes culturels de l'Afrique noire aujorud'hui*. Paris: Présence africaine. (3rd edition).
Dovey, Ceridwen. 2008. *Liens du sang*. Paris: Editions Héloïse d'Ormesson. Translation by Jean Guiboineau.
Du Bois, W. E. B. 2012. *The Conservation of Races*. New York: Dover Publications.
Ducret, André. 2011. Le concept de « configuration » et ses implications empiriques: Elias avec et contre Weber. *Sociologies* [online]. http://sociologies.revues.org/3459.
Durkheim, Emile. 2008. *Les formes élémentaires de la vie religieuse. Le système totémique en Australie*. Paris: PUF.
Dussel, Enrique. 1995. *Teologia de la Liberacion. Un panorama de su desarrollo*. Mexico: Potrerillos Editores S.A. de C.V.
Dussel, Enrique. 1996. *Filosofia de la Liberacion*. Bogota: Editorial Nueva América.
Dussel, Enrique. 2002. *L'éthique de la libération à l'ère de la mondialisation et de l'exclusion*. Paris: L'Harmattan. Translation by Albert Kasanda Lumembu.
Eboussi Eboussi-Boulaga, Fabien. 1977. *La crise du Muntu. Authenticité africaine et philosophie*. Paris: Présence africaine.
Eboussi-Boulaga, Fabien. 1993. *Les conférences nationales en Afrique noire. Une affaire à suivre*. Paris: Karthala.
Eboussi-Boulaga, Fabien. 2000. The Topic of Change. In Karp, Ivan and Masolo, D. A. (eds), *African Philosophy as Cultural Inquiry*. Bloomington andIndianapolis: Indiana University Press, pp. 187–214.
Ela, Jean-Marc. 1980. *Le cri de l'homme africain*. Paris: L'Harmattan.
Ela, Jean-Marc. 2003. *Repenser la théologie africaine. Le Dieu qui libère*. Paris: Karthala.
Elias, Norbert. 1985. *La société de cour*. Paris: Flammarion. French translation by P. Kammnitzer and Jeanne Etoré.
English, Parker and Kibujjo, Kalumba M. (eds). 1996. *African Philosophy: A Classical Approach*. New Jersey: Prentice Hall.

Englund, Harri. 1996. Between God and Kamuzu: The Transition to Multi-Party Politics in Central Malawi. In Werbner, R. and Ranger, T. (eds), *Postcolonial Identities in Africa*. London and New Jersey: Zed Books Ltd., pp. 107–135.

Etounga-Manguelle, Daniel. 1991. *L'Afrique a-t-elle besoin d'un programme d'ajustement culturel?* Paris: L'Harmattan.

Eze, Emmanuel Chukwudi (ed.). 1997. *Postcolonial African Philosophy: A Critical Reader*. Massachusetts: Blackwell Publishers.

Fanon, Frantz. 1975. *Peau noire, masques blancs*. Paris: Le Seuil.

Fanon, Frantz. 1979. *Les damnés de la terre*. Paris: Maspero.

Faye, Jean-Pierre. 1996. *Le siècle des idéologies*. Paris: Armand Colin.

Fillieule, Olivier and Pechu, Cécile. 1993. *Lutter ensemble. Théories de l'action collective*. Paris: L'Harmattan.

Fornet-Betancourt, Raul. 2011. *La philosophie interculturelle. Penser autrement le monde*. Paris: L'Atelier. French translation by Albert Kasanda.

Foulquié, Paul. 1992. *Dictionnaire de la langue philosophique*. Paris: PUF.

Freud, Sigmund. 1995. *L'avenir d'une illusion*. Paris: Points Essais.

Gatsi, Jean. 2001. *La société civile au Cameroun*. Yaoundé: Presses Universitaires d'Afrique.

Gauchet, Marcel. 1989. *Le désenchantement du monde. Une histoire politique de la religion*. Paris: Gallimard.

Gélinas, Jacques. 1994. *ET si le Tiers Monde s'autofinançait. De l'endettement à l'épargne*. Montréal: Les Editions Ecosociété.

Gérard, Jacques E. 1969. *Les fondements syncrétiques du Kitawala*. Brussels: Livre Africain et C.R.I.S.P.

Gilis, Charles-André. 1960. *Kimbangu, fondateur d'église*. Brussels: Editions de la librairie encyclopédique.

Gordon, Lewis R. 2008. *An Introduction to Africana Philosophy*. Cambridge: Cambridge University Press.

Graness, Anke. 2012. What is Global Justice? Henry Odera Oruka's Contribution to the Current Debate. *Journal on African Philosophy*, No. 6, pp. 31–46.

Gyekye, K. 1987. *An Essay on African Philosophical Thought. The Akan Conceptual Scheme*. London: Cambridge University Press.

Gyekye, Kwame. 1997. *Tradition and Modernity: Philosophical Reflections on the African Experience*. New York andOxford: Oxford University Press.

Hallen, Barry. 2002. *A Short History of African Philosophy*. Bloomington and Indianapolis: Indiana University Press.

Harbeson, John W. 1994. Civil Society and the Study of African Politics: A Preliminary Assessment. In Harbesson, John W., Rothchild, Donald and Chazan, Naomi (eds), *Civil Society and the State in Africa*. Boulder and Covent Garden: Lynne Rienner Publishers, Inc., pp. 285–300.

Haubert, Maxime and Rey, Pierre Philippe (eds). 2000. *Les sociétés civiles face au marché. Le changement social dans le monde postcolonial*. Paris: Karthala.

Held, David. 2006. *Models of Democracy*. Cambridge and Malden: Polity Press.

Hersch, Jeanne. 1993. *L'étonnemement philosophique. Une histoire de la philosophie*. Paris: Gallimard.

Hibou, Béatrice (ed.). 1999. *La privatisation des états*. Paris: Karthala.

Honneth, Axel. 2000. *La lutte pour la reconnaissance*. Paris: Gallimard. Translation by Pierre Rusch.

Hountondji, Paulin. 1970. Remarques sur la philosophie africaine contemporaine. *Diogène*, No. 71, pp. 120–140.

Hountondji, Paulin. 1983. *African Philosophy: Myth and Reality*. Bloomington and Indianapolis: Indiana University Press.

Hountondji, Paulin. 2004. Knowledge as a Development Issue. In Wiredu, Kwasi (ed.), *A Companion to African Philosophy*. Maryland and Oxford: Blackwell Publishing, pp. 529–537.
Hountondji, Paulin. 2012. Ehnophilosophie: le mot et la chose. http://rekhseba.weebly.com/uploads/4/2/7/7/42771435/p.j._hountondji.pdf (accessed 12 February 2015).
Houtart, François. 1998. La société civile: enjeu des luttes sociales pour l'hégémonie. *Alternatives Sud*, Vol. V, pp. 5–19.
Houtart, François (ed.). 2005. *La société civile socialement engagée en République démocratique du Congo*. Paris: L'Harmattan.
Houtart, François. 2006. L'état actuel de la théologie de la libération. www.forumdesalternatives.org/juin (accessed 9 September 2016).
Huntington, Samuel. 1966. *The Clash of Civilizations and the Remaking of the World Order*. New York: Simon & Schuster.
Iliffe, John. 1998. *Africa. Historia de un continente*. Cambridge: Cambridge University Press. Spanish translation by Maria Barberán.
Imbo, Samuel Oluoch. 1998. *An Introduction to African Philosophy*. Maryland: Rowman and Littlefield.
Jordan, Tim. 2003. *S'engager! Les nouveaux militants, activistes, agitateurs* …. Paris: Editions Autrement. French translation by Sophie Saurot.
Kabarhuza, B. H., Mugumo, F. M. and Shuku, N. Y. 2003. *La société civile Congolaise. Etat des lieux et perspectives*. Brussels: Colophon.
Kabou, Axelle. 1991. *Et si l'Afrique réfusait le développement*. Paris: L'Harmattan.
Kaczynski, G. Jercy. 1979. Formacion y funciones de los movimientos religiosos congolenos. In Entralgo, Armando (ed.), *Africa. Religion*. Havana: Editorial de ciencias sociales, pp. 143–205.
Kagame, Alexis. 1956. *La philosophie bantu-rwandaise de l'être*. Brussels: Académie royale des sciences coloniales.
Kalulambi, Pongo Martin. 1997. *Etre Luba au XXè siècle. Identité chrétienne et ethnicité au Congo*. Paris: Karthala.
Kaphagawani, Didier N. 2000. What is African Philosophy? In Coetze, P.H. and Roux, J.P. (eds), *The African Philosophy Reader*. London: Routledge, pp. 86–98.
Karp, Ivan and Masolo, D. A. (eds). 2000. *African Philosophy as Cultural Inquiry*. Bloomington and Indianapolis: Indiana University Press.
Kasanda, Albert. 2000. La mondialisation et la résistance culturelle en Afrique, du vertige d'une utopie à la tentation ddu réalisme. In Cetri (ed.), *Cultures et mondialisation. Résistances et alternatives*. Paris: pp. 31–45.
Kasanda, Albert. 2003. Leurres et lueures de la philosophie africaine. In Kasanda, Albert (ed), *Pour une pensée africaine émancipatrice*. Paris: L'Harmattan, pp. 7–20.
Kasanda, Albert. 2005. Considérations sur la société civile congolaise: un apport conceptuel. In Houtart, François (ed.), *La société civile socialement engagée en République démocratique du Congo*. Paris: L'Harmattan, pp. 9–22.
Kasanda, Albert. 2011. Congolese Women's Power and Powerlessness in the Political Landscape. In Horakova, H., Nugent, P, Skalnik, P. (eds). *Africa: Power and Powerlessness*. Berlin: Lit Verlag, pp. 75–91.
Kasanda, Albert. 2013a. Aid or Justice? A questioning about World Solidarity from an African Perspective. *Journal of East-West Thought*, Vol. 3, No. 3, pp. 41–61.
Kasanda, Albert (ed.). 2013b. *Dialogue interculturel. Cheminer ensemble vers un autre monde possible*. Paris: L'Harmattan.
Kasanda, Albert. 2015. Analyzing African Social and Political philosophy: Trends and Challenges. *Journal of East-West Thought*, Vol. 5, No. 2, pp. 29–50.
Kasanda, Albert. 2016. Exploring Pan-Africanism's Theories: From Race-based Solidarity to Political Unity and Beyond. *Journal of African Cultural Studies*, Vol. 28, No. 2, pp. 179–195.

Kasereka, Kavwahirchi. 2015. Reconstruire la philosophie africaine: à la recherche des lieux d'ancrage d'une pensé du futur. *International Journal of Francophone Studies*, Vol. 18, No. 2–3, pp. 311–337.

Kebede, Messay. 2004. *Africa's Quest for a Philosophy of Decolonization*. Amsterdam: Rodobi B.V.

Keita, Lansana (ed.). 2011. *Philosophy and African Development: Theory and Practice*. Dakar: Codesria.

Kelman, Gaston. 2005. *Au-delà du Noir et du Blanc*. Paris: Max Milo.

Kervegan, Jean-François. 1996. Démocratie. In Raynaud, Philippe and Rials, Stéphane (eds), *Dictionnaire de philosophie politiquue*. Paris: PUF, pp. 127–133.

Keucheyan, Razmig. 2010. *Hémisphère gauche. Une cartographie des nouvellees pensées critiques*. Paris: Editions de La Découverte.

Kintges, Karen. 2011. Freedom and Spirituality. In Taylor, Dianna (ed), *Michel Foucault, Key Concepts*. Durham: Acumen, pp. 99–110.

Kiros, Teodoros (ed.). 2001. *Explorations in African Political Thought: Identity, Community, Ethics*. New York andLondon: Routledge.

Klein, Naomi. 2002. *La tyrannie des marques*. Paris: Babel. French translation by Michel Saint-Germain.

Kodjo-Grandvaux, Séverine. 2013. *Philosophies africaines*. Paris: Présence Africaine.

Kouruma, Ahmadou. 1998. *En attendant le vote des bêtes sauvages*. Paris: Seuil.

Lajul, Wilfred. 2013. *African Philosophy: Critical Dimensions*. Kampala: Fountain Publishers.

Laléyê, Issiaka Prosper. 1970. *La conception de la personne dans la pensée traditionnelle Yoruba. Approche phénoménologique*. Bern: H. Lang.

Langley, Ayodele. 1979. *Ideologies of Liberation in Black Africa*. London: Ed. Rex Collings.

Latouche, Serge. 2004. *Survivre au développement*. Paris: Mille et une nuit.

Leleux, Claudine. 1997. *La démocratie moderne. Les grandes théories*. Paris: Les Editions du Cerf.

Lévi-Strauss, Claude. 2007. *Race et Histoire*. Paris: Gallimard.

Lopes, Filomeno. 2001. *Filosofia intorno al fuoco. Il pensiero africano contemporaneo tra memoria e futuro*. Bologne: Editrice Missionera Italiana.

Lopes, Filomena. 2009. *E se l'Africa scomparisse dal mappamondo? Una reflession filosofica*. Rome: Armando Editore.

Lott, Tommy. 1997. Du Bois on the Invention of Race. In Pittman, J. P. (ed.), *African-American Perspectives and Philosophical Traditions*. New York and London: Routledge, pp. 166–187.

Maalouf, Amin. 1998. *Les identités meurtrières*. Paris: Grasset et Fasquelle.

Mamdani, Mahmoud. 1996. *Citizen and Subject: Contemporary Africa and the Legacy of Late Colonialism*. Princeton: Princeton University Press.

Mandela, Nelson. 2013. *Long Walk to Freedom*. London: Abacus.

Martin, Guy. 2012. *African Political Thought*. New York: Palgrave McMillan.

Martinez Montiel, Luz Maria (ed.). 1995a. *Presencia africana en el Caribe*. Mexico, D.F.: Conaculta.

Martinez Montiel, Luz Maria (ed.). 1995b. *Presencia africana en Mexico*. Mexico, D.F.: Conaculta.

Matthieu, Lilian. 2004. *Comment lutter? Sociologie des mouvements sociaux*. Paris: Editions Textuel.

Masolo, Dismas A. 1994. *African Philosophy in Sarch of Identity*. Edinburgh: Edinburgh University Press.

Masolo, Dismas A. 2010. *Self and Community in a Changing World*. Bloomington and Indiana: Indiana University Press.

Mazrui, Ali A. 2001. Ideology and African Political Culture. In Kiros, Teodoros (ed.), *Explorations in African Political Thought: Identity, Community, Ethics*. New York and London: Routledge, pp. 97–131.

Mbembe, Achille. 1988. *Afriques indociles: Christianisme, pouvoir et état en société post-coloniale.* Paris: Karthala.
Mbembe, Achille. 1991. *Le politique par le bas. Contribution à une problématique de la démocratie en Afrique noire.* Paris: Karthala.
Mbembe, Achille. 2000. A propos des écritures africaines de soi. *Politique afriacine*, No. 77, pp. 16–43.
Mbembe, Achille. 2005. Afropolitanisme. www.africultures.com/php/?nav=article&no=4248 (accessed 26 January 2016).
Mbembe, Achille. 2013. *Critique de la raison nègre.* Paris: La Découverte.
Mbiti, John. 1970. *African Religions and Philosophy.* New York: Doubleday.
M'bokolo, Elikia. 1985. *L'Afrique au XXè siècle. Le continent convoité.* Paris: Seuil.
Mbonimpa, Melchior. 1989. *Idéologies de l'indépendence africaine.* Paris: L'Harmattan.
Mbuyi, Kabunda Badi. 1993. *La Integración Africana. Problemas y Perspectivas.* Madrid: Agencia Española de Cooperación Internacional.
Melberg, Arne. 1995. *Theories of Mimesis.* Cambridge: Cambridge University Press.
Memmi, Albert. 1985. *Portrait du colonisé. Portrait du colonisateur.* Paris: Gallimard.
Miller, Christopher. 1998. *Nationalists and Nomads: Essays on Francophone African Literature and Culture.* Chicago and London: University of Chicago Press.
Monga, Célestin. 2009. *Nihilisme et négritude.* Paris: PUF.
Mora, Gerardo. 2004. ¿Etnofilosofia o universalismo? *Revista Intersedes.* Vol. V, No. 8, pp. 1–15.
More, Mabogo P. 2004. Philosophy in South Africa Under and After Apartheid. In Wiredu, Kwasi (ed.), *A Companion to African Philosophy.* Malden and Oxford: Blackwell Publishing, pp. 149–160.
Mosley, A. G. 1995. Negritude, Nationalism and Nativism: Racists or Racialists? In Mosley, A. G. (ed.), *African Philosophy: Selected Readings.* New Jersey: Prentice Hall, pp. 216–235.
Mudimbe, V. Y. 1988. *The Invention of Africa: Gnosis, Philosophy, and the Order of Knowledge.* Bloomington and Indianapolis: Indiana University Press.
Musila, A. Grace. 2016. Part-Time Africans, Europolitans and "Africa Lite". *Journal of African Cultural Studies*, Vol. 28, No. 1, pp. 109–113.
Mwene-Batende. 1982. *Mouvements messianiques et protestation politique. Le cas du Kitawala chez les Kumu du Zaïre.* Kinshasa: Publications de la Faculté Catholique.
Ngandu-Nkashama, Pius. 1998. *La pensée politique des mouvements religieux en Afrique.* Paris: L'Harmattan.
Ngoma-Binda, Phambu. 2013. *La pensée politique africaine contemporaine.* Paris: L'Harmattan.
Ngugi wa Thiong'o. 1986. *Decolonizing the Mind: The Politics of Languages in African Literature.* London, Nairobi, Harare: James Currey, Heinemann Kenya and Zimbabwe Publishing House.
Ngugi wa Thiong'o. 1993. *Moving the Centre: The Struggle for Cultural Freedoms.* Nairobi, Oxford and New Hampshire: East African Publishers, James Currey and Heinemann.
Njoku, Francis O. 2004. *Development and African Philosophy: A Theoretical Reconstruction of African Socio-political Economy.* New York, Lincoln, and Shangai: iUniverse.
Nkombe, Oleko and Smet, A. J. 1980. Panorama de la philosophie africaine contemporaine. In Smet, A. J. (ed.), *Histoire la philosophie africaine contemporaine. Courants et problèmes.* Kinshasa: Faculté de théologie catholique, pp. 273–294.
Nkrumah, Kwame. 1963. *Africa Must Unite.* New York: Frederick A. Praeger.
Nkrumah, Kwame. 1970. *Consciencism: Philosophy and Ideology for De-colonization.* USA: Library of Congress.
Nouss, Alexis. 2005. *Plaidoyer pour un monde métis.* Paris: Les éditions Textuel.
Nouss, Alexis and Laplantine, François. 2001. *Métissages.* Paris: Editions Pauvert.

Obenga, Théophile. 1990. *La philosophie africaine de la période pharaonique: 2780–330 avant notre ère*. Paris: L'Harmattan.
Obenga, Théophile. 1993. *Origine commune de l'Egypte ancien, du copte et des langues négro-africaines modernes. Introduction à la linguistique historique africaine*. Paris: L'Harmattan.
Odera, Oruka Henri. 1976. *Punishment and Terrorism in Africa*. Nairobi: East African Literature Bureau.
Odera, Oruka Henri. 1991. Sagacity in African Philosophy. In Serequeberhan, Tsenay (ed.), *African Philosophy: The Essential Readings*. Saint Paul, Minnesota: Paragon House, pp. 47–62.
Odera, Oruka Henri. 1997. *Practical Philosophy: In Search of an Ethical Minimum*. Nairobi and Kampala: East African Educational Publishers.
Odera, Oruka Henri. 1998. *Ethics*. Nairobi: Nairobi University Press.
Okolo, M. S. C. 2007. *African Literature as Political Philosophy*. Dakar, London and New York: Codesria and Zed Books.
Osaghae, Eghosa E. 1998. Rescuing the Post-Colonial State in Africa: A Reconceptualisation of the Role of Civil Society. *Quest*, Special issue, Etat et société civile en Afrique. Actes du Colloque Internationale Interdisciplinaire, ed. Yacouba Konate. Abidjan (13/18 July). Vol. 12, No. 1, pp. 269–282.
Osha, Sanya. 2005. *Kwasi Wiredu and Beyond: The Text, Writing and Thought in Africa*. Dakar: Codesria Book Series.
Ouologuem, Yambo. 2003. *Lettre à la France Nègre*. Paris: Le Serpent à Plumes.
Ousmane, Sembene. 1970. *God's Bits of Wood*. London: Heinemann. Translation by Frances Price.
Ousmane, Sembene. 1972. *The Money-order with White Genesis*. London: Heinemann. Translation by Clive Wake.
Outlaw, Lucius T. 1996. *On Race and Philosophy*. New York: Routledge.
Perrett, Thierry. 1994. *Afrique voyage en démocratie*. Paris: L'Harmattan.
Pirotte, Gautier. 2007. *La notion de société civile*. Paris: La Découverte.
Pirotte, Gautier. 2010. La notion de société civile dans les politiques et pratiques du développement. *Revue de la Regulation* [online] 7, Spring. http://regulation.revues.org/7787 (accessed 21 May 2016).
Pittman, John P. (ed.). 1997. *African-American Perspectives and Philosophical Traditions*. New York andLondon: Routledge.
Platon. 1950. *Oeuvres completes I*. Paris: Gallimard. Translation and notes by Léon Robin with the collaboration of M.-J. Moreau.
Pogge, Thomas. 2008. *World Poverty and Human Right: Cosmopolitan Responsibilities and Reforms*. Cambridge: Cambridge Polity Press.
Poizat, Jean-Claude. 2003. *Hannah Arendt, une introduction*. Paris: La Découverte.
Ramose, Mogobe B. 1999. *African Philosophy Through Ubuntu*. Harare: Mond Books.
Raynaud, Philipppe and Rials, Stéphane. 1996. *Dictionnaire de philosophie politique*. Paris: PUF.
Rettová, Alena. 2013a. Les défis de la philosophie interculturelle aux temps postcolonial et postcommuniste. In Kasanda, Albert (ed.), *Dialogue intercuturel. Cheminer vers un autre monde possible*. Paris: L'Harmattan, pp. 73–111.
Rettová, Alena. 2013b. *Chanter l'existence: La poésie de Sando Marteau et ses horizons philosophiques*. Stredokluky: Zdenek Susa. French translation by Albert Kasanda.
Ritzer, George (ed). 2007. *The Globalization of Nothing*. Thousand Oaks, London and New Delhi: Pine Forge Press.
Ritzer, George. 2007. Globalization: A New Conceptualization. In Ritzer, George (ed), *The Globalization of Nothing*. Thousand Oaks, London and New Delhi: Pine Forge Press, pp. 1–33.
Rivière, Claude. 1997. *Socio-anthropologie des religions*. Paris: Armand Colin.

Sanchez, R. David. 1999. *Filosofia, derecho y liberacion en América latina*. Bilbao: Desclée De Brouwer.
Sartre, Jean-Paul. 2005. Orphée noire. In Senghor, Léopold Sedar (ed.), *Anthologie de la nouvelle poésie nègre et malgache*. Paris: PUF.
Selasi, Taiye. 2005. Bye-Bye Babar. http://thelip.robertsharp.co.uk/?p=76 (accessed 20 January 2016).
Semprini, Andréa. 1997. *Le multiculturalisme*. Paris: PUF.
Senghor, Léopold Sédar. 1964. *Liberté 1. Négritude et humanisme*. Paris: Editions du Seuil.
Senghor, Léopold Sedar. 1995. On Negrohood: Psychology of the African Negro. In Mosley, A. G. (ed), *African Philosophy: Selected Readings*. New Jersey: Prentice Hall, pp. 117–127.
Serequeberhan, Tsenay. (ed.). 1991. *African Philosophy. The Essential Readings*. Minnesota: Parangon House.
Serequeberhan, Tsenay. 1994. *The Hermeneutics of African Philosophy*. London and New York: Routledge.
Shutte, Augustine. 1998. African and European Philosophising: Senghor's Civilization of the Universal. In Coetzee, P. H. and Roux, A. P. J. (eds), *The African Philosophy Reader*. London and New York: Routledge, pp. 428–437.
Sithole, Masipula. 1998. Civil Society and the Struggle for Democracy in Zimbabwe. *Quest*, Special issue, Etat et société civile en Afrique. Actes du Colloque Internationale Interdisciplinaire, ed. Yacouba Konate. Abidjan (13/18 July). Vol. 12, No. 1, pp. 27–38.
Smart, Ninian. 2001. *World Philosophies*. London and New York: Routledge.
Smet, Alphonse Joseph. 1980. *Histoire de la philosophie africaine contemporaine. Courants et problèmes*. Kinshasa: Facultés de théologie catholique (Book 5).
Smith, Stephen. 2003. *Négrologie. Pourquoi l'Afrique meurt*. Paris: Calmann-Lévy.
Soglo, Godwin. 1993. *Foundations of African Philosophy: A Definitive Analysis of Conceptual Issues in African Thought*. Ibadan: Ibadan University Press.
Soyinka, W. 1976. *Myth, Literature and the African World*. Cambridge: Cambridge University Press.
Stewart, Gary. 2003. *Rumba on the River. A History of the Popular Music of the Two Congos*. London andNew York: Verso.
Strauss, Léo. 1992. *Qu'est-ce que la philosophie politique?* Paris: PUF. French translation by Olivier Sedeyn.
Taiwo, Olufémi. 2004. Post-Independence African Political Philosophy. In Wiredu, Kwasi (ed.), *A Companion to African Philosophy*. Malden andOxford: Blackwell Publishing, pp. 243–259.
Taiwo, Olúfẹ́mi. 2014. *Africa Must Be Modern: A Manifesto*. Ebook. Bloomington andIndianapolis: Indiana University Press.
Taylor, Charles. 1994. *Multiculturalisme. Différence et démocratie*. Paris: Flammarion. French translation by D.-A. Canal.
Tchebwa, Manda. 1996. *Terre de la chanson. La musique zaïroise hier et aujourd'hui*. Louvain-la-Neuve: Duculot.
Teffo, J. 2004. Democracy, Kingship, and Consensus: A South African Perspective. In Wiredu, K. (ed.) *A Companion to African Philosophy*. Oxford: Blackwell Publishing, pp. 443–449.
Tempels, Placide. 1949. *La Philosophie bantoue*. Paris: Présence Africaine. French translation by A. Rubens.
Thomas, Louis-Vincent. 1965. *Les ideologies négro-africaines d'aujourd'hui*. Dakar: Collection Philosophie et Sciences Sociales.
Thomas, Lynn M. 2011. Modernity's Failings, Political Claims, and Intermediate Concepts. *American Historical Review*, Vol. 116, No. 3, pp. 727–740.

Thoraval, Joël. 1994. De la philosophie en Chine à la "Chine" dans la philosophie. Existe-t-il une philosophie chinoise? *Esprit*, No. 201, pp. 5–39.
Touraine, Alain. 1997. *Pouvons-nous vivre ensemble? Egaux et différents*. Paris: Fayard.
Towa, Marcien. 1971. *Essai sur la problématique philosophique dans l'Afrique actuelle*. Yaoundé: Editions Clé.
Traoré, Aminata D. 1999. *L'étau. L'Afrique dans un monde sans frontiers*. Paris: Actes Sud.
Tripp, A. M., Casimiro, I., Kwesiga, J. and Mungwa, A. 2009. *Africans Women's Movements. Transforming Political Landscapes*. Cambridge: Cambridge University Press.
Tutu, Desmond. 1999. *No Future without Forgiveness*. London: Rider.
Van Bilsen, Jef. 1994. *Congo, 1945–1965, la fin d'une colonie*. Brussels: Editions du CRISP. Translation by Serge Govaert.
Van Parys, Jean-Marie. 1993. *Une approche simple de la philosophie africaine*. Kimwenza: Publications Canisius.
Wagner, Peter. 2015. *African, American and European Trajectories of Modernity: Past Oppression, Future Justice?* Edinburgh: Edinburgh University Press.
Wamala, Edouard. 2004. Government by Consensus: An Analysis of a Traditional Form of Democracy. In Wiredu, Kwasi (ed.), *A Companion to African Philosophy*. Malden and Oxford: Blackwell Publishing, pp. 435–442.
Wamba-Dia-Wamba, Ernest. 1992. Beyond Elite Politics of Democracy in Africa. *Quest*, Vol. 6, No. 2, pp. 29–42.
Warnier, Jean-Pierre. 1999. *La mondialisation de la culture*. Paris: La Découverte.
Washington, Booker T. 2012. *Up from Slavery: An Autobiography*. Public Domain Book.
Weber, Max. 1994. *L'éthique protestante et l'esprit du capitalisme*. Paris: Plon.
Wesseling, Henri. 1996. *Le partage de l'Afrique: 1880–1914*. Paris: Denoël. French translation by Patrick Grilli.
White, Bob W. 2008. *Rumba Rules: The Politics of Dance Music in Mobutu's Zaïre*. Durham andLondon: Duke University Press.
Wieviorka, Michel. 2005. *La différence. Identités culturelles: enjeux, débats et politiques*. Paris: L'aube.
Willame, Jean-Claude. 1996. Trajectoires de la démocratie, gouvernance: concepts de base pour l'analyse. *Cahiers africains*, No. 23–24, pp. 9–25.
Wiredu, Kwasi. 1986. The Question of Violence in Contemporary African Political Thought. *Praxis International*, Vol. 6, No. 3, pp. 373–381.
Wiredu, Kwasi. 1996. *Cultural Universals and Particulars: An Africa Perspective*. Bloomington andIndianapolis: Indiana University Press.
Wiredu, Kwasi. 1997. Democracy and Consensus in African Traditional Politics: A Plea for a Non-Party Polity. In Eze, Emmanuel Chukwudi (ed.), *Postcolonial African Philosophy: A Critical Reader*. Massachusets andOxford: Blackwell Publishers Inc., pp. 303–312.
Wiredu, Kwasi. 1991. On Defining African Philosophy. In Sequeberhan, Tsenay (ed.), *African Philosophy: The Essential Readings*. Minnesota: Parangon House, pp. 87–110.
Wiredu, Kwasi. 1992. The Ghanaian Tradition of Philosophy. In Wiredu, K. and Gyekye, K. (eds), *Person and Community*. Washington, DC: The Council for Research in Values and Philosophy, pp. 1–12.
Wiredu, Kwasi. 1998. The State, Civil Society and Democracy in Africa. *Quest*, Special issue, Etat et société civile en Afrique. Actes du Colloque Internationale Interdisciplinaire, ed. Yacouba Konate. Abidjan (13/18 July). Vol. 12, No. 1, pp. 241–252.
Wiredu, Kwasi. 2000. Our Problem of Knowledge: Brief Reflections on Knowledge and Development in Africa. In Karp, Ivan and Masolo, D. A. (eds), *African Philosophy as Cultural Inquiry*. Bloomington andIndianapolis: Indiana University Press, pp. 187–214.

Wiredu, Kwasi (ed.). 2004. *A Companion to African Philosophy*. Malden and Oxford: Blackwell Publishing. Young, Crawford. 1982. *Ideology and Development in Africa*. New Haven and London: Yale University Press.

Young, Crawford. 1994. In Search of Civil Society. In Harbeson, John W., Rothchild, Donald and Chazan, Naomi (eds), *Civil Society and the State in Africa*. Boulder and Covent Garden: Lynne Rienner Publisher, Inc., pp. 33–50.

Zewde, Bahru. 2008. The Concept of Japanization in the Intellectual History of Modern Ethiopia. In *Society, State and History. Selected Essays*. Adis Ababa: Adis Ababa Universirty Press, pp. 198–216.

INDEX

Accardo, A. 56
accountability 25, 101, 114, 123, 126
Accra 76
Achebe, C. 13–17, 61, 158
Adotevi, S. S. xii, 7, 46–47, 61, 142, 158; negritude 50, 54–56
African civil society 14–15, 106–12, 113–19, 120–27, 143–44
African diaspora Xii-xiii, 31, 38, 63, 65, 71; pan-African movement 80, 141,
African emancipation 3, 33, 40, 52, 55–56, 60; sovereignty 61, 63–64, 75, 84, 88, 91; democracy 103, 136–137
African humanism 2, 6, 7, 40, 46, 75
African identity xii, 35, 40, 49, 58, 64; afropolitanism and cosmopolitanism72, 79, 80, 83, 86, 129; African cultures and globalization 138–139, 140
African personality 2, 36, 64, 74–76
African regeneration xii, 35, 38, 53
African religions 19, 46
African renaissance 36, 53
African revival 23, 34, 65
African socialism 2–3, 6–7, 27–28, 40, 46, 81; *See also Ujamaa*
African Union (AU), xiii, 75, 143
Afropolitanism xiv, 63, 81–83, 129, 131, 137–40
Ahidjo, A. 109
Akan 25, 41
Ake, C. 90, 91
Alabama 67

Alexandra 16, 156
Amin Dada, I. 15, 99
Amselle, J.-L. 99, 100, 137
Apartheid xv, 87n9,119, 135–36, 145–46, 147; pluralistic society and nationalism 149, 150, 152, 154, 156
Appiah xiii, 5–6, 13, 15–16, 27, 41; ethnophilosophy and pan-Africanism 47, 65, 71–73,75–76, 80–81, 84; democracy and civil society 90, 93, 100, 117, 122, 132; cosmopolitanism 137
Aquinas 110
Arab world 66, 77–78, 80
Arendt, H. 5, 7, 48, 94, 132–33
Aristotle 5, 13, 110
art x, xii, 12, 13, 20, 30
Australia 32
Awolowo, O. 74

Balai citoyen xv, 123
Banda, K. 15, 16, 74, 92–94
Bantu Philosophy 6
Barber, B. 52, 129–130
Baudrillard, J. 140n1
Bayart, J.-F. 39, 60, 99–100, 109
Bell, R.H. 6, 45, 47, 72
Ben Bella, A. 92
Bénot, Y. 7–8
Berlin Conference xi, xiv, 90, 143
Bernstein, L. 148
Bhabha, H. 57, 77, 102
Bidima, J.-G. 6–7, 13, 22n4, 41, 46, 53; cultural diversity 128, 151

Blyden, E.W. xii, 23, 31, 34–39n4, 64–70, 142
Bodunrin, P. 3
Boele van Hensbroek, P. 32, 37
Bofane, I. K. J.14
Bokassa I, J. B.15
Bona, R. 20
Booth, W. 87
Bourdieu, P. 51, 56
Bratton, M. 107, 111–13, 126
Breytenbach, W. 119–20, 123
Brink, A. 14
Brown, L. M. 10 n3, 14, 23
Burkina Faso 6, 95, 124
Burundi 6

Cabral, A. 3, 15, 24
Calvitt Clark, J. 38
Cameroon 95, 122
Campbell, D. 25
Canada 32
Casely Hayford, J. E. xii, 23, 31, 37
Casimiro, I. 123, 126
Castro, F. 86n4
Cerutti Guldberg, H. 22n3
Césaire, A. 3, 13, 33, 48, 53, 55–56, 121; philosophy of resistance 121
Chabal, P. 108, 111
Chad 78, 122
Cham 34, 147
Charles Quint 134
Cherki, A. 76, 78
Chilembwe, J. 87, 120
China 134
Chraïbi, D. 13
CNN 129
Coca-Cola 129
Colas, D. 8
Colombia 66
colonialism xiii, xv, 2, 13, 47, 52; Africa's domination 55, 60, 66, 70, 73, 76; African civil society 117, 119–120, 129, 136, 142
colonization xi, xiv, 6, 16, 19, 23; African modernity 31, 34, 37–38, 46–47, 53–54, 57–58; violence 60–61, 64, 66, 70, 76, 79–80; Berlin Conference 90, 119–122, 134, 145
Compaoré, B. 6, 95, 124
Compromise of Atlanta 67, 68–69, 72
consciencism 9, 64, 75–76
consensus xii, 23, 26, 28–31, 38, 94; African traditional mode of governance 96–99, 103, 106, 113, 118, 141; *Ubuntu* 155
Cooper, A. J. 64–65, 67–69, 72, 84, 86, 142; *See also* African Diaspora

Corcuff, P. 56
cosmopolitanism xiii, 63, 81, 87, 137, 139
Costa Rica 66
Crummel, A. 31
Cuba 86
cultural pluralism 128, 129, 139, 144

Dabiri, E. 83, 139
Daloz, J. P. 108, 111
Danish Antilles 34
De Boeck, F. 17
decolonization 64, 66, 70, 121–22
De Gaulle, C. 33
de Klerk, F. 152
Delacampagne, C. 32, 51, 147, 156
de Las Casas, B. 134
democracy xii, xiv, xv, 4, 5, 10; precolonial legacy 19, 23, 24, 26–27, 29, 34; African metamorphosis 61, 76–77, 82, 88–98, 100–104, 106; African civil society 110–12, 114, 119, 122–26, 139, 143–45; Mandela and struggle for democray 147, 149, 152
Democratic Republic of Congo 6, 17, 22, 25, 120, 125; *See also* Zaïre
Derrida, J. 156
de Sepulveda, J. G. 134
Destutt de Tracy 8
Diagne, S. B. 19, 22
Diamond, L. 112
diarchy xiv, 94, 104, 143
differentialism 129, 133–37, 139, 144
Diop, C. A. 36, 46
Disneyland 129
Dominican Republic 66
Doutreloux, A. 43
Dovey, C. 14
Drewal, M. T. 21
Du Bois, W. E. B. 56, 64, 67–68, 75, 84, 143; and pan-Africanism 71–73
Durkheim, E. 17
Dussel, E. 17, 18, 62

Eboussi-Boulaga, F. 29, 46–48, 100, 123
Edinburgh 32
Egypt 46, 78
Ela, J. M. 19
Elias, N. 86
emotion xiii, 12–13, 20, 41, 47, 49; beyond the antagonism between emotion and reason 50–51, 56–57, 142
endorsement xiii, 41, 47, 58–60, 142
English, P. 1, 22, 28, 62, 149–52
Englund, H. 16, 92, 93
Enlightenment 129, 134–35

equity 5, 98, 123, 126, 129, 131
Ethiopia 37–38, 70, 138
ethnophilosophy xii, 13, 22n1, 29, 61–62, 142; recycling ethnophilosophy 40–48
Etounga-Manguelle, D. 24
Evans-Pritchard, E. E. 25
Eyadema, N. 92
Eze, E. M. 46, 97, 134–135

Fanon, F. xii-xiii, 1, 3, 16–17, 39, 53; the negritude 56–59; pan-Africanism 64, 66, 68, 76–78, 84, 90; approaching to violence 59–61, 212, 142–143, 153
Faye, J.-P. 9
Filimbi xv, 123–25
Fillieule, O. 5
Fornet-Betancourt, R. 52, 66
Fortes 25
Foucault, M. 18
Foulquié, P. 8
France 29, 33, 68, 86
Freetown 31
Freire, P. 45–46
Freud, S. 17

Gaddafi, M. xiii, 64,77–78, 79, 143
Ganda 26
Gandhi, M. 60, 87, 142, 148, 153–54
Garvey, M. xiii, 64, 67, 69, 70–72, 75; Africa for Africans 84, 87n8, 142, 148
Gauchet, M. 17
Gbabo, L. 6
Gélinas, J. 85
gender xv, 5, 7, 27, 49, 123; and African identity 129, 156–57n3
Gérard, J. 9
Ghana 25, 66, 76, 90
Gilis, C.-A. 9
global market xiv-xv, 116, 126, 131, 133, 137; African traditional modes of governance 143
global justice 64–65, 83, 85–86, 91
globalization xiii, xv, 16, 27, 34, 36; cultural homogenization 40, 52, 63, 79, 82–83, 85; neoliberal democracy 103–04, 107, 125, 127–29, 130, 133–35; cultural heterogeneity 137, 139–40, 144, 154
Gobineau 32
God 8, 17, 19, 34, 69, 93
Gordon, L. 16, 57, 58, 66–71, 73, 77; neoliberalism's goal and colonial modes of governance 84, 86, 119, 136
Graness, A. 49

Guinea 33, 66
Gyekye, K. 5–6, 15, 23–29, 45, 90, 96; African precolonial values and traditions 100, 102, 117–18

Hallen, B. 103
Hamidou Kane, C. 13
Harbeson, J. W. 107, 111
Haubert, M. 108
Hayward, G. W. 68
Hegel, F. 45–46, 56, 126–27, 142
Heidegger, M. 45–46, 142
Held, D. xvi, 10, 24, 27, 89, 98; the Lockean social contract 157n2
Heraclitus 92
Herero-Nama 120
Hersch, J. 92
Hobbes, T. xiv, 5, 89, 126–27
Homogenization xv, 128–29, 131, 134–35, 137, 139; And cultural purity 144
Horton, J. B. xii, 23, 31–33, 38; See also Africanus
Hountondji, P. xii, 3, 6, 40–44, 46, 61–62; Nkrumah consciousness 75–76, 142
Houphouët-Boigny, F. 93, 109
Houtart, F. 17, 115, 126
Hrubec, M. x
Human rights xv, 5, 34, 49,63, 65–66; African states and human rights 85–86, 89, 95, 98, 101, 110–12; African civil society and human rights 123–27, 156
Huntington, S. 134

Ideology xi-xii, 1–2, 7–10, 17–18, 28; race 35, 41, 54, 73, 82, 92; African political philosophy 141
Iliffe, J. 31, 90
Imbo, S. O. 45–46
India 89, 134
Ivory Coast 6, 137

Jamaica 69, 70–71, 87
Japan 37–38
Jim Crow 72, 87
Johannesburg 82, 83, 147, 150, 152
Jordan, T. 5

Kabange Numbi see Sando Marteau
Kabarhuza, B. H. 123, 126
Kabou, A. 24
Kabundi 157n4
Kagame, A. 45–46
Kalulambi, M. 105

Kant, E. 142
Kaphagawani, D. N. 41
Karp, I. 15
Kasanda, A. xvi, 6, 27, 49, 51, 86;
  global justice and identity 91,
  131, 147
Kasa-Vubu, J. 33
Kasereka, K. 6
Kathrada 148
Kaunda, K. 15, 40, 46, 93
Kebede, M. 46, 52, 56–59, 65
Keita, L. 127
Kelman, G. 62, 80–81, 83
Kenyatta, J. 15, 74, 92–93
Kervegan, J.-F. 89, 110
Keucheyan, R. 56
Kibujjo, K. 1, 22, 28, 62
Kimbanguism 9, 19
Kinshasa 17, 131–32
Kintges, K. 18
Kitawala 9
Klein, N. 140 n 1
Kliptown 149
Kodjo-Grandvaux, S. 24, 41
Kourouma, A. 14
Kumalo, S. 87
Kwesiga, J. 123, 126

Labu Tansi, S. 132
Lajul, W. 1, 3, 15, 45, 47, 51;
  ethnophlosophy and one party-rule 62n2,
  92, 95, 105
Laléyê, I. P. 46
Langley, A. 7
Laplantine, F; 137
Latouche, S. 127
Leleux, C. 157
Libya 77–78
Lincoln, A. 75
literature x, xii, 2–3, 12–14, 35–36, 43;
  negritude and Afropolitanism 46, 53,
  68, 138
Loba, A. 13
Locke, J. xii, xiv, 5, 89, 126–127, 150;
  social contract 157n2
Lockerbie 78
Lokua Kanza 20
London 32, 138
Lopes, F. 1
Lovelu 25
Luba 25, 157
Lubumbashi 22
LUCHA xv, 123, 125
Lugard, F. J. D. (Lord) 119, 136
Lumumba, P. E. 33, 125

Maalouf, A. 80
Maji-Maji 120
Malawi 92–93, 122
Mali 66
Malula, J. A. 33
Mamdani, M. 119–120, 135–36
Manchester xiii, 73, 74, 143
Mandela, N. xv, 36, 125, 145–57
Martin, G. x, 33, 73, 75, 91
Martinez Montiel, M. L. 66
Marx, K. 8, 17, 53
Masolo, D. A. 15
Matsouanism 9, 19
Matthieu, L. 5
Mazrui, A. 11, 15, 66
Mbeki, T. 36, 149
Mbembe, A. xiii, 16, 19, 27, 31, 40;
  la circulation des mondes 57, 64–65, 77,
  79–83, 85, 87; Afropolitanism and
  differentialism 110, 129, 131,
  134–40, 147
Mbiti, J. 15, 45–46
M'Bokolo, E. 33, 90, 99–00, 137
Mbonimpa, M. 7
Mbuyi, K. B. 66, 75
McDonaldization 130
McDonalds 129
Meiji 38
Melberg, A. 12
Memmi, A. 86, 135, 147
Messiah 19, 70
Mexico 67
Mobutu, S.S. 15, 92, 94, 105, 109
modernization 23, 32, 37, 56, 92, 115;
  development 131
Monga, C. 20–21, 61
Mongo Beti 13
Mora, G. 45
More, M. P. 146, 153–55
Morocco 78
Moses 70
Mosley, A. G. 51
Mphahlele, E. 13
Mudimbe, V. Y. 13, 22, 24, 33–36,
  39, 47; the negritude 49, 52–53,
  56–57, 65, 110, 112; African
  differentialism 134
multi-partyism 88, 92, 98–01, 143
Mungwa, A. 123, 126
Museveni, Y. 96, 98
music x, xii, 12–13, 20–22, 124, 131;
  Afropolitanism 38, 141
Musila, A. G. 81–84
Mvezo 147
Mwene-Batende 19

NAACP 71
Napoléon Bonaparte 8
Nasser, A. G. 78
National Sovereign Conference 100, 123
Nazism 9
Ndebele 25, 155
Negritude xii, xiii, 2, 7–9, 36, 40; alterity 41, 46–50, 52–59, 61–62, 83, 139; identity discourse 142
Ngandu Nkashama, P. 19
Ngoma-Binda, P. 1, 7, 9–10, 39, 78
Ngugi wa Thiong'o 62
Nguni 155
Nguyen van Chien, T. 70
Nietzsche, F. 56
Njoku, F. O. 127
Nkombe, O. 2, 9
Nkrumah, K.1, 3, 6, 15, 24, 28; ethnophilosophy 40–42, 44, 46, 61, 64, 68; Pan-Africanism 73–76, 79, 84, 87, 90, 92–93; the African postcolonial state 109, 122, 142–43
Noah 147
no-party rule xiv, 88, 97, 104, 118, 143
non-violence 60, 68, 74, 95, 124, 142; Mandela 53–54
Nouss, A. 27, 64–65, 72, 80–81, 137
Nyerere, J. K. 1, 15, 24, 92–93, 143; *See also* African socialism

Obenga, T. 46
Odera, O. H. 4–5, 22–24, 41, 49, 61, 91; equity and people's capacity building 133
Okolo, M.S.C. 12–14
Oluwole, 45–46
oneness 12, 15, 92
ontology xi, 2, 6–7, 9, 10, 47–48; African social and political philosophy 141
Osaghae, E.E. 126
otherness xii, 18, 46, 52, 57–58, 60–61; nativism and one party-rule 92, 136–37, 146–47
Otlet, P. 87
Ouloguem, Y. 14
Outlaw, L. 63, 66–67, 72–73
Oyono, F. 13

Padmore, G. 74
Pan-African Congress xiii, 66, 68, 71, 73–74, 143
pan-Africanism xiii, 2, 36, 63–66, 68, 71–79; critique and defence of pan-Africanism 81–86, 139, 142–43
pan-Arabism 78
Papua 66

Parmenide 51, 92
Pechu, C. 5
Pennsylvania 40–41, 76
Pericles 89
Perret, T. 123
Peter, Abrahams 74, 87
Picasso, P. 110
Pirotte, G. 109, 111–14, 126
Pittman, J. P. 66
Plato xii, 5, 7, 12–13, 89
Plissart, M. F. 17, 132
powerless 15–16, 31, 49, 59, 77, 85; discrimination and equity 131, 140
Prague x

racial solidarity xiii, 82
Ramose, M. B. 102–03
Rastafarianism 70
Rawls, J. 5
Raynaud, P. 157
Rettová, A. 13–14, 21–22
Rey, P.-P. 108
Rials, S. 157
Ritzer, G. 130, 134
Rivière, C. 19
Rivonia 149–51
Robben Island 153, 155–56
Rousseau, J.-J. xiv, 5, 89, 126–27
ruse 68, 150–52, 157

Sanchez, D. 17–18
Sando Marteau 14, 22
Sankara, T. 95, 124
Sartre, J.-P. 14, 49, 53–54, 56
Scott, G. 87
Sefrioui, A. 13
Sekou Touré, A. 33, 92–93
Selasi, T. xiii, 81, 129, 131, 137–40
Sembene, O. 13–14
Semprini, A. 36, 86, 111
Senghor, L. S. xii, xiii, 1, 3, 6, 15; ethnophilosophy 24, 27, 36, 40–41, 45–47, 49–56; the right to be different 61, 142
Serequeberhan, T. 1, 3–4, 61
Sharpeville 153
Shutte, A. 52
Sierra Leone 31, 32, 37, 120
Simiyu, V. G. 29
Sisulu, W. 147
Sithole, M. 28–29, 112, 122
Smet, A. J. 1–2, 7–9, 40, 43, 67–68, 70–71; Garvey and Du Bois 73, 87
Smith, S. 24, 39, 101
social exclusion 7, 10, 84, 156

Socrates 5
Solomon (the King) 70
South Africa 16, 36, 87, 119, 136, 139; apartheid, violence and resistance 140 n2, 145–52, 154–56 See also Mandela
Soweto 16, 147, 153, 156
Soyinka, W. 14
Stalinism 9
Stewart, G. 22, 131
Stimmung 132
Strauss, L. 7
Sudan 78
Swahili 14–15, 22, 27, 124
Swati 155
Sylvain, B. 67
Syria 78
Syrte 78–79

Tafari Makonen 70
Taiwo, O. 85, 90–91, 102
Tchebwa, M. 22, 131
Teffo, J. 105, 118
Tembula, N. 87
Tempels, P. xii, 6, 45, 48
theory of worth 69
Thomas, L.-V. 7, 8, 31, 34, 124
Thoraval, J. 62
Thuku, H. 120
Togo 92, 95, 122
Touraine, A. 127
Towa, M. xii, 40–41, 43–44, 46, 49, 59; ethnophilosophy 61, 142
Transkei 147
Transvaal 25
Traoré, A. D. 85, 91, 100, 116
Tripp, M. 123, 126
Tshisekedi, E. 94
Tsvangirai, M. 94
Tunisia 78
Tutu, D. 5, 135

Ubuntu 5, 155, 156
Ujamaa, 7, 9, 27, 46
UK 29
UNIA 69–71
United States of Africa xiii, 74, 143

Van Bilsen, J. 33
Van Parys, J. M. 41
Venezuela 66
violence 14, 41, 55–56, 58–59, 60–61, 68; governance 97–98, 122, 124, 140n2, 142, 149; self-defence 154–56

Wagner, Peter xvi
Wamala 23–24, 26–27, 30, 96, 100, 105; precolonial values and traditions 118
Wamba-dia-Wamba, E. 102–04
Washington xiii, 64, 67–69, 72, 106, 113; black people empowerment 142
Weber, M. 17, 130
Weltanschauung 42, 49, 142
Wesseling, H. 31, 90
Western Europe 28
Willame, C. 90, 99, 100–01, 126
Williams, H. S. 67, 73
Wiredu, K. 3, 6, 15, 23–24, 30–31, 45; no party-rule 61, 93, 96–98, 100, 102, 117–18; people's capacity building 133
wisdom 4, 7, 12, 15–16, 21, 30; paradigm of governance 41, 48, 97
World Bank xiv, 84–85, 99–100

Y en-a-marre xv, 123
Young, C. xv, 7–8, 111, 118, 121–24

Zaïre 92, 94–95, 105n1, 122,
Zambia 122
Zea, L. 18, 45–46
Zewde, B. 38
Zimbabwe 25, 94, 122, 147, 154